Advertising: Critical Approaches

Advertising: Critical Approaches explores a broad range of critical theories and perspectives to shed new light on the organization, workings and effects of the advertising industry today. Chris Wharton presents the social, cultural and economic role of advertising across history, with chapters tracking the process of advertising from production to reception.

Split into three parts covering foundations, frameworks and applications, the book's chapters explore a range of areas that are central to the development of modern advertising, including:

- advertising history
- cultural, critical and political economy approaches to advertising
- texts in advertising
- the reception of advertising
- advertising in the home and outdoor advertising
- consumer culture.

Case studies explore the diverse uses of advertising throughout history, from Ostia and the Square of the Corporations in the ancient Roman world to the UK Border Agency's 'Go Home' campaign and contemporary City branding throughout Europe.

Assessing the impact that the works of key critical thinkers including Marx, Morris, Lyotard, Barthes, Saussure, Williams and Hall have had on our understanding of consumption and advertising's societal impact, *Advertising: Critical Approaches* illuminates and enhances our understanding and engagement with one of the most vital cultural and economic forces in contemporary society.

Chris Wharton is Senior Lecturer in advertising and culture in the Faculty of Art, Design and Social Sciences at Northumbria University, UK.

Advertising
Critical Approaches

Chris Wharton

With a political economy of advertising chapter by Jonathan Hardy

LONDON AND NEW YORK

First published 2015
by Routledge
2 Park Square, Milton Park, Abingdon, Oxon OX14 4RN

and by Routledge
711 Third Avenue, New York, NY 10017

Routledge is an imprint of the Taylor & Francis Group, an informa business

British Library Cataloguing in Publication Data
A catalogue record for this book is available from the British Library

Library of Congress Cataloging-in-Publication Data
Wharton, Chris (Lecturer in advertising and media)
Advertising : critical approaches / Chris Wharton.
pages cm
1. Advertising. I. Title.
HF5823.W466 2015
659.1–dc23
2014016029

ISBN: 978-0-415-53522-9 (hbk)
ISBN: 978-0-415-53523-6 (pbk)
ISBN: 978-0-203-39314-7 (ebk)

Typeset in Sabon
by Taylor and Francis Books

Printed and bound in Great Britain by
TJ International Ltd, Padstow, Cornwall

Contents

List of illustrations

Figures

Table

Plates

Note on contributor

Jonathan Hardy is Senior Lecturer in Media Studies and Programme Leader for BA Media Studies. He teaches on the Advertising and Journalism undergraduate degree programmes and on the postgraduate MA Global Media and MA Media Studies.

Acknowledgements

I would like to thank Vanessa Maughan for assistance with imagery, editorial advice and the 'William Morris' contribution to Chapter 3; Dr Jonathan Hardy both for his advice and for Chapter 4, 'Political Economy Approaches to Advertising'; and Professor John Fenwick for his collaborative work on policy and culture in cities. Thanks also to Professor John Armitage for advice on 'speed' and Hilary Fawcett on 'feminist issues'; and to Catherine Orange for editorial advice and Robert Orange for photographic support. I would also like to thank Niall Kennedy and Aileen Storry of Taylor & Francis for their patience and support.

I would like to thank the people and organizations who have helped in the production of this book, for their advice and assistance in the tracing of imagery, granting of permissions and reproduction of items. Staff from AB Inbev UK Ltd, Advertising Archives, Advertising Standards Authority, Bridgeman Art Library, Bettmann/Corbis, Bodleian Library, British Museum, Courtauld Gallery, John Lewis Stores, Lafarge, Pluto Press and Samson Rope Technologies merit a special mention. Every effort has been made to trace and contact copyright holders. The publishers would be pleased to hear from any copyright holder so that acknowledgements may be amended.

Introduction

Advertising plays a significant part in many people's lives. The advertising industry is involved in a wide range of activities from promotion, publicity and finance to planning, research and creativity. It creates specialized, highly rewarded employment on the top floor of global corporations and lower-paid work at the street level of advertising display. The industry creates work and income for many people and substantial profits for a few. Advertising operates as a 'selling mechanism for corporate capitalism', creating advertisements that help move the goods, and contributes to a culture of consumption that eases their passage. It generates knowledge and information on a global scale, a feature of everyday life where resources and commodities are plentiful. Where they are scarce the presence of global advertising is merely an irrelevance.

Most parts of the world are touched by advertising. Countries with high levels of industrial and technological development, inhabited by populations with reasonable standards of living, are often perceived to be saturated by it. Advertising is not only an industry, an underlying mechanism, but one that surfaces in people's everyday lives through an increasing range of technologies. It still appears in traditional form on the side of old buildings as fading hand-painted letters and images, and it surfaces on the applications and networks of today's handheld mobile devices. Its visible and audible presence is widely sensed and it is very much a part of modern culture. Advertising is pervasive but occurs in different media forms. Television, radio and cinema advertising need media technology, presentation and audiences; and commercial media need advertising, not least for the funding it provides. Advertising has changed shape and appearance many times since it was first recognized way back in history as a feature of human experience. It is for us today a very contemporary experience: it has a presence in the here and now. As a 'now' experience, it can appear as a full-page advertisement in a newspaper or magazine or as a discreetly tweeted product endorsement by a celebrity footballer on social media. The context and environment in which the advertisement occurs are important, as indeed is the appearance of the advertisement itself. As a series of 'nows', an advertisement may be experienced as one of a cluster of billboard advertisements. As part of a series of broadcast 'nows' it may be characterized as an aspect of advertising flow like the succession of ads that appear on the Internet, television and radio. Advertising flows as sound and visible form across media screens and through homes, workplaces and leisure outlets. This flow weaves its way into the everyday, from home-based domestic life to activity organized around work, leisure and consumption. Advertising is an important aspect of consumer culture; it also features in people's sense of identity and society – how we see ourselves and others.

This book approaches the study of advertising from a critical perspective. It recognizes the significant place that advertising has in a capitalist economy as a means to sell, provide information and in many instances channel goods and services towards people who need them. It also creates wants and desires and encourages associated lifestyles. In these pages advertising is approached critically as a product of changing times – economies, societies and technologies. Critical approaches reflect on the purpose and place of advertising in the economy and social order. Advertising should not be taken for granted: it is neither inevitable nor immutable in its current forms. The book uses different perspectives and borrows from a range of disciplines: from historical studies to political economy, and from art history to urban sociology. Its general field of enquiry is represented by the critical strand of cultural studies. The book is presented in three parts: 'Foundations', 'Frameworks' and 'Applications'. Each part contains a number of case studies which provide a focus for the themes and ideas introduced as part of the wider discussion.

Foundations

The first section, 'Foundations', is made up of five chapters and provides an overview that sets the scene for contemporary advertising. Chapter 1, 'The Nature of Advertising History', explores the significance of advertising history as an important area of enquiry in itself and one that provides an understanding of how contemporary advertising has been shaped by the past. It considers the questions of historiography, of how advertising history is compiled and what *kind* of story it tells. The chapter explores some of the different approaches taken and considers issues of historical method and the significance of different source material to a history of advertising.

Chapter 2, 'Historical Outline', offers an account of some of advertising's main developments. Taking a broad historical sweep, it explores shifts in advertising content over time, examples of technological change and the shifting relationship between advertising and culture. It looks at early forms of promotion from the ancient world, with a case study drawn from the first/second century AD, a mosaic still in situ at the ancient Roman port of Ostia. The case study poses several general questions about the nature of historical material, its relevance to this kind of enquiry and, more specifically, what constituted advertising and promotion in the past. This chapter considers the significance of technological change to the development of advertising. For instance, the introduction of movable type printing in the fifteenth century had an effect on commerce and advertising as well as on communication more generally. Similarly the development of photography in the early nineteenth century was important to newsprint advertising and imagery. In addition to technological development, the creation of advertising agencies in the late nineteenth century had an impact on the organization of advertising production. Radio and television and, more recently, the spread of the Internet, digital and mobile technology in the twentieth and twenty-first centuries have contributed to contemporary advertising.

The establishment of a market society in Britain in conjunction with agricultural and industrial developments involving widespread social and economic change is addressed in Chapter 3, 'Market Society and Its Critics'. New urban centres, transport networks and forms of work were the basis for industrial mass production. Commodities were bought and sold according to market mechanisms and many new kinds of products became available. Trademarks, a form of early branding, became commonplace, and these are considered as contemporary cultural forms but often with deep historical connections. Changes in advertising practice were associated with the newly formed advertising agencies and the creation of advertisements in new media forms such as radio, cinema and television. The working practices and social conditions of the nineteenth-century market economy were met by a range of critical responses. Matthew Arnold was concerned about the value of culture and the nature of social order, while William Morris addressed the production of consumer objects, their quality and aesthetic value. He was also concerned with the quality of life for both producers and consumers in a mass, industrial society. Karl Marx explored the workings of capitalism and the market society through a form of political economy and addressed the nature of alienation and the exploitation of working people.

Jonathan Hardy in Chapter 4, 'Political Economy Approaches to Advertising', shows how political economy scholars have called attention to circumstances beyond advertising texts, to the economic and political dimensions of the advertising industries, in order to explain the power and influence of advertising. A political economy of advertising explores its funding, production, distribution and regulation. Hardy argues that political economy's most distinctive contribution has been to address how advertising finance as a major source of media funding influences media content, media provision and access to communications. The chapter explores the strengths and limitations of political-economy perspectives and offers guidelines for analysis of advertiser influences on communications.

The final chapter in this section, Chapter 5, 'Cultural and Critical Approaches', explores twentieth-century cultural thought about advertising, beginning with an account of the 'culture and civilization' approach associated with F.R. Leavis. In this tradition of thought culture was perceived as an elite preserve and popular culture as an inferior form of expression. Advertising was viewed as part of popular culture and deemed to have little cultural merit. This gave rise to concern about advertising promoting undesirable attitudes and having negative effects in a mass society. These were also, in many ways, the concerns of the Frankfurt School, who considered the political effects of manipulation and false consciousness in a capitalist economy and society where mass culture was closely aligned with mass media. Advertising was viewed as an important part of this. Ideology and hegemony were seen to be essential features of capitalist social stability, with advertising playing an important part in promoting this. In addition this chapter explores post and late-modern concepts that have been applied to advertising, many of which challenge traditional thinking. The chapter outlines the work of the Birmingham Centre for Contemporary Cultural Studies which was important to the study of popular and mass culture. Advertising studies benefitted from this, and Stuart Hall's encoding/decoding model of communication has become the basis for the advertising framework outlined in the middle section of this book.

Frameworks

The second section of the book is entitled 'Frameworks'. Its three chapters in turn explore the encoding or production of advertising; advertisements as texts in a range of different media forms and social spaces; and finally the reception and decoding of advertisements by audiences. These three components – encoding, texts and reception – form what is referred to throughout this book as the *advertising framework*. This term is used to both delineate and indicate the connection between the three essential elements of the advertising process. In Chapter 6, 'Advertising Framework and Encoding', the relationship between the three components of the advertising framework is depicted in a linear pattern. This emphasizes the sequential nature of encoding and reception through time (see Figure 6.1). Later in the chapter the advertising framework is conceived as a circuit or loop in which cultural ideas, images and representations circulate and are formed, selected and incorporated into advertising campaigns (see Figure 6.2). Cultural engagement is acknowledged as more than mere passive reception. Social media is significant in creating a sense of engagement but advertising encoding largely occurs in advertising agencies. Encoding of cultural ideas is explored through a case study of a Pantene hair product advertisement widely promoted before and during the London Olympics of 2012. The chapter concludes with an exploration of particular cultural strands concerning celebrity, sport and in particular women encoded in the Pantene advertising campaign.

Chapter 7, 'Texts', offers an analysis of different approaches to advertising texts as the central part of the advertising framework. The term 'text' can be applied to a wide range of cultural products and activities that include images, words, sounds or other signifying elements that form a series of advertising patterns, shapes and narratives. Advertising texts also have specific qualities relating to sales and promotion and are produced by the advertising encoding process. In this chapter approaches are based on art historical, sociological and cultural perspectives. This includes content analysis as an approach to understanding the prevalence and frequency of advertising texts in different media and in different social and cultural environments. This is contrasted with textual analysis, which includes formal analysis, interpretation of visual and symbolic elements in the art historical tradition and the semiotic interpretation of signs as elucidated by Barthes, Peirce and others. The chapter considers advertising texts as key ideological elements and acknowledges the importance of different technologies and contexts that support them. Textual and content analysis are explored in combination and as applied to a case study surveying car advertising over a specific period of time.

Reception and decoding of advertisements is explored in Chapter 8, 'Reception', from three different perspectives: effects studies, uses and gratifications and the 'decoding' aspect of the advertising framework. The first two are drawn from opposing positions of twentieth-century media reception theory. Effects studies emphasizes what advertisements do to people; uses and gratifications, what people do with advertisements. In isolation, these are considered to be inadequate explanations of an audience's relation to advertising messages. The chapter outlines in detail a series of potential decodings ranging from a preferred reading in which the receiver largely accepts the advertising message to an oppositional reading where it is rejected. These are explored in a case study of a jewellery advertisement from 2012. Decoding is understood as a result not only of an advertising text, but of a wider set of economic, social and cultural circumstances. Class, gender, ethnicity, religion, sexuality and other social factors are identified as part of people's lived experience, and advertising both draws on and speaks to these experiences. The social and political contexts of decoding are examined in recent and current decades.

Applications

The book's third section is made up of four chapters and explores *applications*. It considers further features of advertising presentation and reception by applying the advertising framework to different settings and circumstances. In particular it examines contemporary culture and considers the place and significance of advertising-driven consumer culture.

Chapters 9 and 10 examine the 'spaces and places' where advertising is received and decoded, establishing differences between public and private spheres and how these are linked in the study of advertising in public and private space. Chapter 9, 'Advertising in the Home', looks at the private, domestic space of the home and how advertising is an important part of that environment. People view and listen to advertisements in the home and advertisers make constant references to people and their home life in their advertising campaigns. Consequently this chapter explores domestic life and the environment in which it occurs. There are three aspects to this – home, household and family. The chapter considers home as a material and symbolic space, family as a set of close kinship relations and the household as a social and economic category.

A range of advertising media including radio, newsprint and the Internet are received in the home. It features an assortment of screens delivering both television and advertising on personal computers, laptops, smartphones and tablets. The television set is still a prominent feature of the home and an important source of screen advertising. It gives rise to different viewing and reception scenarios in which both individual and household viewing occurs. People like to talk about television programmes and advertisements, and 'television talk' is a common feature of the household and often carried beyond its walls. But in the home this mingles with wider conversations and activities taking place there, and becomes integrated into what is termed a 'household flow' – making television a domesticated and very potent form of advertising. The household or family share not only a home space but a local culture, which is important in the reception of advertising. Advertising diffusion is a term used to describe the spread of advertising messages among groups of people, with 'word of mouth' advertising perhaps the best-known expression of this. In addition Internet social media sites are increasingly becoming important conduits for advertising diffusion. Diffusion occurs both in the home and in the outdoor environment.

The next chapter in this section looks at advertising and the urban, outdoor environment of largely public spaces. Chapter 10, 'Outdoor Advertising', explores urban settings in which outdoor or out-of-home advertising occurs. Outdoor advertising refers to advertising in public spaces, such as billboards and adshells, electronic panels and mobile advertising carried by public transport. Out-of-home includes advertising that appears on personal, mobile and handheld devices. Outdoor, public areas of cities and towns are important to the advertising industry. They form a very specific context within which advertising reception occurs, not least because time spent in outdoor urban space is experienced differently to that of indoor domestic space. The speed and frenetic movement of crowds and traffic and the pace of contemporary consumer activity play an important part in the reception of outdoor advertising. Its very visible presence is a prominent feature of outdoor town and city space.

'Neat' or 'cool' capitalism are terms used to describe contemporary culture and the economy that supports it. This is particularly associated with young urban consumers. However, disenchantment with it and aspects of contemporary politics have turned in recent years into large-scale global protest. At the same time wider audiences for outdoor advertising exist and these include urban workers and consumers and people engaged in urban leisure. This chapter explores the measurement of advertising effectiveness and interpretive time. It concludes with a case study of an advertising campaign relating to immigration commissioned by the UK Border Agency in 2013. This took the form of an outdoor, mobile 'advan' campaign targeted at a number of areas of London which resulted in widespread opposition, much of which was organized through Twitter and other forms of social media.

Sound and vision are important aspects in creating advertisements and significant features of advertising reception. Chapter 11 explores different 'modes of viewing' advertisements. It considers how people are encouraged to look at advertisements and how they choose to view them. In particular it deals with the viewing of television and Internet advertising, compared with billboard advertising. Three modes of advertising viewing are identified: the look, the gaze and the glance. Viewing is marked by the length of time over which it occurs and the different kinds of concentration and attention involved. This results from a range of factors which include advertising design, medium, viewing context and other environmental features. Modes of viewing are shown to be important to advertising reception and its effectiveness.

This chapter also explores sound as an aspect of radio advertising and as an important element of television, Internet, tablet, mobile and other forms of advertising. It forms the sole means through which the message is delivered in radio advertising, but when accompanied by imagery it functions in other ways. It can draw or return a person's attention to the whole audio-visual advertising text, and it enables engagement with advertising while the listener is involved in other activities. Sound, whether alone or accompanied by visual and textual elements, lends a potency and intimacy to advertising form. Advertising sound, particularly in a bounded space like that of the home, contributes to the sense of self; it speaks not just to 'anyone' but to 'someone'.

Chapter 12, 'Consumer Culture', explores contemporary consumer culture in which commodities, advertising and branding are increasingly socially significant in what is often referred to as a 'society dominated by consumption' (Ritzer and Jurgenson 2010: 16). Consumer society is shaped by the largely eighteenth- and nineteenth-century development of a market economy, industrial mass production and consumption. Consumer culture involves a wide range of activities and experiences: from engagement with the consumer goods and publicity images often dominating urban public spaces to the advertising signs and logos that weave through private life, covering a wide variety and number of surfaces.

This chapter looks at various threads of consumer culture, acknowledging it as a shared way of life, but one in which access to it is unevenly distributed and dependent on a range of economic, social and political factors. It is an important component of social identity, but many other aspects such as class, gender and ethnicity are of at least equal importance. Branding, an increasingly prevalent advertising phenomenon, has contributed to a deeper, more intense form of concentrated or hyperconsumption. This involves reference to needs, wants and satisfactions, driven by what Zygmunt Bauman has referred to as the 'consuming desire of consuming' (2001: 13). Urban centres have become potent symbols of consumer culture, and the final section of this chapter considers how cities are not only intense places of consumption but have themselves become branded objects and experiences. Place marketing takes the built environment of a city, the history and lived culture of its people as a product and gives it the the branding treatment. Branding is explored as a series of marketing strategies involving packaging, logos, brand identity and image.

In the final analysis advertisements sell us things in the form, and using the 'platforms', best suited to the task. The advertising industry markets commodities in the most effective and profitable way possible, making choices from prevailing economic, social, cultural and technological circumstances. In order to do this, advertising needs to seek out people's real lives and existences and speak to their needs and desires. Advertisements sell us things, but in order to be successful advertising needs to sell us a view of the world and by implication a view of ourselves, our relations with others and the world we live in. Advertising both reflects that world and shapes it.

As in the past, today's advertising strategies are based on creative choices and are selected from available ideas, materials and technologies. These involve questions about advertising form (how advertising appears as visual and textual language on screens, pages, posters, etc), content (how the nature of the message about products, people and values is conveyed), the method of delivery (television, newsprint, mobile or other means) and how to shape environments and circumstances of reception. These are also the areas of analysis of the *advertising framework* outlined in the middle section of this book and which underpin the book's overall approach to advertising and advertisements.

Technological development from print to photography has enabled advertising to adapt and in some cases transform both its content and way of engaging and speaking to the public. Advertising constantly endeavours to find new innovative forms, important to the successful marketing of goods. It sells itself through innovation, claiming creativity as its core. But its ability to innovate is limited by other factors not least developments in technology and society. The image of Sir Tim Berners-Lee, inventor of the World Wide Web, sitting behind a computer and tweeting the message 'this is for everyone' to an audience of millions is one of the memorable images from the opening ceremony of the 2012 London Olympics. Yet the advertising industry appears to consider the Internet, mobile and developing communication technologies as existing for its own purpose of creating and conveying new forms of advertising. Indeed the volume and variety of screens increases by the day. In public spaces high-definition digital advertising screens animate narratives more fragmented yet more vivid that the world surrounding them. On the private screens of smartphones and mobile devices advertising apps create seemingly endless product connections and increased exposure to brands as well as creating service links and enabling the direct purchase of goods. Interactive web advertising, including user-generated content, weaves through contemporary communication networks, but largely leaves undisturbed existing social frameworks in which the relations of power, wealth and other social resources define lives and life chances. The social and cultural possibilities and consequences of a rapidly evolving technology remain uncertain for advertising and consumption and for the general well-being and direction of society.

Many recent studies of advertising and consumption stress people's active engagement in the process of choosing and selecting consumer goods. The presentation of self through fashion, taste and the creation of lifestyle projects, sometimes lived and sometimes imagined, frequently operates beyond the limit of allocated resources. The idea of hyperactive consumers and advertising audiences, has become a central feature in the marketing of consumer culture. However, consumer goods and distribution systems have limitations; even choice itself is limited. Choice, as we have seen, is made within social and economic frameworks and limited by access to the range of available and allocated resources.

Advertising both reflects the world and shapes it. Yet the here and now is never enough, the advertising 'offer' is nearly always a choice to be made for the future. As we make these choices, a series of questions is posed by critical approaches to advertising. How freely do people buy into a world constantly shaped, packaged and organized under the advertising sign? How does advertising operate? What kind of a world does it help shape, and in whose interest?

Part I

Foundations

1 The nature of advertising history

Introduction

This chapter looks at the importance of history to an understanding of advertising. The history of advertising is first and foremost about uncovering advertising as it occurred in the past. Identifying the form that it took as an arrangement of words or pictures and the messages it conveyed is an important aspect of this too. So also is a wider understanding of advertising's economic and social purpose in different places and at different times. *Advertising* often refers to the *process* of promoting things, the wider activity of representing commodities to the public, whereas *advertisements* are the outcome of this process, the apparent visible and sometimes audible references to brands and products. Many writers on advertising make the point that what happened in the past and how, why and when people decided to advertise their products, services or ideas to 'the public' is an interesting area of enquiry. Advertisements from the past are often encountered as reproductions in history books and as objects of interest in local art galleries and museums. The Museum of Brands, Packaging and Advertising in Notting Hill, London is specifically dedicated to advertising and its history. Other museums, such as the Museum of Roman Civilization in the city of Rome, include examples of historical advertising among their many exhibits. A more recent addition to the collection of historical advertising can be found at the History of Advertising Trust's online gallery (www.hatads.org.uk).

Advertising and advertisements from the past are not only confined to museums and galleries. Past advertisements can still be glimpsed in the places they were first installed, for instance in the streets we walk down on our way to the shops or to our place of work. Advertisements painted on the outside of buildings in the nineteenth and early twentieth centuries, creating what were at the time vibrant images and texts, are now fading from view. These have become known as 'ghost signs'. In addition, radio and television advertising slogans from the twentieth century, such as 'Go to work on an egg!', created for the Egg Marketing Board, or 'Don't forget the fruit gums, Mum!' for Rowntree's, still exist as recordings and echo through lived memory. Important developments in the history of advertising, such as the formation of advertising agencies in the nineteenth and twentieth centuries and the division of labour between visualizers and copywriters, still have a presence in the contemporary practice of advertising production.

Quite often promotions and advertisements created in the past speak to the modern world with a perplexing combination of the familiar and the strange. Penny coins from 1903 displayed in the British Museum have the Suffragette slogan 'Votes for women' stamped on the coin face and serve as an example of historical political advertising that

Figure 1.1 'Phillips Charles', wall sign, Liverpool, 2012. Photographed by the author.

circulated on the loose change of the day. In addition to what are still today important and ongoing global political questions, the coins raise issues about what might be included in a history of advertising and promotion. Do they count as an element of advertising or merely as a form of political promotion? This is one of the questions that the history of advertising poses. Advertising history also has to take account of the wider changes and developments that have occurred over time, and it is also about continuity. The history of advertising is a rewarding and important area of enquiry and this is reflected in the numerous studies that have been produced (Elliott 1962; Hindley & Hindley 1972; Williams 1980; Nevett 1982; McFall 2004; Tungate 2007). This and the next chapter make reference to these.

In considering change and continuity we come to appreciate the extent to which contemporary advertising has been shaped by the past. In addition to the crucial questions that a history of advertising might pose about what happened in the past, when it occurred and who was involved we might include additional enquiries about why these things occurred and what consequences they have for contemporary and future society? For instance Liz McFall in her book *Advertising: A Cultural Economy* explores the idea that as advertising developed its techniques and expanded into new promotional areas across the nineteenth and twentieth centuries it became more persuasive over time. The 'persuasiveness thesis', as it is termed, became a widely held view of advertising, emphasizing the difference between an advertising based on information and one based on persuasion (McFall 2004: 46). By considering the evidence, and the way historians have handled that evidence, McFall is able to challenge the idea that 'Persuasiveness is

Figure 1.2 Penny coin with Suffragette slogan 'Votes for women', 1903. Reproduced courtesy of the Trustees of the British Museum.

widely characterised as an index of all the ways in which contemporary advertising is supposed to be different from its historical antecedents' (McFall 2004: 45). In doing so McFall not only casts a light on the nature of advertising in times gone by, she also opens up an enquiry into the nature of contemporary advertising.

In addition to exploring advertising and advertisements as history, this chapter also considers questions of historiography. By this we mean that the chapter not only concerns itself with the story that the history of advertising tells, but asks questions about how that story is put together, how it is written and therefore what *kind* of story it tells. The chapter offers an overview of some of the different approaches taken and looks briefly at some existing histories. It considers issues of method, the significance of different kinds of source material and the nature of historical evidence.

Understanding the past

One of the key requirements for the study of advertising is to recognize what we mean by the term 'advertising'. What are we including in the activity that we call advertising and what are we excluding? Defining our terms in order to survey and understand current practices – the advertising of our own times – is a complex enough operation. To do so in order to identify and comprehend activity from the past is more difficult. Caution is required in applying today's terms or ideas retrospectively. Which activities and events that occurred in the past might be explained by the modern, widely used term *advertising*? In current use, as has already been suggested, the word refers to a large-scale industry that includes research as well as creative practice. It also refers to a range of advertising texts and images, communicated across a range of media, from handbills to handhelds. It is worth considering that forms of promotion which occurred in the past might not have been labelled as advertising.

Indeed the use of language to describe the activities and the announcements associated with the promotion of goods and services might be the beginning of a historical enquiry. When was the term advertising first used? In what context did it appear and what did it indicate? The word appears in the title of several early writings by philosopher and essayist Francis Bacon. For example, his essay *An Advertisement Touching the Controversy of the Church of England*, written in 1589, articulated ideas about religion and its organization rather than referring to the promoting of products. The word also appears in the plays of William Shakespeare. *Troilus and Cressida* is the tragic story of a pair of lovers set in the ancient conflict between Greece and Troy and was most likely written in 1602. The word *advertised* is used by the Trojan prince Hector, who has challenged the commanders of the Greek forces encamped outside Troy to engage in battle. Discovering that this is not to be the case he announces that 'I am advertised their great general slept.' In this instance 'advertised' appears to correspond to something like advised or informed in the sense of 'I have been made aware of'. This is of interest in the context of a drama that makes great play on the nature of 'value', 'worth' and 'price', both in terms of people and things. These themes are explored – not in the setting of Shakespeare's play or in the context of the Elizabethan audience for whom they were written – but in relation to contemporary advertising in subsequent chapters of this book.

In the past a variety of English words were used to refer to what we are likely today to call advertising in one or other of its various forms. Early adverts were often referred to as *puffs*, *bubbles*, *blasts*, *devices* or even *impertinences*. So we can see that a wide variety of words carrying a range of different connotations were used to indicate an advertisement. A consideration of the context in which these terms were used and by whom adds to our understanding of their use. The term *advertiser* was being used in the late seventeenth century and *advertisement* by the eighteenth century (Elliott 1962). Indeed Dr Johnson's *Dictionary of the English Language*, produced in 1755, refers to an *Advertiser* as 'he that gives intelligence or information' but also as the name of a 'paper in which advertisements appear.' Johnson's famous aphorism, published in 1759, is worth quoting here not only as an example of the use of the term but for the sentiment it expresses, which still feels true today: 'Promise, large promise, is the soul of an advertisement' (Johnson quoted in Williams 1980: 172). The more general term *campaign*, with less emphasis on the single advert and more on the wider process of promotion of goods and services, became common in the early twentieth century (McFall 2004: 154–7). In recent years the term *branding* has in many circumstances come to be used instead of *advertising* (Danesi 2006).

Language is important to our historical understanding. It labels and describes processes, objects and people. In our enquiry the 'process' is that of advertising, the 'objects' are advertisements and of course it is people who do the advertising. The activity of promotion and advertising – not just the naming of it – has occupied a considerable number of people over the years. This activity is intrinsically linked to economic activity – investing capital and securing incomes, status and social position. It is also associated with culture and leisure. There is a close relationship between advertising and language and more widely between art, culture and advertising (Wharton 2013). Advertising relies on art, design, music and fashion, along with cinema, television and other technologies for the skills and ideas people bring to the industry. At the same time culture and the arts, such as the theatre, galleries and opera, benefit from the income advertising provides and the publicity it generates for events and activities. Furthermore we need to take seriously the close link between advertising and culture because advertising has over time used culture to give meaning, status and often legitimacy to its products and also to the way in which it promotes them. For instance advertising draws on familiar works of art, styles and themes as sources of creativity and as a way of attaching cultural authority to the promoted product. This can be seen in the use of Pablo Picasso's signature to market the Citroën Picasso car and, combined with humour, in Persil's use of the Impressionist painting style to sell its washing powder in the 1990s. *Culture* refers not only to galleries and theatre companies such as the Royal Shakespeare Company and Tate Modern or to the artistic practices or works of art they present. In a more prosaic manner *culture* refers to the way people live their lives. An attempt to understand culture is one of the keys we hold in unlocking the advertising past.

In the same vein, the close link between advertising and various media technologies needs to be acknowledged and explored as part of historical enquiry. It is difficult, for example, to imagine contemporary advertising without the newsprint media or the electronic media of television and radio. So before we can pose our important historical questions – such as 'when did advertising first occur?' – we might need to consider a range of qualifying questions. For instance in the case of identifying the earliest advert we would need to define an advertisement, what form it takes and what activity it involves. In order to do this we would need to compare and contrast our 'advert' with other contemporary objects, activities and technologies.

The history of advertising – like any history – raises a number of questions. Indeed the questions of what should be included in a history of advertising and why are perhaps two of the most important questions we can pose. This chapter opens up a discussion of these issues so that our understanding of advertising history, and any historical enquiry we may subsequently undertake, can develop in a critical and questioning manner.

History and historiography

In this section of the chapter we deal with some of the wider issues that underpin the foundation of the history of advertising. *Historiography* is the term given to these kinds of issues, considerations and concerns. The term is used in two ways. First, historiography can refer to *a body of work*, a set of histories: books, articles, web pages and even popular cultural representations about a specific and specialized area of human endeavour, in this case, advertising. Second, the term *historiography* refers to the *methods* we use to explore the past and the sources we drawn on. In other words it is how we go about history and how the history of advertising is compiled.

We like to think – in our everyday commonsense understanding of the world – that history exists independently of the questions we ask about the past. In this view advertising history is a series of facts – out there, in the past, just waiting to be discovered. But a history is as much the creation of the nature of the questions we ask as it is a series of facts, objects, events or even people who have had a significant presence in the past. As the historian E.H. Carr put it: 'facts of history cannot be purely objective, since they become facts of history only in virtue of the significance attached to them by the historian' (1961: 120). A concern with the 'facts' of history is similar to the questions posed in advertising research about the objects of research enquiry. So we can say that the accumulated historical questions and the answers that are forthcoming are an important part of the construction of history, of our understanding of advertising's past. This is what Spalding and Parker refer to as the 'distinction between the past and a description of it'

(2007: 1). Such issues are explored in the academic world as questions of historiography and in this chapter as the historiography of advertising.

Different histories of advertising have approached their subject in different ways. For example, Mark Tungate's *Adland: A Global History of Advertising* (2007) gives us an insight into advertising's past. It is also a useful example of the way a history of advertising can be structured and written. Tungate's book takes a wide and general chronological narrative both historically and geographically. It begins its story in the early days of advertising and encompasses it in the widest global terms. Stephanie O'Donohoe, reviewing this book for the *International Journal of Advertising*, acknowledges Tungate's ability as a storyteller and explains that the 'stories serve not only to entertain, but also to humanise and contextualise the work of advertising's key figures' (O'Donohoe 2008: 172–3). The history unfolds, according to O'Donohoe, not just around 'key players', but through 'key moments' and around 'key developments'. This is a useful indication of the kind of history that is being presented here. We might add 'places' to this 'stock-in-trade' historical list of players, moments and developments. Traditionally, in a European-centred history of advertising, Rome, Athens and Thebes feature prominently as the places in which some of the earliest forms of advertising occurred. Later in the history of advertising the industrial cities of Britain, France and the US are presented as sites of advertising innovation. Increasingly other geographies and cultures can be added to this list as history is presented in a less Western-centric manner. This reflects multicultural and global interests in recent academic study in the areas of cultural studies, feminism and postmodernism. Similarly an understanding of 'key moments' in advertising history can be extended into a wider consideration of historical periods and eras. Specific forms of advertising communication, such as the outdoor system of billboards and posters, stem from technical developments in printing. Movable-type printing was itself an outcome of and contributor to the economic, social and intellectual organization of the late European medieval world.

Approaches and themes

A variety of approaches may be taken to the history of advertising. The story may, for instance, be told essentially as a series of **technological developments** where, for instance, printing in fifteenth-century Europe and the nineteenth-century newsprint technology that developed from it is presented as transforming the practice of advertising. It enabled widespread mass production of newspapers and multiple and easily reproducible copies of advertisements. The development of photography and later cinema and television created new forms of advertising and transported advertisements into new public and private spaces. Similarly radio and more recently Internet and mobile technology have further transformed the nature of advertising. This approach is known as a technological determinist view, one that emphasizes technological development over and above other explanations of social and cultural change. It can marginalize or even exclude other compatible and complimentary explanations. It can be a techno-optimistic view, emphasizing the positive effects that technology has on society, or conversely a techno-pessimistic one that underlines the negative effects of technology (Fuchs 2012). In either case technological determinism overvalues the part that technology plays in social change. In its most extreme form technological determinism reduces social change to one explanatory factor and is therefore labelled reductionist. The alternative to this is to recognize that technology shapes society in complex ways. Fuchs suggests that the relationship between technology and society is best viewed as a dialectical relationship in which 'society conditions the invention, design and engineering of technology, and technology shapes society ... ' (2012: 387).

An **economic and social history** of advertising looks not only at technological developments that have impacted on advertising but is concerned with the general processes of society. It is about understanding 'the intersections between technological, economic, social and political forces' (Couldry 2012: 13). It is concerned with the underlying economic forces that shape society and culture and the changes that occur across time. Advertising is a significant element of each of these areas, as a significant aspect of a modern economy and a key feature of social and cultural experience. At the same time developments in advertising practice are viewed as outcomes of the changes that occur in the economy and in subsequent social relations. For instance mass production and consumption associated with the expanded urban industrial societies in the nineteenth and twentieth centuries were accompanied by significant change in the advertising industry with the coming of advertising agencies.

A further approach that might be taken to advertising history is to look at the **appearance of adverts** – to ask how they come to look like they do, and how and why they change over time. What are the stylistic and formal conventions at play in an advertising campaign? For instance advertisements for washing powders Daz and Omo from the mid-twentieth century displayed similar but different design characteristics, engaging readers and viewers in different ways (see Plates 1 and 2). Art history poses similar questions about the making, display, understanding and appreciation of paintings and other forms of art. Art history explores the conditions in which paintings are commissioned and produced; the nature and significance of what they represent; and the prevailing stylistic and formal circumstances with which they can be compared and contrasted over time. Like this aspect of the history of advertising, art history is concerned with the changes in styles and themes that occur and attempts to understand this as part of historical change. This approach may well also pose questions about industry and technology, regulations and different mediums but it is essentially about the appearance of the advertisement.

Alternatively the history of advertising can be told as a series of **regulations**. These are laws and conventions applied to advertising that limit where and when adverts can be shown and what kind of content might be permissible. This can be statutory, which means that government, such as the British Parliament, has written these restrictions on advertising into law. On the other hand it can be self-regulatory: this means that the advertising industry oversees and limits its own behaviour. Raymond Williams suggests that because of problems associated with the amount of fly posting in London in the 1830s, a London act was passed that prohibited posting an advertisement without consent (1980: 175). This is an early example of statutory regulation. In 1962 the Advertising Standards Authority (ASA) was created to oversee the British Code of Advertising Practice. This was a form of self-regulation (Hardy 2009: 75). These things can be seen to change the way advertising appears and its wider relation with the economic and cultural aspects of society. The introduction of or changes made to advertising regulation provide important historical markers in the development of advertising.

Historiography, then, is about how history is compiled. A history of advertising is written up from the material gathered for that purpose. What is included and excluded and the reasons or rationale for doing so are highly significant. A process of selection takes place and this occurs even at the earliest stage of the procedure. For instance in

Chapter 2 we consider certain mosaics found in the ancient Roman city of Ostia. These are discussed as being significant to the history of advertising but other similar images found nearby on the same archaeological site are excluded. This judgement is based both on content and location: what the mosaics depicted and where they were to be seen. Particular events and objects supported by certain explanations and interpretations are privileged over others and these come to form the story of advertising. Historical material is not self-selecting, nor does the past speak for itself.

Historical material needs to be organized and presented in order for it to make sense. This is also a significant part of the process. Order and narrative become an important factor in writing and presenting history. White (1980) has suggested that *all* history is presented according to certain narratives. These are usually organized chronologically, and this approach emphasizes a continuous story where things or events are linked through time. This forms a coherent and easy-to-follow history of advertising. In this approach there is a propensity to describe events rather than analyse them. This can result in an over-emphasis on individuals and individual achievements, inventions and innovations rather than a more general, but less tangible appreciation of the social and economic circumstances that give rise to innovation. In many ways this form of story-telling is inescapable, essential to the way humans organize and reflect upon their experiences. However we need to be aware of the complexity of causal factors that give rise to certain events and to historical change. This is in contrast to the view that things or events inevitably give rise or lead on to subsequent things. A cautious and conscientious history will distinguish between necessary and sufficient causes. For instance, photography, a new means of representing the world developed in the early part of the nineteenth century, was perhaps a necessary feature in the creation of a new picture-based advertising in the mid and later part of the century. But other factors were involved, such as developments in printing, newspaper layout, the development of advertising agencies and general expansion of the economy. Therefore photography can be said to be a necessary but insufficient cause for the development of the new pictorial advertising of the late nineteenth century. In other words, photography was important to this advertising development but more was involved than a single, isolated causal relation.

Critics of certain kinds of historical writing often refer to the 'Whig interpretation of history'. This alludes to a group of English historians of the nineteenth century who recounted the history of their country as a series of progressive events that led inevitably to the present. Spalding and Parker describe it thus: 'the Whig historians emphasised – their later critics were to say they over emphasised – history as a story, continuity, a development and, by implication, a progress towards a free liberal, enlightened present' (2007: 13). In this view the present is considered, to borrow Voltaire's famous phrase, as 'the best of all possible worlds'. Something similar has been identified in the telling of advertising history. McFall suggests that many historical analyses present 'advertisements to have attained their current form as a function of a gradual, incremental, evolutionary process' (2004: 98). In this view the present-day advertising world is viewed as the best possible outcome of the past. This view tends to discourage critical appraisal of the outcomes of the past and encourages an unexamined and self-congratulatory view of the present state of advertising.

This uncritical approach has a number of connected strands. One strand presents contemporary advertising in a postmodern cultural and technological setting. Technological developments of the past such as photography, radio, cinema and television have incrementally contributed to the current idea of convergence at the centre of which is the

Internet and handheld and virtual technology. Advertising saturation is an accepted feature of this and is presented as a natural outcome of historical development. In this view people are depicted as free choosing individuals, their social and political freedoms partly constituted by the operation of a consumer democracy, one well served by the prevailing culture and technology. Alongside this, current advertising regulation is presented as the outcome of a gradual process emanating from the early nineteenth century and resulting in the media-regulation body Ofcom and the advertising regulatory regime of the ASA. The ASA, which operates the Codes of Advertising Practice, has fashioned itself as the accessible and responsive regulator and adjudicator of moral and ethical issues associated with advertising. In this view advertising is managed progressively to the benefit of producers and consumers alike, recognizing the wider interests of citizens, state and the economy. There are at times differences of opinion between various social and economic interest groups. This takes the form of a series of contested matters, for instance around advertising representation of women or the effects of advertising on children. Food and health issues such as alcohol and tobacco consumption are further topics often discussed and debated with political and media elites intermittently intervening. Nevertheless, with a few exceptions, a general social consensus around the presence, content and spread of contemporary advertising appears to hold. Critics will contend that advertising in its current form represents a particular kind of economy and society, one marked by social division and deep economic inequality.

Other kinds of historical writing can inform our understanding of the approach that historians take to the writing of history. In the field of art and culture, Modernists have for example been criticized for establishing metanarratives or 'big stories' that offer overarching explanations of artistic and cultural development. In the history of art this

OK, so we're better at
removing bad ads
than making good ones.

Here at the Advertising Standards Authority,
we judge ads on whether they're harmful, misleading,
or offensive. Not on whether they're funny, clever or
they look good. Which is just as well, really.

Telephone 020 7492 2222 www.asa.org.uk

Figure 1.3 ASA, 'Ok, so we're better … ' press advertisement, 2005. Reproduced courtesy of the Advertising Standards Authority.

has taken the form of explaining changes in the appearance of modern painting from the middle of the nineteenth century to the middle of the twentieth century as becoming progressively more abstract. To offer a further example from the area of social and economic history, Marxist historians have stressed the predominance of economics and social class to explain continuity and change at the heart of historical development. Michel Foucault suggested a postmodern approach in which discontinuity is stressed as an aspect of historiography. Genealogy according to McFall is a type of historical method that 'attempts to reveal the historical contingency of objects ... it proffers a challenge to teleological accounts that view historical movement as a singular process of transformation in response to "universal" forces' (McFall 2004: 104; Jordanova 2006). For instance the creation of television didn't necessarily lead to television advertising in the form that we are most familiar with today, the string of advertisements between programmes. In the early days, television advertising – in America – was about programme sponsorship and product placement.

Sources and materials

This section looks at the material that historians and in particular advertising historians draw on in writing history. This is usually referred to as source material or sources. These are conventionally divided into two categories: primary and secondary sources. Primary source material is characterized as the raw material, documents or direct evidence produced in the period being studied. In advertising studies this may take the form of advertisements and other media-produced or designed objects. Primary sources might include contemporary comments such as written evidence about an advert or about the process of advertising. Laws prohibiting advertising or contracts permitting it would fall into this category. Primary source material has a sense of originality and directness to it that as Jordanova suggests might 'imply a special kind of authority' (2006: 40), but this is not to suggest that primary source material speaks for itself. Primary sources require special attention – they need to be interpreted. Secondary sources in historical enquiry are those presented by historians or others that offer a commentary on the past. This may be a written historical account of advertising or some other description or analysis, such as a television, radio or internet reference. The distinction between a primary and secondary source is fundamental to historical enquiry but the difference in practice may not be so easy to make (Tosh 2006: 60).

Secondary sources

Secondary source material, documents and reflections recorded after the event or accounts that comment upon the original source are to be distinguished from primary source material. The books we consult on the history of advertising are for us secondary sources, but may well contain first-hand, primary source accounts. In addition histories of advertising often have quite different approaches, and they take different formats.

Quite often a historical account of advertising may be included in a book with a wider subject matter. For instance Gorman and McLean's well-known textbook *Media and Society into the Twenty-first Century* is generally about twentieth- and twenty-first-century media and society. It gives prominence to advertising as an important aspect of this and includes a chapter 'The Rise of Advertising' that charts the formation of modern advertising (Gorman & McLean 2009). Some writing about the history of advertising comes as a preface to a book or article that goes on to discuss a specific aspect of advertising. Raymond Williams's much-cited account of advertising is a good example of this. 'Advertising the Magic System' (1980) explores the place and function of advertising in the late 1970s, but Williams begins his account with a brief look at the history of advertising. Some histories such as Nevett's *Advertising in Britain: A History* provide a broad sweep of the history of advertising from its early days to the time of writing (1982).

Periodization

Writers choose to start their histories at different times and in different places. Some historical accounts place a great deal of emphasis on particular themes, events or occurrences – such as the development of advertising agencies in the nineteenth century – where others may view this as less important. The material that is included in historical accounts will differ according to the writer's interests, perspectives and ideologies, and this will impact on the periods of history they choose to discuss. Raymond Williams, for instance, began his account with reference to a 3000-year-old papyrus from Thebes, but his real interest was advertising after the Second World War (1980: 170). Gorman and McLean (2009) and Pasic Falk (1997) situate modern advertising in the second half of the nineteenth century. Elliott (1962) and Nevett (1982) tend to concentrate on the post-Caxton period of English advertising history.

Authors generally offer a rationale for their choice of periodization. Falk emphasizes the difference between the premodern practice of 'informing potential clients and customers of the existence and availability of a certain product' and the early modern intention to 'stimulate demand' (1997: 65). Williams agrees that the intention of the historian should be to trace the development of certain trends that lead to the 'institutionalised system of commercial information and persuasion' (1980: 170). For Leiss *et al.*, the important markers in the development of advertising are between 'traditional and industrial societies' and from industrial to consumer societies, as well as the developments that occur within consumer societies (2005: 33). Iain MacRury (2009a: 127) offers a wide-ranging and clear-cut advertising periodization which falls under the headings of proto-modern advertising (1600–1780), early-modern advertising (1780–1880), modern advertising (1880–1950) and late-modern advertising (1950–90). In this last phase we see modern advertising agency functions operating on a global scale and the consolidation and widespread use of media technologies in the interest of advertising. The history of advertising is divided up into periods for a variety of reasons. This might be in order to create manageable 'portions' of history which are easier to imagine and understand than dealing with a large and complex whole. In some cases key events such as the development of printing might provide a pre- and post-event periodization or it might be to do with the description of a period such as premodern, modern or postmodern (Jordanova 2006). This is not without its difficulties as these terms are often used by different writers in different ways.

Primary sources

This section considers the nature and status of source material. Source material is to be recognized primarily within its original context and its relevance understood, as far as is possible, within that context. This might include attempting to understand the direct meaning that an object like an advertisement might have had for contemporary people; the role of organizations and institutions in the promotion of products; or less tangibly the repercussions of an advertising process on the social structure in which people lived. This section then makes the distinction between primary and secondary source material. The question of evidence, proof and interpretation is also considered.

Source material for a history of advertising inevitably includes an analysis of advertisements from the past. For some critics the history of advertising is overly centred on advertisements rather than the process of advertising. For instance advertising slogans and images from the first-century AD world of Roman Pompeii or Ostia, the port of ancient Rome, pose interesting issues about status and interpretation of historical objects. Many of these have been discovered in situ, still positioned where the people who made the advertisements intended them to be viewed by a contemporary audience. Still situated in their original positions, these provide a clear case of a primary source. We can identify, scrutinize and interpret them not only *in* the place they were intended to function but as *part* of that place. The topographical context adds to our interpretation of the object. However a primary source might be reproduced as an image in a book or as an exhibit in a museum where much of its original contemporary context is absent. This can create a challenge and can cause complexity for the historian of advertising.

A radio advert from the early part of the twentieth century provides a further interesting but quite different example of an advertising primary source. Despite many changes and developments in technology it is still possible for today's historian to experience the same radio advertising text broadcast almost 100 years ago. However what might be missing is the context of other radio adverts and radio programmes that accompanied and contextualized the advert.

In both of these examples – the Roman advert and the early radio advert – the people who now view or listen to the advert are a quite different set of people inhabiting different economies and cultures to those for whom the advertisement was first devised. So despite being confident – assuming that the advertising text is authentic and not a fake – that the advert is a primary source what we cannot provide for our historical understanding are the people and their sensibilities for whom the advert was intended. We cannot go out on a field trip and interview the people of the past: the people who could provide contemporary interpretations. If we are lucky contemporary primary source accounts and descriptions might still be available. In the absence of these the historian can attempt to reconstruct the circumstances and context of advertising reception. In doing this the historian attempts to understand the culture in which the historical advertisements were both produced and received. This is done by comparing and contrasting the advert against a range of other artefacts and forms of evidence. This might include other adverts from the time or other forms of visual material. It might also involve investigating the statements and claims, the nature of the visual, spoken or written language that is used in the advertisement in comparison to that of other similar artefacts from the period. Putting all these elements together we can create a picture of how the advertisement might have been received at the time.

What we see as constituting our evidence for the history of advertising is only partial. We can only fully study what still exists from previous periods and our knowledge is derived from these surviving primary sources. The exception is where a document describes and perhaps offers an assessment or even analysis of the item that has either disappeared from history or not yet come to light. This poses a range of questions for the historian. Why do some sources survive and others disappear? Could it be that particular kinds of evidence survive and that these lend themselves to certain forms of interpretation? What other types of evidence have not survived? Has a process of selection – hidden from the historical researcher of the twenty-first century – taken place? Does the process of selection and conservation – and these questions are true for all advertising primary source material – favour certain types of evidence?

It would be foolish to suppose that what we see on the streets of Pompeii in the second decade of the twenty-first century is a full record of the advertising and promotional material produced and operating before Vesuvius erupted and buried the city in volcanic ash in 79 AD. Neither can we be certain that it is necessarily typical of other Roman settlements of the first century AD. Pompeii and its sister archaeological site of Herculaneum lay largely hidden and unexcavated for many years. What cannot be ascertained is what was lost in the pilfering of the site and the early, less-methodical archaeological digs that have taken place. Our evidence from this site is likely to be partial – yet it is from this that a broader understanding of the role and nature of advertising in the ancient world is drawn and from this that generalizations about advertising are made. Could historians be missing a lot of primary source evidence that might alter knowledge of the ancient world, its economy and promotional activity?

A third example of advertising primary sources can be drawn from the more recent past. Traces of old advertisements, many from the industrial period of the nineteenth and early twentieth centuries, can often be discerned painted directly on the walls of old buildings. In some cases signs have remained constantly visible but with the advertising texts and images weathered and fading with time. These have become known as 'ghostsigns' (Ghostsigns 2011). Some historic wall advertisements only become visible as facades are removed revealing older, pre-existing signs. When buildings are demolished new sight lines are created revealing previously unnoticed signs. The goods and services being promoted may no longer exist, but the signs are interesting in themselves. They provide primary source evidence of earlier outdoor advertising and the way in which goods were advertised. However only certain buildings have survived and some walls have been cleaned of advertising or the advertisements have faded, almost beyond recognition. Conversely some advertising sites have been painted over, often with new advertising signs which may paradoxically preserve the older signs beneath. Whatever the circumstances of this process of preservation it involves an element of selection. Some outdoor advertisements are maintained in situ and may become primary source material for historical advertising enquiry. Others are not and this and the reasons for it need to be taken into account when these adverts are used as evidence of earlier advertising forms and content.

Evidence, interpretation and proof

We might wish to include a variety of other contemporary documents or texts such as newspaper accounts, local government records, photographs or sketches. Television, radio, video and other media records might also be included in our source material. These might provide information or evaluation of a campaign or a particular type of advertising. They may well offer an invaluable contemporary account of a campaign providing primary source material revealing social and cultural attitudes towards advertising (Tosh 2006). For instance the Advertising Standards Authority's adjudications and assessment of advertisements across a range of media provide primary historical material that comments on advertising and its content. This includes not only adjudications but also evidence and complaints submitted by the public about advertising campaigns. This material provides important insights into cultural values, attitudes and expectations held by the public. These will be useful to future historians attempting to reconstruct the past when their period of study is no longer part of living memory. This kind of evidence can be understood as 'witting or unwitting testimony', providing information about cultural values and the advertisements people choose to comment upon. Witting evidence is a conscious and deliberate intervention in the contemporary world and can take the form of a stated complaint against an advertisement, but this might also provide unwitting evidence about general cultural and social values (Tosh 2006: 106).

Evidence is central to the history of advertising. The close relation between evidence and historical narrative is one of the things that distinguishes academic historical accounts from literary or media forms. There is a keen difference between historical narrative grounded in evidence which supports reasoned interpretation and storytelling based on assumption, the needs of the medium or the market. However evidence, even substantial evidence, is not the same as proof. Historians talk of 'weighing the evidence' which may not be conclusive but points with some certainty in a particular direction. Proof on the other hand is generally conclusive and unqualified. It states with certainty that something has happened in a certain way and this or that significance should be drawn from it (Anderson 2012). The emphasis on evidence underlines the importance of interpretation – facts do not speak for themselves.

All historical source material requires interpretation and advertising is no exception (Jordanova 2006: 160; Tosh 2006: 145). Interpretation is present at each stage of advertising history. It is there at the outset, in the selection of available sources and in the description and analyses applied to them. It is present in the narrative in the telling of the story of advertising history. The reader or viewer of secondary source material interprets the evidence as it is presented to them. Numerous skills are present in this process which are closely tied to the idea of objectivity: for example, making claims that can be supported by the evidence and the ability to make connections between things. Also important to the process but perhaps more mundane are writing and critical reading skills.

Conclusion

The history of advertising is an important aspect of advertising studies. It is an interesting area of enquiry in itself and provides a valuable understanding of the nature of the contemporary advertising industry and its products. Questions of historiography are to do with how the history of advertising is compiled and written, what is included in a historical account and why it is important to this. The nature of historical evidence and interpretation and the distinction between primary and secondary sources are also therefore significant. There are different types of advertising history presenting history in different ways and taking a wide variety of approaches to themes and periodization. The following chapter explores further some of these themes with reference to advertising and promotion in different historical periods.

2 Historical outline

Introduction

This chapter opens with an exploration of advertising in the ancient world, in particular the Roman Empire, and examines examples of advertising and publicity from the cities of Rome, Pompeii and Ostia. The chapter considers the nature of this kind of communication and assesses whether or not it can be viewed as advertising as we understand it in the modern era. The chapter continues by exploring technological change, in particular the introduction of movable-type printing in the fifteenth century and the effect this had on commerce and advertising. Further technological developments in printing and in photography, fundamental to the creation of modern newsprint advertising, are examined. This is shown to be a necessary component of modern advertising. It exists alongside radio, television and the Internet as important features of contemporary advertising. Different forms of rapidly developing Internet advertising are explored. A key element, necessary to making advertising a central aspect of consumer capitalism, was the creation of the advertising agency.

Promotion before printing

Some histories of advertising begin their examination of the subject with reference to the ancient past of early civilizations, city states and empires – in the period of history in which the transition from the Roman Republic to the Roman Empire of Augustus Caesar occurred (Cunliffe 2008). The birth of Christ is presumed to have been at this time and this created the historical dating system of BC (Before Christ) to indicate dates prior to this and AD (Anno Domini) to indicate dates subsequent to it. However these same periods are also referred to as BCE (Before the Common Era) in place of BC and CE (Common Era) in place of AD.

Writers on the history of advertising have started at different historical points. For instance Raymond Williams began his account of the history of advertising with reference to 'the three thousand year old papyrus from Thebes, offering a reward for a runaway slave' (1980: 170) and T.R. Nevett alludes to the use of signs and public announcements in ancient Athens (1982: 3). But it is Rome – at first the republic and later the early empire of the first century – that offers the most tangible evidence of publicity in the ancient world. Sign writing, one of the oldest forms of promoting goods and services, was preserved among the ruins of Pompeii and nearby Herculaneum, both Roman towns buried under a layer of volcanic ash after the eruption of Mount Vesuvius in 79 AD in what is now southern Italy. These 'trade signs' have been discussed as historical finds in a variety of archaeological accounts of Pompeii's excavations (Sage 1916; Maiuri 1960: 188).

Promotion in Pompeii

The town of Pompeii in the first century AD was a complex and thriving economic and cultural space, a place of home, work and leisure. Evidence of this exists in the theatres, bars and shops, temples, bathhouses, houses and gardens that line the excavated streets. Workshops where goods were produced front the streets. The road system (as in most Roman settlements) extended beyond the forum and out from the town, connecting it with the empire and wider economic activity. Roads enabled the widespread exchange of goods and information. Pompeian consumers could buy goods from the fixed shops and workshops lining the streets; from permanent and occasional markets or from hawkers and street stalls that operated in Roman towns (Holleran 2012). Pompeii has also revealed an array of advertising. Trade signs of this period took the form of painted wooden signboards. They could also be displayed as frescoes, which were paintings created on interior or exterior wall plaster, or as stone carvings. They also appeared as mosaics, which were created on walls or the floor by a careful arrangement of marble or other small pieces of stone into images and words. This was of course well before the period of movable-type printing and the large-scale production of posters and handbills that it enabled. It would be almost two millennia before photography and the moving images of television, cinema and other screens carried advertisements for everyday goods. One advert in Pompeii offers a property to rent and boasts that it offers 'an elegant bath suite for prestige clients, tabernae, mezzanine lodgings and upper floor apartments on a five year contract' (Beard 2008: 110).

Many other forms of promotion are visible in Pompeii, predominantly for goods and foodstuffs. In addition electoral slogans – an attempt to promote a particular candidate in an election – were painted onto walls, often in the same style and created by the same hand as advertisements for gladiatorial games. The games, held in the amphitheatre at Pompeii, were one of the cultural highlights of the town (Wallace-Hadrill 1994). The content of these advertisements indicate the significance of goods and activities such as gladiatorial events, the use of bars and the sale of food stuffs to everyday life and how advertising and promotion was an important element of these activities (Beard 2008).

It is not just the range of adverts and the types of goods and services represented that is of interest in Pompeii, Herculaneum and other Roman towns and cities such as Ostia (Holleran 2012). The way the adverts were produced, as well as where they were situated, is of interest to a historian of advertising. Signs were painted onto the facades and outside walls of shops and bars with names and images advertising or promoting the premises that lay behind. One bar in Pompeii displays a picture of a phoenix as an identifying sign. The phoenix in classical mythology was the bird that rose from the ashes, and its image is placed next to a slogan that reads: 'The phoenix is happy and so can you be. This is the bar owned by Euxinus, "Mr Hospitality"' (Beard 2008: 225). The association of the product with the lure of happiness is not, it would appear, a modern advertising strategy. At Pompeii the sale of wine was advertised at the entrance to bars, and one bar at least offered its produce at different prices presumably reflecting the quality of the wine on offer (Holleran 2012: 147).

The painting of signs and the creation of images of food and drink were also found inside bars and were painted directly onto fresh plaster using similar techniques as the muralists who created the frescoes that decorated the wealthy homes of Roman towns and cities. The

Figure 2.1 Phoenix pub named signboard, Hexham, 2014. Photographed by the author.

Figure 2.2 Phoenix pub sign, Hexham, 2014. Photographed by the author.

Figure 2.3 Sign for the thermopolium (taverna) depicting a phoenix and inscription 'Phoenix Felix et Tu', Pompeii, 1st century BC to 79 AD (fresco). Reproduced courtesy of the Bridgeman Art Library.

interior artwork that adorned the homes of Roman citizens in this period is identified by art historians as falling into different styles of painting. These styles were defined by the manner in which painting was carried out in addition to the subject matter of the paintings. Some frescoes were heavily illusionistic in design, depicting architectural elements or creating decorative or figurative scenes. Many of the interior images of the commercial premises depict food and drink: hanging game birds, a variety of vegetables, loaves of bread and beakers of wine can still be seen in situ painted on the walls of the bars.

But the question for the historian of advertising is not so much about style or what exactly is being depicted, but what significance was attached to these images at the time? So the important questions that need to be posed of these images are the same that can be asked of adverts from any historical period. These are questions of intention, function and interpretation. Were the images in Roman bars intended to promote the wares or to encourage consumption once a consumer was on the premises? Or were they quite simply an appropriate and pleasing element of design to enhance the atmosphere associated with a bar or tavern? If the latter, do they count as adverts? Similar images are recorded in private Roman houses of the same period. These 'still life' scenes created in fresco or in highly colourful mosaic form also depict food stuffs, fruit, game etc. Many have been removed from their original settings and can be viewed in the Naples Archaeological Museum. For instance 'still life' frescoes from a large villa in Pompeii known as the House of Julia Felix depict eggs, seafood, thrushes and domestic utensils (see Plate 3).

That similar images from bars, shops and taverns were also to be found in what were known to be private houses suggests caution is required in interpreting the bar images as promotional or advertising material (Sage 1916: 205–6). Research in the history of advertising needs to draw on contextual material and specific knowledge of the places where the images were intended to be seen.

It was not just frescoes that were used to depict and perhaps advertise consumer goods in ancient Rome. Mosaics, the arrangement of tesserae or little pieces of stone, marble or glass formed into decorative patterns and images, appear to have been used to promote a range of goods. They were also one of the main forms of private interior design. Mosaics might cover the floor of an outdoor pavement area or form a passage between buildings or rooms within a building. They might be highly decorative or quite plain and simple in design. Designs on promotional mosaics, as in the more decorative, domestic mosaics, included a wide range of images of animals, humans and gods. They had geometric borders surrounding more representational images. Some mosaics were wholly geometric in design. Styles changed according to place and across time. Mosaics might be completed in contrasting black and white or include a wide range of colours. The size of the tesserae was also important to the quality and nature of the design. Mosaics carrying promotional messages were often made out of large pieces of tesserae in comparison to more refined and detailed decorative work which was created from smaller pieces. A good example of a promotional mosaic is a liquamen or garum (fish oil) promotion found in a building at Pompeii. The black-and-white mosaic featured an image of a jar of the product in each corner.

Case study – Ostia and the Square of the Corporations

Other objects and places interesting to the history of advertising survive from the Roman era and provide examples that might be interpreted as evidence of early advertising. Ostia, the port of the ancient city of Rome, was situated downstream from the city at the mouth of the River Tiber. The course of the river has altered and the coast line receded since ancient times, placing the port of Ostia today inland by some three or four kilometres. In ancient times its fortifications, shipbuilding and commercial activities were vital to the Roman republic and later empire, and it was here that imported goods such as grain, wine, oil and fruit were landed, stored or transferred on to Rome (Cunliffe 2008). Much of Ostia Antica has been excavated and is again visible. Turning off from the Decumanus Maximus, the main street of Ostia, is the Piazzale delle Corporazione, sometimes called the Square of the Corporations or the Forum of the Guilds. Here are situated the remains of a series of shops and offices; the floor mosaics bear inscriptions referring to guilds or corporation, shippers and traders. Reference is also made to the ports and places from where goods and materials were transported to Rome. The guilds referred to represent traders in grain, wood, flax and rope and other materials necessary to a bustling city of one million people. The mosaic inscriptions are accompanied by a variety of images of ships, lighthouses, dolphins and fish related to the nature of transportation. The references to each product, place and trader are placed in front of the remains of rooms that make up a portico or porch that faces onto an open area. These rooms were most likely commercial offices dealing with transportation and the texts and symbols functioned as a form of advertising.

The Square of the Corporation's mosaics are in black and white and are of a modest quality of design compared to other more colourful and elaborate mosaics and frescoes which can still be seen in situ at Ostia. Over 50 different mosaics survive in the Square, which was altered several times in antiquity. On at least one occasion the floor level was raised to bring the area into line with surrounding buildings. Consequently the mosaics have been difficult to date but are likely to be from the first and second century AD. One mosaic refers to the shippers and traders, presumably of grain, from Karalis, modern Cagliari in Sardinia, and bears an image of a ship and two grain measures (see Figure 2.4). The lettering and images are in black and set against a white background which is framed by a black border. This gives visual emphasis to the relationship between the inscription and images and marks them out from other similar designs in close proximity across which people visiting the complex would have walked.

Design

A key design consideration that occurs throughout advertising history is how to be recognizable as a form of promotion but distinguishable from other similar forms. The two-line inscription, 'NAVICVL ET NEGOTIANTES KARALITANI', is in black mosaic lettering and is contained within a further black border which is itself emphasized by two inward-pointing triangles that function like modern-day

Figure 2.4 Mosaic, Square of the Corporations, Ostia, Italy: 'Navicul et negotiantes Karalitani', 1st/2nd century AD. Photographed by the author.

directional arrows (Figure 2.4). These direct the eye to the 'shipping, trading and place' information. Below this is the image of the ship flanked by two grain measures half the height of the ship. This is not therefore a design that is primarily concerned with verisimilitude or realistic 'true to life' representation. However if we read the grain measures as 'in front' of the ship this might place the ship spatially beyond the measures creating a sense of distance. Is this how the image would have been read in antiquity? Was this a consideration for the people walking through the square in the second century? The ship with its white sail divided into 28 parts is created from black mosaic tesserae with white delineations and two oars or rudders, one shown 'behind' the boat, which is positioned slightly off centre in the design. This gives a sense of depth. The three black lines positioned below the boat suggest both the presence of 'sea' and possibly movement and direction. These simple naturalistic elements appear crudely executed in comparison with other Ostia mosaics and with other mosaics associated with trade in the Square of the Corporations. Nevertheless, we can assume they functioned as recognizable promotional signs.

Interpretation

So the important questions that might be posed by the advertising historian include: What was the function of these words and images, and what were they intended to signify? How were they received by people passing through the Square? And what was the nature of the promotion? At one end of the spectrum we might interpret these mosaics purely as design, clearly context related, but essentially intended to fill a space with something interesting and perhaps visually pleasing. Maybe they signified wealth, position or prestige although the quality is inferior to other similar items found in the town. Or was this about providing information – the basic 'what's on offer' and 'where you can get it' info that was to develop over time and features as an important consideration of advertising history? If so, how does this relate to recognition; to memory; to existing knowledge and even identity? Perhaps the mosaics merely delineated space, creating a place where certain people met and trade-related activities were carried out. The uniform use of black and white might also have suggested a form of place or activity branding. The signs might have been governed by the 'corporate' nature of the square or by rules applied to promotions and how goods could be promoted in this type of commercial area of a town or city. At the other end of the spectrum, can we read these mosaics as advertising services and perhaps even specific goods? It is difficult to know with certainty what the status and function of these objects was. But posing the questions, generated as they are by historical objects and spaces, triggers the historical imagination and takes us some way into an exploration of what constituted an advertisement in ancient times.

Contexts and comparisons

A further set of questions might refer to context. What other visual and textual material contemporary with the Corporation mosaics can we compare them to? For example, mosaics in Ostia and other Roman towns and cities were used for many purposes. Mosaics decorate the floors of temples and private houses. They can have a religious purpose or function as a display of wealth, power or prestige or simply provide a decorative flooring to a highly designed environment of frescoed ceilings and walls. How do the 'advertising' mosaics compare with these? What other comparable objects can be found in situ, displayed in museums or mentioned in historical records?

A more difficult but also more interesting question is, what might a person of the time have compared these to – images on buildings, architectural features, paintings, other mosaics, designs on household or personal items such as pottery or jewellery? In other words, what were the contemporary frames of reference within which these mosaics were understood? Images of ships were part of everyday visual culture with galleys and other types of ship depicted on coins of the first century BC and on public monuments like Trajan's Column in Rome erected in 113 AD (see Figures 2.5 and 2.6). These had a public propaganda role in representing the state and its social elite but pictures of ships and seascapes also appear in frescoes in the gardens and private rooms of Pompeii homes. These images – and the references they created for people – were features of a society heavily reliant on the sea for travel, trade and communication. Perhaps the ubiquity of the car on today's streets and in the adverts might be the starting point for a contemporary comparison. At the bustling port and shipyard of Ostia, the referent was also a real feature of the lives, work and social relations of its people. The Square of the Corporations was only a short distance from the river and sea and the masts of ships unloading and loading their produce are likely to have been visible from it.

Two general questions arise from an engagement with the ancient, classical world and the promotional signs uncovered at places like Ostia, Rome and Pompeii. One is the way that advertising fits with other aspects of life and culture where the decorative arts, political signs and the advertising of a range of goods exist side by side. These

Figure 2.5 Ship from Trajan's column, Rome erected 113 AD. Photographed by the author.

Figure 2.6 Loaded ship from Trajan's column, Rome erected 113 AD. Photographed by the author.

seem to share not only the same public spaces – streets, walkways and commercial premises – but also similar creative techniques such as the fresco and mosaic. The second is how are these signs different to the other representations produced in the medium. These questions can be posed of any medium used for advertising purposes and of the adverts themselves produced at different moments in history. In posing and attempting to answer these questions we come to consider not just the advertising of the past but how it 'fits' into the wider social, cultural and economic life of a period. And therefore we come to study a wider conception of history.

Technological change and advertising – printing

Advertising is largely dependent on the media space that different media forms create and make available. In a contemporary context this might relate to the advertising space newspapers provide, or the advertising slots on television and cinema screens. The latest manifestation is advertising colonizing the Internet. In all these cases advertising is dependent on the technological developments that made the host media forms possible in the first place. Each media form creates different kinds of advertising – billboard advertising takes a quite different form to newsprint advertising. In the ancient word, the promotion of a product or commodity was dependent on the knowledge, skills and art associated with the making of frescoes and mosaics.

Advertising of the ancient past is largely known from texts and images found in public spaces. These were fixed – a fresco was painted on wall plaster or inscriptions were cut into stone as a single item. An important development in the history of advertising was that of movable-type printing. Book production in fifteenth-century Europe was transformed by the setting up of Guttenberg's press at Mainz in modern Germany in the 1450s. This technological development enabled books like the famous 42-line Bible to be produced. This was a major departure in book production from the labour-intensive, hand-produced books like the illuminated Lindisfarne Gospels (*c.*700) of the past. Books such as these Christian Bibles had to be borrowed, often transported across great distances to be copied by hand. For instance the Codex Amiatinus, commissioned by Ceolfrith in 692, was produced at the monastery of Monkwearmouth at Jarrow in the north-east of England and was in part based on a Bible brought from Rome. Printing quickly spread throughout Europe and was in effect the beginning of the mass production of books.

In 1478, William Caxton published a printed version of Chaucer's late-fourteenth-century work *The Canterbury Tales* at Westminster in London. This is seen as a milestone in the history of English printing. The account of the pilgrimage from Southwark to St Thomas Becket's tomb at Canterbury Cathedral and the tales the characters relate on the journey made its way to a wider audience through the medium of print. A less renowned and much smaller print job – a single sheet known as *The Pyes of Salisbury* – was produced on Caxton's printing press in 1477 (Figure 2.7). This is often acknowledged in the history of advertising as the first printed advertisement. The text referred to the Pyes of Salisbury, which were a set of instructions intended for the clergy regarding the 'concurrence and occurrence of festivals'. The announcement went on to indicate that these could be found 'good chepe' at the Almonry at Westminster (Elliott 1962). *The Pyes of Salisbury* text is in English but it is followed by a single statement in Latin 'Supplico stet cedula' – please let this document/schedule stand.

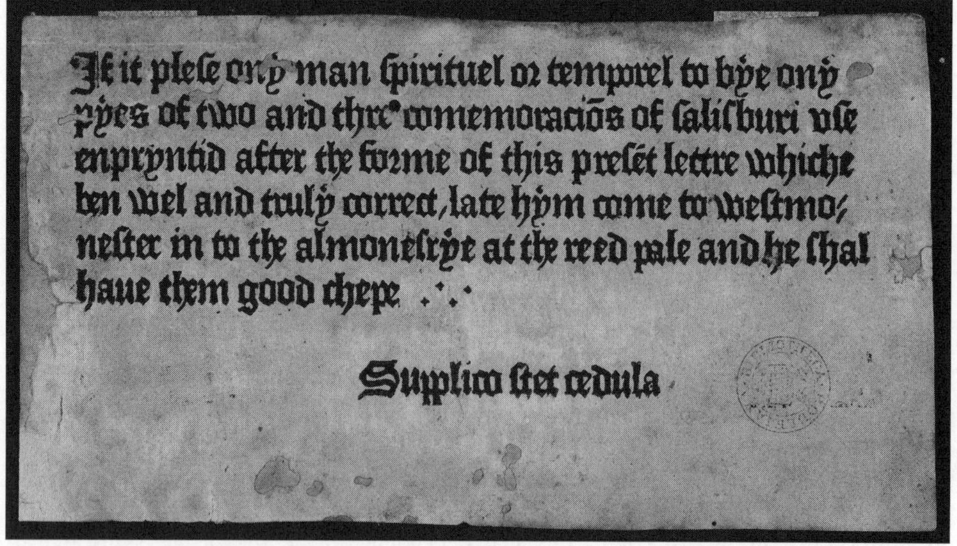

If it plese ony man spirituel or temporel to bye ony
pyes of two and thre comemoracios of salisburi vse
enpryntid after the forme of this preset lettre whiche
ben wel and truly correct, late hym come to westmo-
nester in to the almonesrye at the reed pale and he shal
haue them good chepe .·.

Supplico stet cedula

Figure 2.7 *The Pyes of Salisbury*, William Caxton, 1477. Reproduced by permission of The Bodleian Libraries, University of Oxford: Arch. G e. 37, recto-Caxton's Advertisement.

Multiple copies

What was the intention of this printed announcement and how might it have been interpreted at the time? Although only two copies exist today the fact that it was printed rather than handwritten suggests that multiple copies were produced. The meaning and status of the announcement have been interpreted in different ways. Nevett suggests that the Pyes of Salisbury announcement, although measuring only 136mm × 76mm, more the size of a modern handbill, was used as a poster. The Latin text appears to support this. It was translated in an eighteenth-century annotation to the text as – 'pray do not pull down this advertisement', suggesting that the message was to be displayed on a wall (Nevett 1982). Elliott however considers that classifying it as a poster might be misplaced and the term 'advertisement' used in the eighteenth-century annotation was not in use in the sixteenth century. The use of Latin suggests that this was a phrase in regular use and perhaps a customary way of completing an announcement; 'bills containing advertisements or announcements' were pasted at this time onto the pillars of London's St Paul's Cathedral. Was Caxton's document used in the same way? Evidence suggests then that this document can be categorized as a piece of promotion but questions remain: was it a poster or a handbill? Was it intended to be displayed – and to remain – in a prominent place or to be presented and circulated by hand? These are important considerations for early advertising.

This is, according to Elliott, the earliest example of a broadside still in existence. A broadside or broadsheet was a single sheet of paper printed on one side and often sold on the streets of towns and at public gatherings such as fairs. The broadside was part of a culture – and particularly a visual culture – of popular prints which made images more widely available (Briggs & Burke 2005: 31–3). In circulation from at least the sixteenth century in England and Europe (O'Connell 1999), the subject matter ranged from religious and moral tracts to almanacs combining calendars with astronomical and astrological information. Other prints referred to historical and political events, natural disasters and accounts of executions. By far the most popular were printed ballads. These were the product of urban workshops which operated commercially and circulated prints around the town's population and further afield. Printed handbills advertising a range of goods should be understood as an aspect of this circulation of popular information.

The development of typographic (movable type) print in the fifteenth century in Europe enabled handbills, broadsides and posters to be created more economically and with more detail than xylographic (hand-cut woodblock) techniques had previously allowed. Trade cards were another popular form of printed publicity (see McFall 2004: 167). These were small printed advertisements providing the name and trade of the proprietor, details of the premises where the goods were sold and sometimes images of the items for sale. Commodities on sale at George Wildey's store on 'the Corner of Ludgate-street, next St Pauls', such as spectacles, compasses, telescopes, scissors and other items, were pictured on his trade card of 1720 (O'Connell 1999: 29). Handbills carried advertisements for a range of services and commodities from dubious medical treatments and medicines (Williams 1980) to promoting fairground displays of human or animal 'phenomena' of unusual proportions and shapes. These commercial spectacles might include, for instance, the presentation of exceptionally large or small people or the display of malformed 'monstrous creatures'.

Newspapers and newsprint advertising were further developments of movable-type printing. A good and early example of this was the London-based weekly publication *The Publick Adviser* of 1657, with its reference to shipping schedules and to the sale of commodities such as coffee and chocolate (Elliott 1962: 35). Another London publication, *The*

Merchants Remembrancer from 1681, offered information about imported goods including price quotations for items arriving at the London docks (Elliott 1962). As a framework of publicity it provided a printed schedule of imported goods recently arrived. This functioned in a similar manner to the Ostia promotional mosaics found in the public spaces of the ancient port of Rome. The *Remembrancer* and *Adviser* were followed by similar publications as newspapers developed rapidly in seventeenth- and eighteenth-century England. These developments in advertising reflect the social and economic changes associated with the expansion of trade and empire. They indicate the flow of raw commodities and consumer goods essential to early industrialization and the expansion of consumption and markets. Most commentators, although citing a wide and sometimes bewildering variety of evidence, all agree on the expansion of newsprint advertising across the seventeenth and eighteenth centuries (Nevett 1982; Elliott 1962; Williams 1980; McFall 2004; MacRury 2009a).

Commodity information

Advertising before the early nineteenth century is predominantly informational and textual. In the main it included the essential promotional information telling potential consumers what was being promoted, where it could be found or when it was available. Imagery does occur but this is not the main element of the advertising message. Advertisements up to the middle of the nineteenth century are predominately textual; occasional imagery is supportive of textual information but is not the main element of the advertising message. Whereas today's advertising message is often designed solely around the image or carries a text that supports or reinforces the image. Advertising is a core element of contemporary visual culture

Woodblock to photography

Produced by woodblock printing techniques, early advertising imagery can appear crude and unsophisticated to the twenty-first century viewer. Layout and display are uncomplicated, with an economic use of pictorial form, perspective and depth. Images created to head an announcement or illustrate an advertising text were often reused in further advertisements. Different shipping announcements, for instance, often appeared under the same reused image of a sailing ship. However, on occasion imaginative and design-based techniques were used to create visual impact. Pointing hands and asterisks were a common feature to draw attention to printed text. Design must be seen against the prevailing customs of newsprint production and newspaper design of the time. For example, a strict adherence to the use of columns of printed text created a rigid verticality to the appearance of newspapers, and adverts were contained within this format. Technological limitations were also prevalent, for instance in the quality of the imagery produced. Blocks became worn and rarely produced images of the fine detail created in the hard, close-grained boxwood favoured by engravers like Thomas Bewick (Tattersfield 2009). The use of different kinds and directions of line, the creation of tone, cropping and inclusion of significant forms and above all the basis in observation mark Bewick's illustrations and vignettes out from the mainstream commercial wood-block imagery of the late eighteenth century or from the more detailed copperplate and metal-block imagery produced at the time. One example from Bewick's workshop in Newcastle – an important centre for print in the eighteenth century – is a Chinese tea-drinking scene created to promote 'Davidson Grocer & Tea-dealer Side Newcastle' in which a seated figure dressed in Chinese costume, framed by an arch of palms and other foliage, is served a cup of tea (Figure 2.8). The work is finely detailed, with a combination of naturalistic and decorative detail. An illusion of space suggesting the ground on which the scene takes place is created from just a few etched lines, which complement the overall shape of the design. Bewick's work and the quality of this type of promotional work was exceptional.

Generally speaking the use of steel plates – harder than copper and longer lasting – existed alongside wood engraving as a means of producing advertising imagery in the nineteenth century. Wood engraving became the preferred form of image reproduction for magazine illustration and block printing, and along with the steam press led to a mechanization of printing and the reproduction of advertisements as a feature of newspapers and periodicals (Sperling 2010). The development of photography in the early nineteenth century made possible a range of newspaper representations no longer dependent on hand-drawn images; and the development of photo-chromolithography brought printed colour images to newsprint and to poster advertising.

Outdoor advertising

In addition to technological and commercial limitations, legal and political restrictions such as the stamp and advertising tax were important factors in advertising output (McFall 2004). In addition to newsprint advertising, handbills and posters, other forms of 'outdoor' advertising were visible on the streets of Britain's cities. In the nineteenth century a wide array of placard bearers and sandwich-board men were deployed alongside horse-drawn

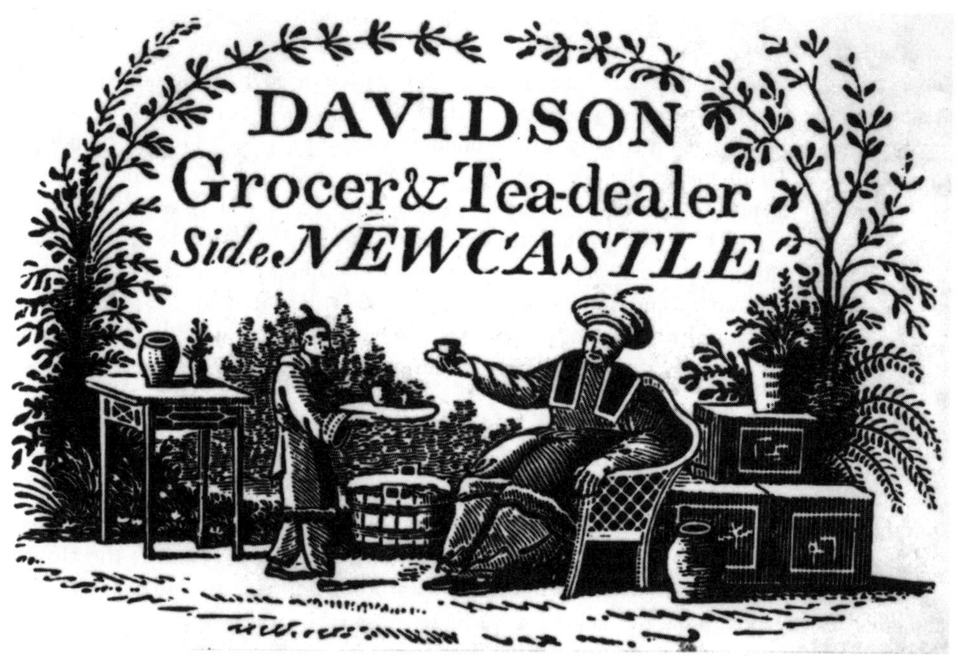

Figure 2.8 Label for Davidson Grocer & Tea-dealer, undated engraving. Reproduced courtesy of © Bettmann/Corbis.

mobile advertising carts. By the mid nineteenth century omnibuses carrying advertising were running through the streets, and buildings were adorned with adverts painted directly onto their surfaces (Wharton 2013: 59) or were covered and re-covered by 'bill stickers' working in teams and competing for available space to paste up their posters (Nevett 1982: 53–6). In the early nineteenth century posters were often pasted on any available surface. This led to a London act being passed in 1837 prohibiting this from happening.

Billboard advertising has developed rapidly in the last couple of decades. From a reliance on the technology of print and photography, outdoor advertising has become more varied in form. Billboards are characterized as front and rear illumination, rotating panels or digital multiadvertisement screens and have been joined on the roadside by ad shells (bus shelters with advertisements) and other forms of street furniture carrying advertisements. Screens have become more comparable in appearance and technology to television or cinema screens and widely used in town and city centres. This is, as we have seen, a similar development to that occurring in the nineteenth century when advertising increased in volume and spread. Artist and designer William Morris was concerned not just by the visual despoiling of towns and cities by excessive advertising but by the 'boards that are stuck about our fields' which come to 'disfigure rural scenery'. 'It is', he claimed in a speech of 1896, 'very piteous, whilst travelling along the railway, to see some pretty piece of scenery disfigured' (Morris 1896). Many similar disparaging comments can be heard today regarding the advertising trucks placed in fields alongside major roads that advertise a variety of goods.

Agencies, space and content

Technological developments such as printing, photography, etc were fundamental to the creation of modern advertising. However a further element was necessary to making advertising a central aspect of consumer capitalism: the creation of the advertising agency. Advertising agents had generally been around since the early 1800s performing basic media functions. The first UK advertising agency, Taylor and Newton, was operating in 1786 and by the close of the nineteenth century several hundred were operating in London (Hindley & Hindley 1972; McFall 2004). The first agencies were media-space dealers securing advertising space for their clients. At first agents secured newspaper space by selling it on and taking a cut of between 10 and 15 per cent. The later practice of 'farming' entailed the agent obtaining all the available advertising space in a newspaper and then selling it on at a higher rate. The agency's role in the advertising process was that of space brokerage, with the manufacturers and retailers producing their own copy. However, they had a further significance: providing local commercial knowledge and trade links for businesses (McFall 2004: 112).

Commodified space

The main function then of the first advertising agencies was to secure and deal in commodified space suitable for advertising. Something similar to the selling of advertising space in the newsprint media was also happening on the streets. Towards the close of the nineteenth century – in part as a result of statutory controls prohibiting the space available for fly posting – designated advertising hoardings were created with builders and property owners charging rent for their use.

The early-nineteenth-century advertising space brokers and the early-twentieth-century advertising agencies were the outcome of a rapidly developing economy based on industrial production. The factories that came to dominate the towns and cities of manufacturing areas symbolized the new organization of work and class relations. Capital and labour, new forms of machine production and the transportation of raw materials and commodities formed the basis of an industrial economy. The mass production of goods helped create mass markets producing commodities and consumption on a global scale. Advertising became a necessary aspect of consumption and a significant element of the developing mass media, creating new forms and transmissions of information, entertainment and social knowledge. Advertising became not only a necessary part of the economy but a very visible cultural presence.

Media, circulation and audience

From the nineteenth and in to the twentieth century advertising agencies came to provide a range of other services in addition to space brokerage. As the media expanded, even the simple function of buying and selling-on media space and time required a broader and more sophisticated level of knowledge. Advertising agencies needed to develop knowhow about circulation and how audiences could be transformed into potential customers for the advertised products.

Newspapers provided much of the media space for nineteenth-century advertising. Indeed the development of advertising is closely linked to that of the newsprint industry – from printing technology to taxes. In 1846, Charles Mitchell published the *Newspaper Press Directory*, 'a guide to advertisers in their selection of journals as mediums more particularly suitable for their announcements' (Gliserman 1969: 10). This was an early form of advertising guide informing and advising potential advertisers as to the circulation, price and political orientation of the papers. Mitchell's directory also included advice on advertising taxes, the law and copyright. In the late 1860s Mitchell's directory was extended to include an index of magazines and periodicals in addition to newspapers.

Newspaper and advertising taxes were progressively introduced during the eighteenth and nineteenth centuries and limited the operation of both the newsprint and advertising industries. However in 1853 the Advertising Tax was abolished and this was followed by the abolition of Stamp Duty on newspapers in 1855.

Full-service agencies

Advertising agencies took different forms, with some concentrating on space brokerage and others on other services (McFall 2004: 114). The 'full-service' agency supplying the various service functions of media planning, research and account management required to mount and direct a successful advertising campaign was in place by the 1920s. These agencies came to offer the advertiser the necessary means to produce an advertisement, and they became crucial not just to the selling of advertising space but to the creation of the advertisement itself. Copywriting is an important element of an advertisement and at that time the writing of the advertising text came to be offered as a free service. It was an inducement and enhancement of the newsprint space on offer. In addition, the agencies began to offer the services of illustrators and then photographers, forming the full 'creative' mechanism of personnel and skills for producing an advertisement. The visual language borrowed from painting, illustration and then photography and film became part of advertising. Artists and writers were quick to put themselves at the service of advertising, and advertisers were to borrow people, ideas and motifs from the arts.

Advertising came to be seen as a creative practice in its own right and the relation between culture and advertising production was strengthened (MacRury 2009a: 145–6; Wharton 2013). In addition to technical and creative skills, the advertising agencies added financial and research functions.

Advertising forms

It is important in our approach to the history of advertising to remember that each type or form of advertising such as television, radio, newsprint or Internet is dependent on the technology of the host medium. From the representation of products and creation of promotional methods to the voice, tone and mode of address, the adverts are shaped by the formal and representational methods of the medium in which they are being presented. The formal attributes of an advertisement such as shape, line, movement, colour, perspective, dimensionality and creation of narrative are attributes of the type of media that give space and time to the advertisement. For example, cinema uses a particular media technology to produce a moving image advertisement, whereas the printed poster advertisement of the billboards is a static one. Consequently these are two very different forms of advertising. Although technology is an enabling mechanism, it also limits the construction and presentation of the advertising message. The form an advertisement takes based on the host media technology is a factor in creating where the advertisement will be seen and the nature of its audience.

Increasingly retailers and advertisers choose from a wide range of possible advertising forms to promote and market their goods and services. The advertising industry has come to use specific terminology to differentiate between different advertising forms. 'Above the line advertising' refers to advertising forms such as television, cinema, radio and print. 'Below the line advertising' is composed of direct mail, retail and point-of-sales displays (Jefkins & Yadin 2000). Online advertising uses an evolving array of email systems, websites, networking and social media sites, including Facebook and Twitter, and search engines offering business services. These tend to blur the distinction between 'above' and 'below' advertising forms and have been termed by MacRury and others as 'through the line advertising', recognizing the importance of the Internet not just as the latest medium to provide advertising but as a potential 'confluence of all media' (Richards quoted in MacRury 2009a: 86). The development of digital technology in the last few decades has contributed to a huge growth in personal computing and expansion of the World Wide Web, as well as developments in telecommunications that gave rise to the notion of media convergence (Dwyer 2010). Media convergence involves the integration of the old into the new. What is known as old or traditional media is composed of radio, television, cinema, billboards, mobile or transit and the newsprint media of magazines, newspapers and directories. Each of these media forms was separate, having its own identity and mode of media delivery. Convergence alters the relationship between these existing technologies and forms. Convergence incorporates old media, which was in the main analogue, into digital 'new media'. New or digital media enables forms of advertising and marketing communication to be distributed through different technologies such as the Internet, mobile phones and tablets (Bainbridge 2013).

Radio, television and the Internet

The remainder of this chapter focuses on the development of three advertising forms: radio, television and the Internet.

Radio

The introduction of radio was an important marker in the development of broadcast media. The mid to late nineteenth century saw the development of the electric telegraph carrying coded text in the 1840s, followed by the telephone later in the century and then the radio telegraph. By the 1920s radio was established as a medium able to carry natural sound, including the human voice and music. In Britain, the British Broadcasting Corporation, created in 1922, became a state corporation in 1927 with a public service remit over the new medium. Radio in Britain was not deemed a suitable vehicle for advertising. Government committees tasked with the regulation of broadcasting chose the licence fee rather than advertising as a way of funding programmes. The newsprint industry, itself heavily dependent on advertising revenue and the foremost advertising platform at the time, lobbied against advertising going to radio. While the BBC developed its public service broadcasting tradition, radio in the US took a different route (Nevett 1982; Leiss *et al.* 2005; Street 2006). By the late 1920s advertising was established on American radio even though there were concerns about the practice from both politicians and advertisers alike. In 1922, the American secretary of state for commerce voiced concerns that the potential of radio to broadcast news, entertainment and education might be 'drowned in advertising chatter, or used for commercial purposes' (Gorman & McLean 2009: 74).

Nevertheless the formal and signifying elements of radio that came into being with its creation are worth considering as aspects of radio advertising. These are the qualities that make radio different to other mediums, such as the poster or cinema. These formal aspects are the enabling and limiting features of the technology – sound is obviously important here. Sound enables a different form of narrative; it tells its story over time while the visual narratives of paintings or photographs – both well used in advertising – are contained within the viewed moment of the frame. Sound – unlike in television advertising – is the only dimension in which the product can be promoted, whereas sound in the cinema or television advert is often used to draw the viewer back to the visual content of the advert. Yet sound – voice, music, scene-setting potential or simply the quality and aesthetic effect of sound in itself – has a greater independence from its means of transmission. Where the image, even in the era of the handheld, is contained by its screen or its specific place of projection, sound is autonomous from its mechanism and can travel across the space of a home in a way that the visual content of an advert cannot. It has a specific and more intimate 'mode of address' than other forms of media and advertising discourse. The sense of 'liveness' – the immediacy of listening in the broadcast moment – is an important element of any media broadcasting and is particularly pronounced in live radio broadcasting (Scannell 1996, 2009) In many ways radio's advertising message is more concentrated, contained within a single dimension and well suited to accompanying other activities. Heard from the household or car radio it can accompany the listener in a variety of tasks and across a range of distances in the way that visual and print media cannot. So in considering sound as a feature of radio broadcasting we must also consider the aesthetics, narrative structure and flow associated with sound (see Chapter 11).

US and UK radio and advertising

A history of advertising needs to take account of the wider context in which the advertising form developed. As McFall put it, the tendency has been to see the creation of modern advertising as an inevitable 'gradual, incremental evolutionary process' (2004: 98), 'but not as part of a journey to a preordained destination' (2004: 192). UK and US radio advertising developed quite differently. In the US, advertising by the late 1920s became a feature of radio as the networks of affiliated stations developed and regular programmes were established securing the audiences that advertisers could appeal to. Radio brought together the potential to combine commercial activity with entertainment and information in new ways. For example, advertisers provided radio 'talks' exploring issues relevant to their products with, for instance, Gillette sponsoring a discussion of facial hair fashion. Sponsorship took other forms and helped develop radio programming in such shows as those of Amos 'n' Andy, created in 1920s America. The early storyline followed the exploits of two farmworkers making their way to Chicago. Subsequent narratives were constructed around dialogues voiced by the same two actors playing multiple parts and creating several social 'types' and 'characters'. Each episode was preceded by a musical introduction and a spoken advertisement. In the summer of 1929 – the year the Great Depression, the twentieth century's economic downturn, began – the show's advert took the form of an announcement that 'improved' Pepsodent would give teeth a 'higher polish and brighter lustre'. In addition to commercial sponsorship other forms of advertising activity were cultivated in the early days of American radio. Products were referred to in drama and comedy and featured in programmes of live music and 'endorsed' by renowned radio personalities. 'Dramatized commercials' – adverts that took the form of mini dramas were produced (Gorman & McLean 2009: 74) and spot advertising became possible with the recording of live programmes and advertisements. Through the deployment of advanced production techniques these could be freed of live imperfections and replayed across different stations.

In the UK things were quite different. The BBC – funded by the licence fee – exercised exclusive control over radio broadcasting. This provided advertising-free programming and radio content independent of commercial influence and control. However commercial radio could still be received in the UK with stations such as Radio Luxembourg and Radio Normandy broadcasting English programmes from mainland Europe. By the 1960s these were joined by the 'pirate' radio stations that broadcast from ships anchored off the coast and therefore outside of British jurisdiction. Radio Caroline situated off the south coast and Radio 270 off the northeast coast were two of the many commercial stations creating a very different radio content to that of the BBC. Pirate programming created a continual stream of nonstop 24-hour pop music, jingles, adverts and, significantly, in the person of the disc jockey, a less formal style of presentation. Reception was enabled by the availability of cheap portable 'personalized' transistor radios and appealed primarily to young people. Listening to the illegal pirate radio became an aspect of teenage identity. 'Tranny [transistor radio] culture' became a signifier of independence from the parent culture. It also provided a targeted route for advertisers into a specific demographic sector and at the same time helped encourage a developing market-based youth culture. This is significant to an exploration of youth subcultures and countercultures and the ongoing debates about mass society and the entrenchment of consumer culture. In 1972 an Act of Parliament enabled independent commercial radio in the UK. The favoured radio advertising form became the spot ad with some programme sponsorship. For radio and other forms of commercial broadcasting the extent to which advertisers and sponsors shape the content and frame the listener's experience is part of a continuing debate (Metykova 2013).

Once developed the media tend to appear as if they are inevitable outcomes of history. The same to a certain extent is true of advertising, in part because it is heavily dependent on the media for transmission. However this is not necessarily so. There are always choices to be made. The different outcomes represented by commercial, advertising-dominated US radio and the non-commercial state provision of the BBC in the UK are good examples. McChesney makes the point that in the early days of radio there was substantial opposition 'to the network-dominated, advertising-subsidized US broadcasting system that emerged between 1928 and 1935' (2008: 158). However the emergence of this system had a profound effect on the entrenchment of advertising in everyday culture and its spread into 'every nook and cranny of American and, indeed, international life' (2008: 180). Monika Metykova among others (Curran 1998; Murdock 2004) has explored the relation between media and advertising and makes the important distinction between the interests of consumers and those of citizens (2013).

Television

Perhaps the most important twentieth-century development in media and advertising is that of television technology in the 1920s. The act of television viewing and the real and symbolic presence of the television apparatus in domestic space has changed and developed over time since the first regular British television broadcasts in 1936 and the first independent television channel began broadcasting advertisements in 1955. Turner and Tay refer to the early television set as 'the hearth of modernity' but recognize that 'television's family audience in the living room has now dispersed ... into the kitchen ... into the bedroom and finally out of the home altogether into the street and onto their mobiles' (2009: 2). Advertising was first seen on TV in the US in the early 1940s, and in Britain a second channel, ITV – not dependent on the licence fee but independent and commercial – was set up in 1954–5. The first British TV advert was in 1955, for Gibbs SR toothpaste; although it was in black and white, it was far removed from the Pepsodent advert delivered solely through the spoken word on American radio of the late 1920s.

By the late 1950s there were more households with television than those that relied solely on the radio for broadcast communication. Up until the 1980s British television had a single commercial channel. In 1982 a second advertising-carrying channel, Channel 4, was set up, and this was followed in 1986 by BSkyB being awarded a satellite franchise. Household time spent engaged with television and the acquisition and organization of its technological equipment, such as video recorders, cassettes, reception, licences, satellite and cable arrangements and subscriptions, became intrinsic elements of household and family expenditure, time and experience. The continuing spread and volume (numbers) of televisions in domestic space was noted by Anne Gray in the late 1980s: 'Many households had more than one television, but second sets were usually small black and white portables in the kitchen or one of the bedrooms, preference was for viewing on the main television set' (Gray 1992: 78). The continuing increase of sets and now other technologies that incorporate television-receiving screens per household results in the multiple penetrations of domestic space and domestic life by television and television advertising (Turner & Tay 2009; Marshall 2009). These pervade and combine with domestic activities and processes carried out in domestic space.

The amount, intensity and level of penetration of television advertising into the home is markedly different to outdoor advertising. Across the range of people in the UK over the age of 4 years, the average amount of time spent watching television amounted to 25 hours, with differences according to age and gender. The amount of time given over to television viewing in 1998 increased for both sexes according to age: under 20 hours per week for the under-15s to almost 40 hours per week for the over 65s. Television viewing might be more accurately described as exposure to the television set and its programmes and advertisements. Studies rarely measure the 'experience' of viewing in the sense of time duration and concentration or quality of viewing. The amount of advertising differs across the spread of commercial channels and according to the time and day of broadcast.

The television has become an object of immense significance in the contemporary home, with nearly 60 per cent of the 25 hours of television viewing time spent on commercial channels. Advertising comprises about 7–8 per cent of commercial-channel viewing time. Nevertheless the annual share of viewing for non-commercial British television in 1998 was 40.8 per cent, with the figure of 57.6 per cent representing the combined commercial, advertising-carrying companies of ITV, Channel 4, Channel 5 and Cable, satellite and RTE Ulster (BARB 2004). Satellite television was received by 13 per cent of households in 1998/99 in the United Kingdom, and Cable television was received by 9 per cent of households (Social Trends 2000). Both of these subscription television services join the Independent Television Channel in broadcasting commercial advertisements as part of their daily programming.

An indication of viewing numbers for advertising channels in 2012 can be gleaned from the Broadcasters Audience Research Board (BARB). The commercial channel ITV1 attracted between 6 and 8 million viewers for each episode of its popular soap *Coronation Street* in the week ending 28 May. This is comparable to similar viewing figures for a selection of BBC programmes, including its popular soap *Eastenders*. However, for television advertising the picture is more complex. As the number of commercial channels increases so does the assumed potential audience for commercial TV fragments (MacRury 2009a: 98–101). Fragmented and shifting audience-demographic profiles are encouraged by the number and type of screens that television advertising can be viewed on, for instance, PCs, laptops and tablets. This has been further complicated by an increase in the forms of transmission with the coming of cable and satellite. The nature of audiences is constantly changing and audience demographics is shifting as numerous providers compete for audiences who have greater channel choice. Subscription and pay-per-view options have changed the nature of the relation between programme providers and audiences. However advertising revenue remains the primary income source for commercial TV companies. As numerous providers compete for audiences, with greater channel choice, audience demographics and the changing nature of audiences are further complicated.

In many instances audiences no longer receive free commercial television viewing in exchange for being subject to a periodic string of advertisements. At the same time technology enabling the television viewer to filter out specific product advertisements or to eliminate advertising completely continues to advance. For instance, Spotify, a digital musical streaming system, enables music to be downloaded from a variety of sources and on payment of a subscription removes visual and aural advertising. There is perhaps an interesting paradox at play here: those who can afford to pay to remove adverts are likely to be those who the advertisers wish to attract.

Internet and digital advertising

This section looks at the rise of digital advertising and Internet technology. The impact of the Internet and World Wide Web has enabled advertisers to reach potential consumers in new ways, more quickly, and to target them more precisely. Many think that digital culture is giving rise to a new form of consumer culture organized around online advertising. Digital is a form of electronic media distinguishable from analogue and which 'works by the exchange of digital codes' (Bassey 2009). The first online advertisements appeared in the early 1990s on websites such as Hot Wired in the form of an uncomplicated banner style (Hollis 2005).

Digital advertising is associated with the idea of media convergence, which as discussed earlier involves the integration of old or traditional media such as television, radio, cinema and newsprint media into the new. Older or traditional advertising media forms were separate, having specific formal identities and technological modes of media delivery. Convergence alters the relationship between these existing technologies and forms and incorporates old, mainly analogue media as digital new media. This enables forms of advertising and marketing communication to be distributed through different technologies such as the Internet, mobile phone and gaming devices (Bainbridge 2013).

The flow of advertising across new media also forms a continual stream of online digital advertising such as pop-ups, email and spam that accompany new media content. Digital advertising takes many different forms and contents, and many argue that it is reshaping consumer culture. Some argue that more consumer choice and greater access to online information, often provided by other consumers and users of goods, leads to a more informed consumer culture. Others argue that the extent of Internet marketing and the colonizing of space and time by internet advertising activity is detrimental to culture and non-commercial cultural forms (Wharton 2013).

As Internet commercial culture increases and expands its different types of advertising forms are being categorized by writers on the subject (Austin *et al.* 2007; Reid 2013). Examples are display or banner advertising, which can create an interactive relationship with a user: a real-time connection in which further information is activated by opening up a URL (uniform resource locator) containing an advertising message. Email advertising, commonly known as 'spam', targets huge numbers of Internet users – whether they wish it or not. Viral advertising, sometimes known as buzz marketing, relies on audience engagement with advertising information and is passed on predominantly through email networks (Kasapi 2009); it can be seen as an electronic form of 'word of mouth'. A further example of Internet advertising is where search engines place paid-for advertising along with the results of the computer user's search for information. What search offers over most other forms of digital advertising is reach and its unique ability to connect with the consumer using contextual, behavioural and geo-targeting methods. Search also has the ability to contextualize information, targeting users with advertisements for products and services based on their consumer preferences. Similarly adware programs are used to analyse a computer user's Internet surfing habits. By discovering the type of goods and services that the user is likely to purchase, 'contextual ads' related to this information pop up periodically on the screen. In a similar vein, forms of Internet advertising deliver adverts to computer users based on their past search behaviour. 'Geo-targeting' methods deliver the content of a search to a consumer's specific physical locality and may include the actual street address, the ISP details or the IP address.

Internet consumer culture

Social media, such as Facebook and Twitter, are an important part of the outcome of technological development and plays a large part in the new consumer culture. Primarily used as a personal and private space, advertisers have had difficulty in utilizing it to market brands. Indeed the projection of advertising and marketing communication into that space can have a negative marketing effect. Users can resent the intrusion into social media space and this can be seen as the antithesis of social media.

Mobile technology is increasingly important to developments in advertising (Chapman 2013). A wide range of advertising and marketing communication is now delivered to mobiles, in the form of instant messaging, Bluetooth promotions, barcode scanner promotions, mobile apps and web-based digital marketing. Broadband enabled the Internet to deliver high-speed communication, and a similar advance has occurred in mobile phone technology with the development of high-speed wireless networks 3G and 4G. Mobile phones and smartphones, handhelds and laptops are constantly evolving and changing the way in which advertising makes approaches to the potential consumer, who can be reached wherever they are and whatever other activities they are engaged in (Media *Guardian* 2011). The significance of this lies not just in the fact that the technology is mobile but that user and potential consumer's mobility can be utilized for marketing purposes. The relationship between people and advertisements and between people and the goods they might wish to consume changes. It brings about a deepening of commercial consumer culture, with a spread that transcends boundaries.

This is of importance to out-of-home advertising, which describes not just outdoor advertising such as posters and billboards but also a range of advertising such as radio or Internet advertising when it is received outside of the home environment.

The relationship between the consumer, the economy and the commodities on offer has changed dramatically, with both globalization and technology playing significant parts. The impact of the Internet and World Wide Web has allowed advertisers to reach the consumer more quickly and more precisely. A new form of consumer culture has developed in which product information and shared consumer knowledge are central. Digital culture is becoming an important element of new cultural formulations, and online digi-ads are a significant aspect of this content. This is not only important to consumer culture, it is likely to have deep seated and perhaps as yet unknown ramifications for culture in general.

Conclusion

This chapter has offered a broad sweep of advertising development, including changes in the content of advertising over time, technological change and new forms of culture. It looked at some early forms of promotion and advertising from the ancient world. Examples were drawn from Rome, Pompeii and Ostia during the period of the Roman Empire. Advertising and promotional material were considered an important element of communication, and changes in technology considered important to this development. For instance, the introduction and expansion of printing based on movable type in the fifteenth century was seen to have a profound effect on communication, commerce and advertising. Further advancements in printing alongside the invention of photography in the early nineteenth century were important to newsprint advertising. The creation of the advertising agency and its expansion in the late nineteenth century and the scope and forms of promotion it enabled were further elements necessary in making advertising a central aspect of consumer capitalism. Radio, television and more recently the spread of Internet, digital and mobile technology in the twentieth and twenty-first centuries have created the parameters of contemporary advertising and a constantly developing consumer culture.

3 Market society and its critics

Introduction

This chapter explores the formation of a market society in Britain. Developed over several centuries, it had by the nineteenth century created a world quite distinct from that of previous eras (Spies-Butcher, Paton & Cahill 2012). Market societies are founded on market economies. Markets had been a feature of ancient and feudal societies in which goods were exchanged between producers and consumers. By the nineteenth century the intensity and centrality of markets, partly resulting from agrarian and industrial change, produced an economy which was to give rise to a different social order. As a consequence of this, new social and political relations were created and rapid and fundamental cultural change occurred. The mass production of goods was a significant feature of this economy, which in turn required the mass consumption of goods to complete the circle. New products gave rise to new forms of consumption, and advertising came to play an increasingly important part in the new economy. Changes in the form that advertising took, in part based on innovations and developments in media technology, ensued. Advertising became a part of cultural life, and we can recognize aspects of late-nineteenth-century advertising, promotion and marketing as important features of today's culture. The chapter highlights the use of trademarks, an early version of the logo, as an example of this. Drawn from a range of religious, artistic and mythological sources, trademarks, along with other branding imagery, became significant features of everyday culture and essential to a developing market and consumer society.

Market society was not without its critics. The work of Karl Marx is important to an explanation of the evolution and working of the economics of an industrial market society and its potential for social change. Matthew Arnold's criticism of mass society and culture was quite different but indicated the social concerns and fears apparent at the time. The chapter concludes with a look at the ideas of William Morris and explores his criticism of mass production and consumption.

From agrarian to industrial society

Fundamental agrarian and industrial change occurred in Britain between the seventeenth and nineteenth centuries. The agrarian revolution involved major improvements in agriculture and changes to agricultural production. This in turn gave rise to an increasingly pervasive industrial production centred in the factories and mills that came to dominate the expanding towns and cities especially in the north of Britain. A new organization of work, machine driven and time monitored, created the mass production of commodities, which in conjunction with other factors helped generate mass markets through which the goods were sold. The development of international trade and empire were important features of this.

Agricultural change

Several periods of agrarian change and development have occurred in different parts of the world and at different times in history. Our focus here is on what is usually referred to as the British agrarian revolution. Beginning in the seventeenth century, although some commentators suggest earlier, various scientific and technological developments resulted in an improvement in the productivity of the land and in the quality of livestock. Much improved crop rotation methods resulted in less land lying fallow and unproductive. It has been calculated that 20 per cent of arable land lay fallow in 1700, but by 1900 this had been reduced to 4 per cent (Overton 2012). In addition pasture was converted into arable land, creating land that yielded crops. The introduction of new agricultural equipment, such as threshing machines, and improvements to existing machinery, such as ploughs, increased both efficiency and yield. Through selective breeding, improvements in the quality of livestock resulted in greater quantities of meat. All in all the land in 1850 was more productive than in 1750. In 1750 the population of Britain was 5.7 million, with most people working on the land in what was still an agrarian economy. By 1850 the population had risen to 16.6 million with the number of people working in agriculture falling to 22 per cent of the population (Williamson 2002; Overton 2002).

In pre-capitalist, feudal Britain the household was the central social and economic unit of society, and most household members were engaged primarily in agricultural production. The household 'varied in size according to the wealth and standing of … occupants, but it was where people produced and consumed the necessities of life as well as raising and socialising children' (Spies-Butcher *et al.* 2012: 4). In many parts of Europe the typical peasant or labourer could be distinguished from his or her 'betters' through ownership or non-ownership of land and access to it. Under the feudal system the peasant spent a part of his time providing labour for the lord's estate or an equivalent such as the payment of taxes or tithes (Hobsbawm 1973). However the peasant also had the right to common land on which animals could be grazed and from which firewood could be gathered and wild food foraged. As feudalism broke down, the enclosure of common land as private property created exclusive land ownership and use rights for a minority. According to Eric Hobsbawm, from 1760 onwards 6 million acres of common land were turned into private property by the parliamentary enclosure acts (1973: 188). This gave rise to what he refers to as a 'capitalist agriculture' based on competition. In the process, land had been turned into a commodity and those who previously used the land as a right were now paid wages by landowners in exchange for their labour (Spies-Butcher *et al.* 2012). Some became part of the domestic system working in the home producing textiles as part of the household activity, often renting the machinery and selling on the product of their labour to a merchant class. Many unable to find work moved to the expanding urban centres, funded in part from the increased profits from agriculture, hoping to find work in the new found factories and mills.

Industrialism

Groundbreaking changes in agriculture were followed by similar developments in industrial production which were to contribute to the creation of a market society.

Dramatic scientific and technological breakthroughs are often emphasized in some historical accounts of the industrial revolution. Other histories stress the 'small scale invention and successive improvements and modifications to existing techniques' (Griffin 2010: 99). However the years between 1750 and 1850 would see the growth of industrial Britain. An important marker in this was James Watt's development of the steam engine in the 1760s and 1770s. It was based on Thomas Newcomen's earlier, but less efficient, machine, which had been used to pump water from mines. The steam engine came to replace animal and human sources of energy as well as windmills and waterwheels (Ashworth 2004). The cotton and iron industries became driven by steam, which relied on the burning of coal. In Shropshire, the Darby family developed iron ore smelting utilizing local coking coal, and Abraham Darby's Ironbridge at Coalbrookdale, erected in 1779, became the world's first bridge to be built of cast iron. The bridge spanning the River Severn became the symbol of the industrial revolution. A painting by Phillip de Loutherberg of 1801 depicts the Coalbrookdale valley, lit by the fires of the industrial furnaces and smoke from the chimneys drifting across what had previously been a romantic and pastoral landscape. This is similar in atmosphere to J.M.W. Turner's 'Fighting Temeraire' (1839) (see Figure 3.1 below), a painting characteristic of the period depicting the full-rigged sailing ship the Temeraire being towed to its final berth by a steam-powered tug.[1]

Figure 3.1 J.M.W. Turner, 'Fighting Temeraire', 1839; part of the Art Everywhere project, Newcastle upon Tyne, 2013. Photographed by the author.

Transport and urban life

Transport and travel became more efficient and extensive in the eighteenth and nineteenth centuries with the creation of canals and improvements to waterways, road systems and road surfaces (Ashworth 2004). Steam-powered locomotives running on iron rails steadily replaced horses pulling wagons over wooden rails. Stephenson's Rocket reached speeds of 30 miles per hour in 1829 and the space between long distant places appeared to recede. A ship driven by both sail and steam crossed the Atlantic in 1819. The transport of people, raw materials and finished goods for sale aided both production and the new markets. Often, goods were sold far from the place they were produced. Distance and times changed. The natural markers of shared time following daily and seasonal patterns were challenged by the newly imposed mechanical experience of factory life. Local variations in time gave way to the uniformity of Greenwich Mean Time used by the railway companies wherever they operated in the United Kingdom. As Anthony Howe has suggested: 'this period saw the most dramatic communications revolution before the Internet with canals, railways, steamships and the telegraph dramatically altering speed, time and distance' (Howe 2004: 23; Briggs & Burke 2005).

The new industrial period was marked by the migration of people from rural areas to urban centres with the growth of the major textile towns and industrial cities. Society according to Marx in 1848 was 'splitting up into two great hostile camps … the bourgeoisie and proletariat' replacing the earlier class differences of a feudal society (Marx 1935a: 23). In a market economy, the proletariat or working class had only its labour to sell and as 'hands' men, women and children were set to work in the harsh conditions of the new mechanized mills and factories of the cotton industry in and around Manchester. On the other side of the Pennines, Leeds and Sheffield grew as centres for cloth, coal and steel. Other places specialized in different forms of manufacture: Stoke for its pottery, Birmingham for metalwork and Clydeside for shipbuilding. The populations of Birmingham, Leeds, Sheffield and other cities increased enormously in the first two decades of the nineteenth century. In this period, for instance, the population of Manchester doubled in size (Griffin 2010: 57–8). Working-class people were not of course only confined to these rapidly expanding urban areas. Ports such as London, Hull, Bristol and Liverpool traded in raw materials and commodities destined for developing overseas markets. Large areas of the United Kingdom were given over to the mining of coal, notably Tyneside and Durham, south Wales and Scotland. Production of coal expanded across the nineteenth century with 115,000 employed in the industry in 1831 expanding to over 1 million in 1913 (Floud 1997: 133).

Working-class life

People worked long hours in atrocious working conditions. Across the span of the nineteenth century Parliament passed various Factories and Mines Acts that incrementally moderated the effects of unregulated capital, but generally living conditions in the cities were hazardous and unhealthy. Reflecting on his work *The Condition of the Working Class in England in 1844*, Frederick Engels talked of the 'filth, ruin, and uninhabitableness' of a Manchester he described as a 'Hell upon Earth'. Engels made clear that this was not a natural phenomenon: 'Everything which here arouses horror and indignation is of recent origin, belongs to the industrial epoch' (Engels 1892: 48–53).

Charles Dickens account of 'Coketown', the fictitious town at the heart of his novel *Hard Times* (1854), creates a vivid picture of a northern industrial town in the first half of the nineteenth century. It is worth quoting in some detail:

> It was a town of machinery and tall chimneys, out of which interminable serpents of smoke trailed themselves for ever and ever, and never got uncoiled. It had a black canal in it, and a river that ran purple with ill smelling dye, and vast piles of building full of windows where there was a rattling and a trembling all day long, and where the piston of the steam-engine worked monotonously up and down like the head of an elephant in a state of melancholy madness. It contained several large streets all very like one another, and many small streets still more like one another, inhabited by people equally like one another, who all went in and out at the same hours, with the same sound upon the same pavements, to do the same work, and to whom everyday was the same as yesterday and tomorrow, and every year the counterpart of the last and the next.
>
> (Dickens 1854: 24).

These are powerful descriptions of the living and working conditions associated with industrial production that framed the lives, homes and working spaces of the industrial proletariat. Capitalism also created a further difficulty: the problem of overproduction when more commodities were being produced than could be sold and consumed. It constantly needed to find new markets. Capitalism was developing in other countries but with major differences between European and non-European economies. The leading European countries, including Britain, Portugal, Spain, France, Germany and the Netherlands, over time established colonies around the world, notably in Asia, Africa and the Americas.

Empire and markets

In 1792, the British Empire was made up of 26 colonies; by 1815 this had expanded to 42. At the close of the nineteenth century, the Empire had steadily grown in size and power to become the dominant global force. By the outbreak of the First World War in 1914 the empire covered a fifth of the world's landmass and nearly a quarter of the globe's population (Peers 2004). Empire was important in many ways to nineteenth-century Britain and its economy. It enabled the acquisition of natural resources to facilitate production at home, established profitable places to invest overseas and secured trade through the creation of new markets. It was also important to the spread of industrial techniques and machinery around the world. Indeed Britain was often described as 'the workshop of the world', but as Howe has suggested it 'was also the warehouse, banking hall, shipping agency and insurance office of the world' (2004: 25). Through the agricultural and industrial revolutions England had been transformed from an economy and culture based on peasant farming and self-sufficient communities into an 'industrialised market society and world capitalist power dominating international trade and colonial expansion' (Spies-Butcher *et al.* 2012). This was secured by the establishment of trade but also through coercive and violent means on both land and at sea. It was according to Peers 'an empire that made frequent appeals to ideals of political and legal liberty': for example, Britain was important in the abolition of the slave trade, 'yet depended ultimately on coercion and the suspension of such principles' (2004: 54).[2] The British Empire's economic, military, political and cultural power and position was challenged by other countries, notably the US and Germany, and the wars that ensued in the twentieth century were in part an outcome of its expansion.

World of commodities

Many of the commodities for sale in Britain's shops and markets were produced from raw materials secured from the colonies: 'the soaps which came out of Port Sunlight were from West African palm oil ... Calcutta jute fed the mills of Dundee, the electrical industry as well as the bicycle and later automobile manufacturers turned to Malaya for rubber' (Peers 2004: 68). Mass, factory production made goods cheaper and more widely available. This was given a huge boost at the turn of the nineteenth century by the introduction of the Fordist assembly-line model of production using Taylorist techniques of labour and workplace organization to produce standardized goods. As we have seen, mass distribution using the transport systems of railways, waterways and roads, either created or refined in the industrial period, brought many people new products and services. Department stores began to appear in European and American cities in the nineteenth century. For instance, Le Bon Marché, which opened in Paris in 1852, displayed a wide selection of merchandise offered at fixed prices. The first British branch of the popular American store Woolworth's opened in Liverpool in 1909. Woolworth's offered customers a more direct consumer experience. They were able to select and handle goods without the intercession of sales staff. This changed the relationship between merchandise and purchaser. The self-service supermarkets, discount and cash 'n' carry stores were to follow later towards the latter part of the twentieth century (Strasser 2009). Shopping as a significant social experience became a central and increasingly ubiquitous experience of living in a market society. Even at the turn of the nineteenth century, the volume, range and variety of commodities on offer would have been beyond the imagination of previous generations.

New products and services transformed people's lives: 'gas, electricity, running water, prepared foods, ready-made clothes and factory-made furniture and utensils' changed the domestic and consumer experience (Strasser 2009: 27). Products once produced locally, on a small scale for local consumption, were now produced in industrial quantities and sold on national markets. The developing soap industry is a good example, with soap starting to be produced on a mass scale in the late eighteenth century. Pears accompanied soap production with a range of advertising campaigns to help popularize their products. Similarly with the Lever brothers, William and James, soap advertising became an important form of promotion creating new ways to sell products. Pears' early advertising juxtaposed clean well-scrubbed babies with the famous bar of brown soap and its distinctive lettering. Pears's later advertisement using Millais's acclaimed painting 'Bubbles' featured a dreamy child blowing soap bubbles in the direction of the heavens and made a new connection between the product and other aspects of culture, in this case 'high art' (see Plate 4). This gives an indication of the cross-cultural connections being made between products, advertising and other cultural forms. The advertising effect was generally connected with potential consumer expectations of the benefits and uses of the product. In the case of the soap bar this was an old product being marketed in new ways.

It was of course a very different matter to advertise and sell a totally new product, such as the newly invented automobile. A 'car' was something about which people had little knowledge or experience and the product's potential personal and social effect was underdeveloped. An advert appearing in *Life* magazine in 1908, the year that the first 'affordable' Ford car came off the assembly line, enclosed its advertising text within a decorative frame formed from classical style columns in the fashionable art and design style of Art Nouveau. Natural forms in the shape of trees emerge from column capitals placed on either side of a model stationery car. This newest of products, here acquainted with the latest style in design, was offered for sale alongside a clumsy implication of the outdoors, countryside and escape from the city. The product, like the genre of car advertising, was still in its infancy.

Advertising agencies

Working lives, routines and experiences had changed dramatically with the development of an industrial market society. For those able to afford the abundance of new products and services, life changed in other ways. Less time and labour were spent on making home-produced goods, which were being replaced with shop-bought items. Becoming a consumer entailed a different way of thinking about and considering goods. The advertising industry adopted an intermediary role between production and consumption. As an aspect of consumer culture it informed potential consumers about products. It also provided a market mechanism feeding back information about preferences and patterns of consumption to the companies that produced the goods. Advertising became a necessary aspect of consumption and a significant element of the developing mass media of newsprint, photography, cinema and eventually radio and television. This created new forms and transmissions of information, entertainment and social knowledge about products and patterns of consumption. As part of the rapidly expanding mass media advertising became a very visible presence in people's lives, creating new ways of seeing commodities. Soap bars could be linked to high art, cars to the latest in design motifs. On behalf of consumer capitalism advertising created not only wants but altered perceptions of needs, fashioned new views of specific products which took on meanings far removed from their use value and brought organized consumption close to the centre of social life.

Advertising agencies, which were taking on a more elaborate and creative role, became central to making goods desirable and accommodating them to people's lives. At the same time that goods, both everyday and luxury products, became more plentiful, available and affordable, they came to be marketed in new ways. Branding and trademarks became a recognizable and significant aspect of market society, borrowing ideas, motifs and images from a variety of cultural strands: fine art, mythology and popular culture. Culture became linked to commodities. The branding of goods became part of the sales tactics of the late nineteenth century and many of today's familiar brands such as Bovril, Coca-Cola and Martini were transformed from plain products into brands in the nineteenth century. Significantly this involved packaging – a necessity when transporting goods over distances – being made more distinctive, using recognizable typefaces and creating memorable imagery and slogans. In many ways this was an extension of the naming of products and the trademarking of goods. The distinctive lettering and red triangle of the beer brewing company Bass (Figure 3.2) was the first trademark to be registered in the UK in 1876.

Trademarks and early brands

A common feature of the British public house, a bottle of Bass pale ale, displaying its distinctive red triangle trademark, features alongside champagne bottles and a glass bowl of mandarins in Edouard Manet's famous painting 'A Bar at the Folies Bergère' (see Plate 5). The painting was first shown at the Paris Salon in 1882 and the bottle of beer with its identifiable trademark is one of the features of the painting, creating for its first audiences a sense of naturalism with clear reference to elements of their own contemporary consumer culture. The bottle and other objects that appear on the bar were painted in Manet's studio as a series of still-life sketches and then combined into an overall composition (Bareau 1986). It is a painting that alludes to the contemporary culture of the 1880s and shows the barmaid Suzanne at work and others at leisure. It depicts a Parisian café concert with music, trapeze acts and other elements of popular culture. One of its features is the arrangement of mirrors and reflections and the figure of the barmaid is isolated in her work space and surrounded by her wares. It is an enigmatic painting – not least because of the figure of the man, wearing a top hat and black coat, shown to one side. Suzanne's precise place in the painting and her role as a serving girl has generated different understandings of the painting (Clark 2000). Manet's painting, an example of the rich tradition of nineteenth century French art, has become one of the most celebrated paintings of the period. Manet was considered a leading painter of modern life, creating a realism through his technique and choice of subject matter. The inclusion of the red triangle of the Bass trademark in the painting is important, signifying for its early audiences the present and the everyday.

Samson, the rope makers, provides a further example of a registered trademark (Figure 3.3). Registered with the US government in 1884, the mark featured a depiction of the biblical character Samson wrestling with a lion. The image refers to the tale from the seventh book of the Hebrew Bible and Christian Old Testament where Samson journeys to secure a marriage. In the vineyards of Timnath he encounters the lion, 'a young lion roared against him' (Judges 14:6), and Samson struggling with the beast kills it with his bare hands: he 'rent him as he would have rent a kid and he had nothing in his hand' (Judges 14:14). Biblical stories and images were part of a culture still very much dependent on a shared religious background, which provided a wealth of images and symbols that could be utilized for commercial purposes because of their familiarity. In this case the story of Samson provided an apt symbol of effortless strength for a company operating in the rope-making business and wanting to create a trademark as a form of branding. In the history of culture, Samson is sometimes compared to the Greek mythological character Heracles, sharing a propensity for strength and endurance. Heracles (Hercules in Roman culture) was known for his appetite and pride and is represented in paintings and sculpture carrying a club and wearing a lion skin with the head still attached. A trademark on bags of cement sold in modern-day Greece by the cement company Heracles depicts the bearded face of the hero wearing his lion skin (Figure 3.4).

The story of Samson, drawn from its biblical context and associated with trademarks and advertising brand design, gets retold as part of a visual, popular culture of everyday packaging. In the story Samson returns to find the carcass of the lion he has killed barehanded. He discovers that a swarm of bees have nested in the carcass, producing honey. The story becomes part of a riddle Samson tells at the wedding feast: 'Out of the eater came forth meat and out of the strong came forth sweetness' (Judges 14:14). The last part of the riddle became the text to appear alongside the distinctive green-and-gold design of Lyle's Golden Syrup, which in 1885 started to be sold in cans (Figure 3.5) rather than the casks from which it had been previously dispensed. This reminds us of the importance of packaging not just as a means of containing the commodity, but also as a means of presenting and branding commodities.

Figure 3.2 Bottle of Bass beer. Photographed by the author.

Figure 3.3 Samson trademark. Reproduced courtesy of Samson Rope Technologies Inc.

Figure 3.4 An illustrated image of Heracles, who is featured in the logo for Heracles General Cement Company. Illustration by Vanessa Maughan.

Critics of industrialism and market society

As we have seen, the industrial process beginning in the second half of the eighteenth century fundamentally changed the face of Britain. In the nineteenth century, economic historian and social reformer Arnold Toynbee made popular the term 'industrial revolution' to describe this change. Eric Hobsbawm in the late 1960s was to suggest that 'no change in human life since the invention of agriculture, metallurgy and towns in the New Stone Age has been so profound as the coming of industrialism' (1999 [1968]: xx). The 'change in human life' involved not only people and the wider sense of the economic and social order but the environment. The concentration of manufacturing in cities such as Manchester and Sheffield, the industrialization of rivers like the Tyne and Tees and the cutting of canals and railways across the country transformed the landscape. For many, the nature of work changed as people moved from the countryside into the industrial towns and cities where factory working hours were long and working and living conditions harsh. Arnold Toynbee (1852–83) and other social reformers encouraged the formation of trade unions and cooperatives to represent and serve working people. Robert Owen (1771–1858) was instrumental in the cooperative movement and in creating harmonious working communities based on utopian socialist ideals. Owen was a social reformer agitating for state intervention in regulating working practices. Over the period of the nineteenth century the state progressively intervened, introducing various factory

Figure 3.5 Lyle's Golden Syrup. Photographed by the author.

acts intended to alleviate the harshness of industrial production. The year 1833 marked the beginning of factory inspection, with the working day for under 18s limited to 12 hours and under 13s to 9 hours. Children under 9 could not be employed. By 1847 women and children were limited to 10 hours work per day. This was at first applied to the textile industry and by 1878 limitations were applied to all industries. These and other social reforms eased the harsh working conditions of an industrial society in which human relations were largely expressed in terms of the cash nexus. Market society had helped shape revolutionary forms of production; it had also created new forms of goods and new ways of selling them. All this was not without its critics.

Karl Marx

Most commentators on the nineteenth century acknowledge the critical contribution of Karl Marx (1818–83) to an understanding of the economy and the kind of society and culture that it gave rise to. This is true in a wide range of areas of study, from the political sciences to the arts and culture, including advertising studies. The publication of *The Communist Manifesto* in 1848 offered not only an analysis of the rapid expansion of capitalism and the increased exploitation of the working class but placed this within a historical framework. Furthermore it suggested that future social change would emerge from the antagonism that occurred between capital and labour, between capitalists and workers.

For Marx, history was to be understood as a series of conflicts between different classes of people: 'The history of all hitherto existing societies is the history of class struggles' (1935a: 22). He emphasized how the economy was structured and created different social groups or classes. The two main groups were organized around the economy with a split between those who owned the means of production and those who did not. They had their own particular economic interests that often conflicted. The main struggle that was developing in the nineteenth century centred on resources and how these were distributed. It was also about political power and political rights. The bourgeoisie or ruling class owned most of the resources that provided the materials and the means of production, such as the factories and machinery from which the commodities were produced. The proletariat or working class had only its labour to sell. It produced the commodities and then bought them back with the wages earned. In the process, surplus value was created which was creamed off by the capitalist. Furthermore capitalism was prone to crisis involving overproduction and underconsumption (Fine & Saad-Filho 2004). It expanded rapidly through capital accumulation, but this was likely to be followed by decline in which the poorest suffered the most. Today we refer to this as 'boom and bust'. By and large people were constrained by history and background – people were able to make choices but these were limited. As Marx put it, people 'make their own history but not in the circumstances of their own choosing' (Marx 1935b: 116).

Marx outlines at the outset of *Capital* the working of the system in terms of political economy, describing the wealth of societies as being 'an immense accumulation of commodities'. Marx was keen to explore the production and significance of the commodity to a market society. This has had an enduring importance not only to the analysis of commodities but to an analysis of advertising, which became an important feature of the developing consumer society (Williamson 1978; McFall 2004). Commodities are goods or services at the centre of a market society. Made for profit and exchanged for an agreed price, they have value. 'Use value' is the term that describes the significance the item has in its use: its satisfaction of needs. For instance, a bread loaf is produced from flour, yeast, water and other ingredients, worked into a dough, baked in an oven, and its use value is that of food. Similarly, a chair cut, crafted and assembled from wood has a use value as an item of furniture and functions as a seat. The bread loaf and the chair may function in other ways, for instance providing aesthetic or gastronomic pleasure, however this can be independent of their 'exchange value'. Exchange value is the equivalent monetary value that an item fetches when it is exchanged on a market. This means that the value of a bread loaf or several bread loaves can be compared to that of a chair. However the appearance of goods in a marketplace or their symbolic representation as monetary value disguises the labour that produced them and the nature and conditions of that production. This is what Marx referred to as 'commodity fetishism' – the commodity is given an elevation and significance beyond that of the people and the processes that created it. In Marx's view, according to McFall (2004: 37), 'people make a fetish out of commodities when they see values as inherent in objects, rather than as the result of human actions' (Leiss *et al.* 2005: 252; Odih 2010: 73; Spies-Butcher *et al.* 2012: 32)

Furthermore in Marx's account of a capitalist economy and its workings, human labour is characterized as being alienated. People produce commodities and goods but not directly for their own needs. Through the process of exchange the labour that created the product is itself turned into a commodity. Work is not a pleasure in itself satisfying the workers needs, but becomes, through exchange value, a means towards an end. In this sense the worker becomes alienated from the mode of production. In advanced capitalist production work became highly repetitive and specific, with the worker losing sight of the raw materials from which the commodity was produced and with the overall process of manufacture itself. The end result of labour was largely known in its status as a commodity rather that as an outcome of productive labour (Slater 2008 [1997]: 106).

For Marx the worker is alienated from his or her labour and also from the satisfaction of real needs. Advertising is inherently linked to this process because it is closely involved in the process of exchange and commodification. At an early stage in its development, advertising provided essential information about the sale of commodities. As market society develops into a mass consumer society, advertising takes on a special significance. Needs are increased: as Marx put it, 'the expansion of needs becomes the inventive and ever calculating slave of human, refined, unnatural and imaginary appetites – for private property does not know how to transform crude need into human need. Its idealism is fantasy, caprice and infatuation' (Marx quoted in Slater 2008 [1997]: 110). Advertising is central to providing the visual appearance of a way of life inherent in a consumer society. Advertisements saturate public and private space in volume and frequency. In this argument, advertising overdetermines the significance of commodities in the consumer society and at the same time distorts reality, masking real social experiences with a consumer haze of unattainable plenty. It is for Marxists a very potent form of false consciousness.

The economy and the way in which goods are produced shapes the wider social and cultural life of people. The 'mode of production of material life', as Marx put it, 'conditions the general character of social, political and intellectual processes of life' (Marx 1978 [1859]). This aspect of Marx's explanation is usually referred to as the base/superstructure debate. The economic base is composed of the forces of production (which includes raw materials, the skills and labour of the workers and the technology and tools required) and the relations of production (class positions of workers and bosses). This influences, and in some interpretations determines, the superstructure, which involves such things as education, politics, religion, arts, culture and media, including advertising.

This concern with advertising's power through its language and ideas has persisted into the twenty-first century. Marxism – of which there are many variants – provided the most potent analysis of industrial capitalism and its cultural manifestations, including advertising. Based as it is on a particular understanding of history, the early work of Marx interprets capitalism as a specific stage in history based on a particular mode of production (Marx 1935a).

The recognition of the importance of advertising is not just about the production of material things, such as the manufacture of household goods or of today's ubiquitous car, or about how they are promoted and distributed through markets. Nor is it solely about the economic or social and political consequences that flow from this production. Needless to say, all this is important and informs our study of advertising and these themes constantly recur in subsequent chapters of this book. The study of advertising is also about how it fits into a way of life that is shaped by a particular economy and the social relations that flow from this: capital and labour; employers and employees; producers and consumers. Since the demise of the Soviet bloc in the late 1980s and the 'actually existing socialisms' this particular economic form appears as a taken-for-granted aspect of modern or postmodern life. However, with the recent and continuing global recession, and the reactions against it – from traditionally organized trades unions to newly created and more loosely organized critics, such as the global Occupy movement, the Spanish Indignados and UK Uncut – the acceptance of the dominant form of capitalist economic and social life no longer goes unchallenged.

Matthew Arnold

Matthew Arnold's response to the upheaval of industrialism, the new economy and the society it gave rise to has been both influential and contentious (Collini 2000). Arnold (1822–88) was a poet and a literary and cultural critic who published regularly in the periodicals of his day. Arnold was what was considered at the time 'a man of letters' and although he wrote extensively on political, religious and literary matters he was not the originator of a theoretical system of thought in the sense that Marx was to become. However, his observations and social criticism are important to an understanding of the developing Victorian market society and his ideas continue to have significance to the study of culture. Arnold's name is today usually associated with the 'culture and civilization' tradition of cultural thought and debate, which continued into the twentieth century through the work of F.R. Leavis and Denys Thompson (Giddings 1986; Collini 1994).

In 1869, Arnold brought together previously published essays to form the basis of the book *Culture and Anarchy*. It offered a critique of a post-feudal 'commercial society' as well as a response to the squalid conditions of industrialism, created through the widespread factory system. We have noted the reforms in working hours and conditions passed by Parliament, and these were in many ways a response to political agitation by the working classes and middle-class reformers. Working people were organizing themselves into trades unions and the politics of the early nineteenth century was marked by the Chartist campaign calling for universal suffrage and reform of Parliament. *Culture and Anarchy* was published amid these political and social tensions. The Reform Act of 1867, preceded by intense political agitation and riots and mobilization of troops in London in the previous year, extended the franchise to the urban male working class. In the following year 1868, the Trades Union Congress (TUC) was formed.

Although the main critical thread of *Culture and Anarchy* is neither economic nor predominately sociological, Arnold characterizes mid-nineteenth-century society as three social groups: the aristocracy – he termed the 'Barbarians' – were no longer capable of providing leadership; the middle class – termed the 'Philistines' – were unfit for government because of their worship of machinery and money; and lastly a 'general Populace' composed of working people whose behaviour was perceived as becoming increasingly unruly. Arnold's answer to this problem was 'culture', a body of knowledge understood as 'the best that has been thought and said in the world'. He famously described this as 'sweetness and light' (Storey 1998: 8). This was something to be attained in the pursuit of social harmony and would be 'the great help out of our present difficulties' (Storey 1998: 7). The present difficulties were generally to be understood as the consequences of industrialism and in particular the social and political unrest associated with the male urban working class.

The 'anarchy' of the title of Arnold's book refers to popular culture – that is, to the lived experience and culture of the working classes, which he referred to as the 'raw and uncultivated masses'. The anarchy that Arnold perceived in the world he inhabited was a result of a lack of social leadership but also appears to have been triggered by attempts by working people to improve their own circumstances. Arnold's answer to this, according to Robert Giddings, lay in 'creating a cultivated elite … an aristocracy of the enlightened; supported by a cultivated bourgeoisie; followed by an obedient proletariat' (1986: 20). For culture critic John Storey, Arnold's conception was of a culture intended to 'police the unruly forces of mass society' in which 'the main concern is social order, social authority, won through cultural subordination and deference' (Storey 2009: 21). A call to culture was a response to the social fractures and problems created by industrialism and market society. Ultimately, culture, for Arnold, was a means to maintain social order. Notwithstanding Arnold's stated elitist conviction that 'knowledge and truth in the full sense of the words, are not attainable by the great mass of the human race', culture was also about education and improvement.

According to Stefan Collini, Arnold's take on culture gave recognition to an 'ideal of human life, a standard of excellence … aesthetic, intellectual and moral' rather than culture in general or in the broader sense of a way of life of a people or a social group (Collini 1994: 85). Culture 'as the best that can thought and said in the world' became apparent in the nineteenth century with the provision of new cultural resources, organizations and institutions. From the opening in the 1850s of the British Museum, a showcase for Britain's store of historical objects housed in a purpose built neo-classical building, to the creation of the Victoria and Albert Museum, dedicated to improvements in design and design education: Arnold's notion of culture was put on display. The creation of art galleries, theatres and circulating libraries can be seen as features of a culture based on the 'best that can be thought and said'. This might have had an improving cultural quality but was for many far removed from the everyday experience of working-class life at work or at home.

Arnold's was a conservative response to the developing popular culture of the nineteenth century. For working-class people this was shaped around two areas of experience: first, industrialism, the forms of work and conditions of employment that had been created by it and the political response to it organized through trades unions, political clubs, cooperatives and friendly societies; second, a developing commercial culture that increasingly placed packaged, branded commodities and the places where they were sold within the cultural experience of working people. This was accompanied by a growing commercialization of leisure made possible by an incremental reduction in working hours, an increase in 'free time' and a rise in income. Traditional rural recreations associated with 'feast days and holydays had been marked by pastimes such as ploughing contests, wakes, cockfights and football' associated with rural living gave way to more modern forms (Croll 2004: 397). There was for example a growth in working men's clubs, public houses, music halls, excursions to the seaside alongside the races and fairs (Jones 1974). At one level these events and activities needed to be advertised to attract the required level of participation and at another level they were to become incorporated into the consumer society and the culture of the twentieth century.

William Morris

William Morris (1834–96) is remembered today as a proponent of craft guilds and hand production and against machines, factories and mass production. He was a champion of worker's rights and social justice, and an advocate of enjoyment in art for all people. Morris, like Marx, recognized that the problems of nineteenth-century society were to do with the economy, the nature of production and distribution of wealth. Morris was keen that workers organized themselves through trades unions, making demands on government and employers for fair pay and decent working and living conditions. As we have seen in this chapter, government measures such as factory acts limiting the working week and health and safety legislation improving conditions in mills, mines, factories and workshops were introduced incrementally. Similarly, in the field of political representation workers and their socialist and liberal allies in the middle classes agitated for and eventually achieved universal suffrage. The Chartist movement in the early nineteenth century was important to this campaigning to extend the franchise, as were the Suffragettes in the early twentieth century. William Morris provided a political vision, sometimes labelled 'utopian socialist', that went much further than this. In *News from Nowhere* he imagined life and work based on pleasure and produced through creativity and cooperation.

William Morris is often presented as a contradictory figure – a romantic, socialist and idealist on the one hand and a producer of luxury goods for an upper-class elite on the other. However, interest in and knowledge of arts and culture together with concerns for social well-being and political emancipation are central to Morris as a designer and craftsman, theorist and social commentator. According to E.P. Thompson, 'Morris was not just interested in the quality of art products – but in the manner in which these are made and in the people who made them' (1996: 104).

William Morris together with fellow arts and crafts workers established Morris & Co., a decorative arts business producing furniture, woodwork, fabrics, carpets and stained glass in the 1860s. It was born out of a desire to reinvigorate hand-craft production in reaction to poorly designed, mass-produced goods churned out of factories across Britain at the time. The business provided him with an opportunity to develop his philosophy and practice – to improve the quality of designed objects and the lives of people, both as producers and consumers.

The Great Exhibition

The Great Exhibition of 1851 was conceived as a showcase to celebrate industrial production. It was held in a huge iron-and-glass structure built specifically for the occasion in London's Hyde Park and became known as the Crystal Palace. Although proclaimed a huge success in terms of the revenue it generated and the numbers of people who visited, it was less than enthusiastically received by a number of art and design critics. A scrutiny of the vast array of objects on show identified stylistic incoherence and decline in design standards, inappropriate use of materials, decoration and ornamentation. With the seemingly never-ending innovations in technology and mechanized production, manufacturers believed novelty and ornamentation added value to mass-produced goods and increased profits. An over-reliance on pattern books and little or no understanding of design principles resulted in poorly designed and shoddily made goods leaving the factories heading for the expanding domestic middle-class market. It is against this backdrop that Morris developed his aesthetic, social and political ideas linking design reform with social and political emancipation.

For Morris and his arts and crafts proponents, the alienating effects experienced by factory workers in their daily toil as machine operatives were reflected in the poor quality goods made, advertised and offered for sale to the rapidly expanding middle-class consumer market. As we have seen in Chapter 2 Morris was unhappy with widespread, large-scale advertising, which he considered was spoiling not only the urban but also the rural landscape. Indeed the last public address he made before his death in 1896 was to this effect, delivered to the Society for Checking the Abuses of Public Advertising in London. Nevertheless, he acknowledged the necessity of promotion to the success of Morris & Co., even suggesting that 'beauty is a marketable quality' (Harvey, Press & Maclean 2011: 256).

Useful work

Alienation, as Marx had explained it, was for Morris inherent in the making of factory-produced goods and was also transferred as a form of alienated consumption.

By using high-quality materials and hand-craft production techniques, Morris & Co. goods were costly and labour intensive to produce and by comparison with factory-made goods expensive to buy. Mass-market production with its focus on high turnover and novelty turned consumption into the mere acquisition of goods rather than the thoughtful purchase of things both beautiful and durable – principles at the heart of Morris's practice. In Morris's essay 'Useful Work v. Useless Toil', he clearly identifies the damaging effects of industrial capitalism upon the social relations of production and consumption: 'But think ... of the product of England, the workshop of the world, and will you not be bewildered, as I am, at the thought of the mass of things which no sane man could desire, but which our useless toil makes – and sells?' (Morris 2008 [1888]: 8).

Morris associated luxury with the quality of his products rather than their cost. However, the company's initial success was dependent upon private commissions and the patronage of an economic, social and cultural elite, and it was with some irritation that Morris acknowledges that his success was in part due to having to '[minister] to the swinish luxury of the rich' (Morris quoted in MacCarthy 1995: 210). Yet Morris provided a bespoke personal service to clients – particularly those who were investing in the furnishing or refurbishment of newly acquired or newly built country homes – often resulting in a considerable financial outlay. If Morris & Co. were operating today, the products would be marketed at the luxury-goods end of the interior design market.

By the mid-1870s Morris & Co. had achieved a level of commercial success that enabled it to move to larger premises in Oxford Street. With more space Morris was able to showcase and sell an expanded and more affordable range of standardized products, such as his famous 'Sussex' chairs, which could be purchased by a discerning but less wealthy middle-class consumer. Contrary to popular opinion, Morris was not totally anti-machine: he made use of machinery and mechanized processes for the larger scale production of carpets at the Merton Abbey works. Intelligent use of machinery could increase production without losing the essence of the craft process. Merton Abbey workshop production was different to large-scale commercial practice in that Morris's workers were craftsmen and women, treated as equals and involved in the whole process. From the late 1870s Morris delivered a series of lectures examining the relationship between art and society in which he reinforces the view that art created from a society based on profit produces bad design. 'I don't want art for a few any more than education for a few, or freedom for a few ... what business have we with art at all unless all can share it' (2008 [1888]: 85).

Morris saw art and by extension design not as an elitist pursuit to be practiced by a select few but as vital to all human creativity and development, 'the expression by man of his pleasure in labour' (Morris quoted in Naylor 2004: 149). Even in the humblest of homes good and worthwhile design could be found in everyday objects if 'made by the people for the people as a happiness for the maker and the user' (Morris quoted in Naylor 2004: 150). Morris's design philosophy, of hand-craft production, truth to materials and pleasure for the maker and user was intrinsic to his campaign for social justice and a fair economic system. As a producer of high-quality expensive goods in a capitalist market system, Morris recognized the contradiction of his own position. Both his philosophy and his practice proposed an alternative to the mass market where socialist ideas and practices could help make a society in which people could enjoy freedom and, not least, become creative beings.

Conclusion

This chapter has outlined agrarian and industrial developments occurring in Britain which contributed to the creation of a market society in the nineteenth century. This involved pronounced social and economic change altering the working lives of people in the new circumstance of industrial production. It involved new patterns of work, transportation and the creation of urban centres. From this arose a breadth of new social, cultural and political relations and experiences that constituted a market society. At the centre of this economy was the mass production of commodities, which were bought and sold according to market mechanisms. The mass consumption of goods, like the changes in production techniques, also came to have a profound effect on the way people lived their lives. Many new kinds of products became available. The exchange of goods on a mass market was accompanied by changes in advertising practice and in the appearance of advertising. New media forms developing in the nineteenth century assisted this and provided new channels for the delivery of advertising. Advertising agencies used trademarks and brands as marketing tools, and these along with the proliferation and visibility of advertising became a central part of a developing consumer society and culture. But the market economy of the nineteenth century was not without its critics. Arnold with his concern for culture and order, Marx's political economy and Morris's concerns about the nature of art and craft and the value of its products and life in general were among the many critics of the market society. Responses to industrial, market society and to its nineteenth-century critics can still be heard today.

Notes

1 Turner's painting is shown here represented on a billboard as part of the 2013 Art Everywhere project, which placed images of popular works of art on advertising billboards and electronic panels across Britain. This one appeared opposite the Laing Art Gallery in Newcastle upon Tyne.

2 At the beginning of the century slavery had been an important source of wealth. Although the revolutionary government of France abolished slavery in 1794, it was later restored by the Consulate in 1802. In 1803 Denmark prohibited slave trading. Britain passed Acts of Parliament in 1807 and 1833 to outlaw and abolish it in most parts of the Empire, and France followed suit in 1848.

4 Political economy approaches to advertising

Jonathan Hardy

Introduction

Advertising is a pervasive sensory presence, a major textual genre, a controversial source of imagery and cultural meanings, and a prominent selling mechanism for corporate capitalism. Critical scholarship addresses all these features but it is another key aspect of advertising that has been the focus of the political economy tradition that this chapter explores. As a source of finance to fund media, advertising has a tremendous influence on the nature of the content and services made available.

Critical political economy approaches to media developed from the 1960s in the context of a broad resurgence of radical politics (Wasko 2004: 312–13). Political economists tend to share and amplify critiques of advertising as the leading ideological agency for capitalism, for its role in promoting consumerism and possessive individualism and for its regressive, stereotypical representations of gendered, racial and other identities. But critical political economy (hereafter CPE) researchers developed a more distinctive contribution by addressing how advertising finance as a major source of media funding influences media content, media provision and access to communications. This chapter traces both 'classic' and 'contemporary' approaches to advertising within the political economy tradition. In doing so it seeks to outline key arguments but also to contribute to identifying the revision and renewal of this radical tradition and to invite an assessment of its value and contemporary relevance.

Political economy is concerned with how resources are organized in societies and examines 'the social relations, particularly power relations, that mutually constitute the production, distribution and consumption of resources, including communication resources' (Mosco 2009: 24). Critical political economy generally refers to approaches that place emphasis on the unequal distribution of power in society and are critical of arrangements whereby such inequalities are sustained and reproduced. In media and communication studies, critical political economy approaches developed from the 1970s and form a distinctive subfield characterized by a central claim: that different ways of organizing and financing communications have implications for the range and nature of media content and the ways in which these are consumed and used (Murdock & Golding 2005; Hardy 2010b, 2014). Recognizing that the goods produced by the media industries are at once economic and cultural, this approach calls for attention to the interplay between the symbolic and economic dimensions of the production of meaning. One direction of enquiry leads from media production to meaning making and consumption, but another considers the relationship of media and communication systems to wider forces and processes in society. CPE approaches are not reliant on any particular concepts in exploring these relationships;

rather, the ongoing justification for CPE rests on the quality and salience of its analysis of *problems* in communication and social systems.

A political economy of advertising explores advertising's funding, production, distribution and regulation. This requires study of 'economic' dimensions – how advertising and media sectors function in the production, circulation and consumption of goods and services – 'political' dimensions – how marketing and communications are organized and regulated – and 'symbolic' dimensions – meaning and ideology – to explore the contribution of advertising to the production of meanings, social relations and material practices. These can be distinguished analytically but are bound together in material processes of promotion (McFall 2004). They are also powerfully linked, for instance in the environmental consequences arising from both messages promoting consumption and the material impact of energy-intensive, waste-generating promotional industries (McAllister & West 2013). Advertising has been examined as part of a system of communications that 'engineers consumption to match production and reproduces the ideological system that supports the prevailing status quo' (Faraone 2011: 189). The advertising industry 'involves two interconnected systems of activity that are crucial to Western society', systems of ideology and of media support (Turow & McAllister 2009: 2).

Critical political economy approaches to advertising

The Western CPE tradition asks what role advertising plays within capitalism. The answers given have reflected debates between different tendencies in Marxism, notably in the relative influence given to economics and culture in explaining advertising. To summarize, a tradition of Marxist economic analysis was challenged and revised by influences from critical sociology and cultural Marxism in the 1980s. The subsequent decline of Marxist influence and the ascent of postmodernist and culturalist analyses led to a relative neglect of political economy. Yet there has been a resurgence and revitalization of political economy analysis in the last decade, reflecting renewed concern about the organization, practices and influence of marketing and media businesses.

For various Marxist analysts advertising is a necessary component of modern capitalism whose main function is to stimulate and manage consumer demand in order to increase profits from the sale of goods and services. Baran and Sweezy (1966) examined how companies invest in the 'sales effort' to stimulate demand to keep pace with mass production:

> The function of advertising, perhaps its dominant function today, thus becomes that of waging, on behalf of the producers and sellers of consumer goods, a relentless war against saving and in favour of consumption. And the principal means of carrying out this task are to induce changes in fashion, create new wants, set new standards of status, enforce new norms of propriety.
>
> (1966: 128)

Capitalism's inbuilt drive to overproduction, they argued, required advertising to create demand. Advertising expenditure contributes to the creation of 'monopoly capitalism', whereby a handful of large firms dominate supply in markets. The huge investments made in marketing and promotion act as cost barriers making it more difficult for competitor suppliers to enter the same market. The costs of attaining brand recognition may exceed the resources of smaller firms 'effectively barring them from the market' (Gandy 1982: 630), making branding a 'bulwark of market power' (Sinclair 2011: 210).

Baran and Sweezy's work influenced later generations of political economists. According to Herman and McChesney (1997: 21), 'Advertising and product variation became primary competitive weapons of corporations in place of cut-throat price competition to protect and expand market share'. In oligopolistic markets, where a few firms dominate supply, firms tend to produce similar products and sell them at similar prices. Advertising is undertaken to promote brand values, brand differentiation and brand recognition. Advertising serves as 'a major way to increase or protect market share without engaging in destructive profit-damaging price competition' (McChesney 2013: 42; see also McChesney 2008). With increasing ad clutter, there are intensifying pressures to 'cut through' and extend advertising into new spaces and activities, sustaining advertising as a powerful and pervasive cultural force (McChesney 2013: 41–6).

A great strength of the political economy tradition is that it examines promotion in the service of power and explores how advertising for commercial interests influences media content, encourages acquisitive individualism and promotes a set of values and beliefs about society that amount to 'commercial propaganda' for neoliberal capitalism. However, critical scholarship must avoid offering a totalistic account. For instance, McChesney *et al.* (2011) argue that the 'typical economic unit' of today is the giant corporation and the advertising they discuss is in the service of such firms. Yet this is only one kind of advertising, however dominant and pervasive it may be. Advertising and promotion takes a great many forms and serves different interests across businesses, civil society organizations, groups and individuals. This matters if we are to move beyond overgeneralized condemnations of the *advertising system* to examine the nature and diversity of marketing activities, the detailed political economy of advertising finance and the dynamics of (hyper)commercialization. For instance, the shift of ad spending from local newspapers to the Internet impacted on housing, cars and classified advertising, not (trans)national brand advertising for major corporations.[1] The imbrication of promotional communications into social media involves small firm advertising and diverse forms of promotion (and self-promotion) beyond major brand advertising. The alignments between giant corporations, oligopolistic markets, advertising on their behalf and commercial media influence are very strong but advertisers, markets and media comprise greater heterogeneity than can be reduced to a simple formula describing an *advertising system*.

For Baran and Sweezy advertising served an economic function for manufacturers in creating demand for products, and achieved this through psychological manipulation. Later political economists considered this explanation unsatisfactory, on various grounds. For Dallas Smythe it neglected the commodity production of advertising, media and audiences (see below; Caraway 2011: 695–6). Others criticized Baran and Sweezy for concentrating on the economic dimensions of advertising to the detriment of cultural aspects. The latter was explored by a Western Marxist tradition that included the work of Frankfurt School theorists Theodor Adorno and Max Horkheimer (1997 [1944]). In this tradition, Wolfgang Haug (1986) argued that capitalist accumulation requires the ongoing production and promotion of new wants, packaged and sold to consumers using 'commodity aesthetics', which served to integrate individuals into consumer capitalism. However Haug's theory of ideological manipulation, in what he termed the 'distraction industry' and 'illusion industry', was subsequently criticized as too limited in explaining consumer behavior and commodity gratification (Harms & Kellner 1990).

As Mattelart (1989) explains, the concept of manipulation fell into disfavour in place of a cultural anthropology of use, focusing on the ethnographic examination of actual consumers and their engagements with goods and meanings in everyday life (Certeau 1984).

Other concepts that had informed a generalized Marxian (Marxist-based) critique of advertising were challenged, including that of dominant ideology (Curran 2002b), ideological manipulation and 'false' needs. Marxian critique was weakened and marginalized, but what fell most out of favour was arguably least defensible: critiques of the social function of advertising that were both too narrow and overgeneralized. In its place, critical political analysis provided better explanations derived from studies of the historical development of advertising and consumer cultures, the structures and practices of the advertising industries, regulation and the relationships between media and advertising. Some of the deficiencies of general critiques of the *advertising system* were addressed by analyses of the *advertising industry*, exploring the corporate organization of marketing communications, and of *advertising work*, examining the practices and reflexivity of practitioners. Another area of focus has been the *governance and regulation of advertising*, where CPE scholars have emphasized both the importance of public regulation setting limits on advertising and the efforts of organized lobbying by marketers, marketing agencies and commercial media to extend commercial speech rights and the 'right to advertise'. The fifth main area of analysis has been the *relationship between media and advertising*. Advertising has been an important source of finance for media, influencing media content, the activities and behaviour of media firms and shaping what kinds of communication services are provided.

Historical studies and approaches

The interrelationships between businesses, media, advertising agencies and consumers have been a key focus for CPE scholars. Stuart and Elizabeth Ewen explore the development of modern advertising industries, images and techniques, the birth of consumer society and of the new doctrine of consumptionism in 1920s America (Ewen 2001; Ewen & Ewen 1982; and Ewen 1988). In order to launch new mass-production methods and counter the social conflicts which accompanied them, consumption was presented as the natural expression of democracy, with advertising constructing the domestic family as target for mass-produced consumer goods. Critical scholars have examined such issues as the dramatic rise in marketing to children, including across entertainment media (Kline 1993; Schor 2004), and the extension of commodification into areas formerly governed by non-commercial, public-good values such as libraries, public spaces and universities (Schiller 1989; Klein 2010).

Political economy of advertising industries and practices

There are many aspects of advertising we may choose to investigate but in order to examine marketing practices in any given context we need to attend to the organization and regulation of the businesses involved. The various promotional industries have experienced the same core processes of corporate reorganization that have occurred across media businesses and more generally throughout advanced economies (Turow 2010, 2011). These include processes of corporate growth, conglomeration, globalization, convergence and digitalization (Croteau & Hoynes 2006; Hesmondhalgh 2013). Advertising agency growth accompanied that of transnational corporations and their expansion into foreign markets. The global growth of advertising after 1945 in turn fuelled the expansion of commercial media (Herman & McChesney 1997: 21–2).

There were strong links between US and UK advertising agencies in the early twentieth century but US agencies began to expand their operations overseas in earnest after 1945. The 1980s saw an intensification of growth and consolidation in the global advertising industry (Herman & McChesney 1997: 39). There was a drive among major advertisers to consolidate their advertising accounts, with agencies reorganizing to match the needs of transnational corporations (TNCs). By the early 1990s, seven major global advertising holding companies dominated, with a second tier of large firms dominating continental regions and a third tier of national and subnational firms. Today, four major global groups dominate: WPP Group (British), Interpublic Group (US), Omnicom Group (US) and Publicis (France), the latter two sought a merger in 2013 to create the largest marketing agency before abandoning plans in 2014. These giant holding companies acquired leading national agencies and own transnational advertising agencies (TNAAs), media buying and market research organizations. Over the last five years, advertising growth has shifted from recessionary western economies to developing markets, with China's rapidly expanding advertising market now third largest after the United States and Japan, although the four holding companies exercise considerable influence over highly consolidated, global markets (Sinclair 2011: 32–37). At the level of advertising firms there have been de-convergence as well as convergence trends. The mid-twentieth-century 'full service agency' model has proved unwieldy, with the separation and consolidation of media buying and more recent pressures to provide boutique specialist services for social media and digital marketing (Nixon 2011)

Political economists insist on the need to examine interrelationships between marketing agencies, big business and corporate media. This connects to the wider theme of media and advertising relationships explored below. There has been increasing corporate integration across the sectors, with both media conglomerates and new digital giants like Google building up acquisitions across communications and marketing businesses. Another aspect is the representation of major advertiser interests on the boards of media companies. The tobacco giant Phillip Morris, for instance, held seats on News Corporation's board, while Rupert Murdoch remained on their board for 12 years. Pfizer, the pharmaceutical giant, had directors on the boards of Time Warner, Viacom and Dow Jones. Such corporate interlocking indicates the 'continuing symbiotic relationship between news, advertisers, and advertising' (Bettig & Hall 2012: 165; Bagdikian 2004). The ways in which executive boards influence operations and editorial decisions require specific, situated analysis, as the corporate integration of advertising and media raises profound issues for democracy, media and culture. The communications businesses that promote corporate capitalism and carry out lobbying and public relations, as well as advertising, of behalf of their clients and themselves also influence the political system in other ways, including funding political parties (Mullen 2013: 181). Marketing communications TNCs such as Aegis, Omnicom, WPP, Havas and Interpublic colonize media and political systems across the word (Sussman 2011).

Advertising work

Over the last 40 years of critical writing on advertising, studies of advertisements have predominated. Critical political economists have insisted that such advertising texts should be examined in relation to their conditions and contexts of production. The CPE contribution has thus often combined, to varying degrees, analysis of corporate structures, regulation, marketing strategies and activities with ideology critique of marketing communications messages. This leaves out detailed examination of how actual users/consumers interact with and take meaning from advertisements. The charge of 'reading off' audience responses is a long-standing and important one, but the focus on 'production' is defensible provided it is pursued with recognition of the explanatory limits of such selective analysis. A more damaging critique has been that 'production' too has been read off, through the neglect of a close examination of the work and behaviour of marketers themselves. Nava (1997: 37) rightly identifies a tendency in critical studies of 'theoretical neglect of the production and consumption of advertisements as products in themselves'. The critical stance taken towards marketing practices has reinforced tendencies to neglect engagement with marketing practitioners, work processes and arrangements but it is vital that these are reincorporated. The contribution of critical political economy towards the study of media work, including advertising work, has been limited (Hesmondhalgh 2010) but is growing and is making good some of the gaps and deficiencies criticized. For instance, Sivulka (2009) examines women working in advertising, Turow (2011) uses interviews with practitioners and published data to examine online marketing practices, while various edited collections bring critical perspectives to studies of marketing work and practice (Powell *et al.* 2009; McAllister & West 2013).

Media and advertising

The most distinctive contribution of critical political economy analysis of advertising, I wish to argue, examines the implications of advertising finance for media communications. Advertising is most visible and pervasive as a significant part of the total content and output of media. Advertising is also one of the main means of support for commercial media. There are critical concerns about the amount of advertising carried in media, the placement of advertising, invasiveness and reach, but a core focus of critique concerns the influence of advertising on non-advertising media content. Privately owned commercial media that depend on advertising revenue must compete for advertiser attention and must serve advertiser interests if they are to prosper, argue CPE critics (Herman & McChesney 1997: 6–7). This section traces some classical perspectives and issues before considering how far changing conditions require these to be revised.

The audience as commodity

One of the pioneers of the critical political economy of communications, Dallas Smythe, established a distinctive theory of media and advertising focused on the creation of audiences as commodities (1977, 1981). Critical research, he argued, had been too focused on media content and ideological effects and should address its 'blindspot', the economic role of mass media in advanced capitalism. The primary function of media is to create audiences for sale to capitalist advertisers. Media content, entertainment and news, is the 'free lunch' used to recruit potential members of the audience and to maintain their attention (Smythe 1977: 5):

> The appropriateness of the analogy to the free lunch in the old-time saloon or cocktail bar is manifest: the free lunch consists of materials which whet the prospective audience members' appetites and thus (1) attract and keep them attending to the programme, newspaper or magazine and (2) cultivate a mood conducive to favourable reaction to the explicit and implicit advertisers' messages.

The audience commodity is sold by media to advertisers for a profit. Here Smythe draws on the Marxist labour theory of value and applies it to audience 'work': the profit is derived from the surplus value created by audience 'labour'. Audiences 'work' to produce themselves as the audience commodity, they 'learn to buy particular "brands" of consumer goods, and to spend their income accordingly' (Smythe 1977: 6). Audiences 'work to market ... things to themselves' (Smythe 1981: 4); they 'self-market' (Jhally 1990: 67). In addition, Smythe argued, audiences work in their 'leisure' time to reproduce their own labour power (by relaxing and replenishing energy).

Mattelart (1989: 203) praises Smythe for offering 'one of the first analyses of the organic link between advertising and the way the media function'. Smythe's work inspired and influenced North American political economy analysis and debates (Jhally 1990; Meehan 1993), but was criticized by contemporaries on various grounds. For Smythe, the production and sale of commodity audiences is the core purpose of mass media industries, so by focusing on the production of media meanings, researchers were investigating 'secondary effects' at best (Meehan 1993). This 'blindspot' argument was challenged by Graham Murdock (Murdock 1978), who argued in favour of a cultural materialist tradition, influenced by western Marxism and Raymond Williams in particular, which emphasized that cultural products are at once both economic and symbolic and that critical analysis needed to be responsive to both dimensions. Smythe took free-to-air (FTA) ad-financed television as paradigmatic of mass media. This was drastically narrow, argued Murdock, it failed to apply to sectors where revenue is collected from consumers with minimal dependence on advertising revenue, including cinema, music, comics and books. It did not apply to ad-free public service media, such as the BBC. In response Smythe (1978) highlighted commercial interdependencies and cross-marketing across cultural content industries, and asserted that 'their apparent independence is illusory within the monopoly capitalist system'. Yet the various forms of capitalization across the cultural industries, ad-dependence and commodification processes all matter for analysis, since they influence what kinds of content and services are provided and to whom. The 'blindspot' essay also remains trapped in a functionalist logic to describe a system regarded as functional, necessary and 'successful'. The result is an overly smooth account whereby audiences 'complete' the marketing effort by absorbing advertising messages and then purchasing the goods advertised; the 'main function of the mass media ... is to produce audiences prepared to be dutiful consumers' (Smythe 1994: 250). Later analysts stress the risks and uncertainties of advertising effectiveness that occur at each point from placement, reaching target prospects, through to the impact and persuasiveness of commercial messages.

The audience commodity concept has been critiqued but also modified and developed. Jhally (1990: 72–3) argues that the time purchased by advertisers is 'communications-defined time': 'Media sell *potential* audience-power, but the only thing they can guarantee is the *watching activity* of the audience'. Audience watching time is a form of labour, and exploitation, since watching generates profits to broadcasters from advertising revenue; in Marxist terms, surplus value is expropriated from labour by capital. Jhally acknowledges the argument that characterizing watching as 'labour' is problematic since watching television does not have the characteristics of expended effort, compulsion and exploitation found in wage labour. However, he contends that watching activity is indeed compelled and thus an alienated activity. Others object that watching TV has no wage equivalent, not least since audiences cannot convert the 'salary' received (Fuchs 2012). What might have remained an increasingly arcane debate on the applicability of Marxist labour theory to audience activity has been revived and revitalized in efforts to examine the audience as commodity, and free labour, in contemporary studies of digital media (below).

Another body of research starts from the observation that what marketers purchase is usually *estimated* audience time, constructed through ratings. For Eileen Meehan

(1993: 386), the 'naturalistic assumption' of the audience in Smythe's work 'deflected attention from research into the effects of market pressures on corporate definitions of the commodity audience and commercial measures of audience preferences'. The commodity audience was not natural but manufactured, and analysts should distinguish between the audience as valued and constructed for measurement and the actual audience. Meehan's work (1993, 2002, 2005) examines ratings as a commodity in a highly monopolistic industry dominated by firms such as the Nielsen Corporation in the US. 'Ratings are commodities – products designed to meet the unified demands of buyers' (Meehan 2005: 117–18). She describes interdependent markets for consumers, ratings and programmes that shape business decisions, as distinct from the interests of viewers in their totality. This informs a broader critique of the equation of media supply with consumer demand (Meehan 2005).

Feminist political economists, exploring the relationships between capitalism, gender and class, have examined the construction of the female audience in US radio and television (Meehan & Riordan 2002; Stole 2003). Meehan (2002: 216) describes how the most highly prized commodity audience in postwar US network television was upscale white men, aged 18–34; channels that lost this ratings contest chased 'niche' audiences (women, children, African Americans or Hispanic Americans). Into the 1980s, women remained marginalized as a niche audience despite their influence over domestic consumption and their growing economic equality with men, an outcome reflecting 'the sexism of patriarchy as surely as overvaluing upscale audiences reflects the classism of capitalism' (Meehan 2002: 220).

Many media continue to operate in what economists call a 'dual product market', selling goods ('content') to consumers but also selling media audiences to advertisers (Doyle 2002: 12). This has several important implications, most notably that advertising-financed media respond to advertisers' demands, not simply to consumer demand. This crucial dimension is ignored or downplayed by those who equate 'free markets' with consumer sovereignty or regard media provision as the expression of popular demand. Commercial media do not necessarily give the people what they want; they give what is profitable to provide. Further, they give what the advertising system will support. This classic critique is relevant for ad-financed, 'free' social media whose economic model has affinities with FTA commercial television. The critique needs updating, however, as what is provided is not media content so much as services or software for user communication and (co)creation.

Digital media and 'free' labour

Smythe's audience commodity concept has renewed relevance in contemporary CPE studies of digital media. Many social media services are free to use, but provide platforms for advertising and monetize user's profiles and activity by selling these to marketers. If Smythe alludes to the adage 'there's no such thing as a free lunch', his work resonates with a contemporary adage, 'if you are getting the service for free then you are the product that is being sold' (Pariser 2011; McChesney 2013). The activities of users in building social media profiles, uploading pictures, creating content and communicating can be regarded as work to create an audience commodity that is sold to advertisers. Yet, as Fuchs (2012: 711) highlights:

> The difference between the audience commodity on traditional mass media and on the Internet is that in the latter case the users are also content producers, there is

> user-generated content, the users engage in permanent creative activity, communication, community building and content-production. ... Due to the permanent activity of the recipients and their status as prosumers [producer-consumers], we can say that in the case of corporate social media the audience commodity is an Internet prosumer commodity.

Terranova (2000: 33) analyses the 'free labour' involved in internet activities from content creation to reading and communication; drawing on autonomist Marxist conceptions of immaterial labour, she describes this as 'simultaneously voluntarily given and unwaged, enjoyed and exploited'. Fuchs applies Marxian concepts of labour, value and exploitation in his analysis of the Internet prosumer commodity. Social media time is 'work time' (Fuchs 2012: 72), a form of exploited labour where the surplus value is created by labour but accrued by capital (corporations such as Facebook).

The audience commodity concept fuses two propositions, one of which is largely accepted and the other hugely contentious. The accepted proposition is that audiences are 'sold' to advertisers. No longer reliant on estimations of the audience by ratings agencies, digital media transactions are increasingly based on selling an individual's profile based on their actual behaviour. Here the audience becomes a commodity in the literal sense of a product that is bought and sold; marketers purchase access to individual users, through real-time bidding and micropayments, in order to solicit their attention with marketing messages. Behavioural advertising is based on web-browsing activity conducted over a period of time, while contextual advertising is allied to particular content viewed online and includes retargeting, when advertising is delivered based on website content that a user has just viewed (Internet Advertising Bureau 2009). In behavioural advertising the audience is a commodity that is sold to marketers. Yet instead of the aggregated, imprecise 'audience' of cost-per-thousand targeting, now the commodity is a selective profile of an individual user for which behavioural advertising opportunities are sold.

The contentious proposition concerns audience labour. Caraway (2011) argues this offers an unpalatably passive, fatalistic account of audience agency and neglects working-class resistance and contestation. That may be so, but issues of control remain central. For instance, digital users remain mostly unaware of behavioural advertising as corporations have lobbied successfully for automatic opt in mechanisms to be applied, so 'to suggest users are willing collaborators in their own subjection is a difficult position to maintain in this particular regard' (McStay 2011: 316; Turow 2011). As Mosco (2009: 138) argues, the analogy of audience activity and the labour process is useful because it highlights issues of control and contestation: 'the audience exercises power, but also like labour, it is power circumscribed within terms largely set by capital'. Yet others object to the ethical as well as analytical implications of applying Marxian labour theory to relatively unconstrained and voluntary leisure activities. Comparing my social media usage to labour exploitation risks flattening important distinctions in information capitalism, from the Congolese workers mining Coltan for mobile phones to the health-sapping conditions for many thousands of Chinese workers producing high-tech gadgets. While some call for an expansive concept of labour, attentive to unpaid domestic work (Jhally 1990; Fuchs 2012), critiques risk disparaging voluntary activities and non-commodified 'gift' exchanges (Hesmondhalgh 2010). Another criticism is that claims of exploitation lack sufficient regard for the value and benefits to users of digital services. They do not describe the totality of user engagement with social media nor encompass the competencies involved in navigating 'free' services and benefits, albeit in structurally disadvantaged ways. Yet, for a critical study of advertising, the concept of Internet prosumer *commodification* addresses key aspects of advertising processes. CPE scholars highlight the realization of value by the businesses supplying digital services from the unpaid activities of users. In doing so they advance a critique of a much more incontrovertible aspect of the 'audience commodity' process: the creation of value by monetizing users' activities by selling data and access to marketers.

The evolving business models for commercial social media firms like Facebook involve the generation of income from marketers based on connections to the communications activity, time spend, as well as content produced by users (Turow 2011). Information about users' uploaded data, social networks, their interests, demographic data, their browsing and interaction behaviour is sold to the advertisers as a commodity in increasingly sophisticated ways. These include forms of programmatic (automated) buying including real-time bidding, where digital advertising opportunities are auctioned off in milliseconds through algorithm-driven computer trading, enabling advertisers to reach web users as they browse or smartphone users based on their current location.

Facebook's business model is principally based on advertising finance, although it makes some revenue from games and apps. Facebook offers advertisers targeted advertising based on 'demographic factors such as location, age, gender, education, work history and the interests people have chosen to share on Facebook'. A corporate spokesperson told a BBC reporter (Cellan-Jones 2012):

> Facebook offers the most targeted advertising of any medium. If your business is selling alloy wheels in Manchester, then you can deliver your adverts to men aged 20–30 who live within 10 miles of the city and like *Top Gear* and *Max Power*.

In 2011 Facebook introduced so-called sponsored stories, whereby marketers can purchase 'stories' created when someone likes or comments on a page, and send these to other people who are either friends of the person or connected to the page. Sponsored stories have been described as a way in which Facebook 'turns users into spokespeople for companies and products in ads that are broadcast to their friends' (Hill 2012). In October 2012 Facebook offered $20 million to settle a class action privacy lawsuit challenging the legality of sponsored stories, offering up to $10 each to nearly 125 million users. Previously in 2009, Facebook paid $9.5 million to charities to settle another class action on privacy concerning Beacon, the company's short-lived sharing of users' purchases that caused a storm of protest. In June 2013 Facebook announced a streamlining of its ad products, reducing the 13 types of sponsored stories available as a standalone product and instead directing advertisers to buy one ad format based on the richest social context available (Advertising Age 2013).

For Mosco (2009: 137) Smythe's audience commodity concept must be updated for digital systems 'which measure and monitor precisely each information transaction' representing 'a major refinement in the commodification of viewers over the earlier system of delivering mass audiences'. Andrejevic (2012) identifies exploitation as arising from the work of being watched. Audiences trade personal information for customized offers and in doing so provide an invaluable source of labour in the form of market research. The capacity for such economic monitoring has increased enormously and with it the power imbalance between businesses who control systems of economic surveillance and ordinary audience members/users. On platforms like Google or Facebook 'monitoring becomes an integral component of the online value chain both for sites that rely upon direct payment and for user-generated content sites that rely upon indirect payment (advertising)' so that 'user activity is redoubled on commercial platforms in the form of productive information about user activity' (Andrejevic 2012: 84). There is a further, important aspect. The value of users to advertisers is not a product of their online activities as such, but of their economic worth as prospective buyers. To the analysis of free labour we need to add the analysis of targeting and profiling and the socially divisive consequences of marketers dividing people into targets and waste (Turow 2011).

Advertising influences on media

To fully understand media we need to understand how media content and services are financed and paid for. A rich tradition of CPE work on media finance and advertising shares with mainstream media economics a concern to examine the resources for media firms, matters of growing importance and complexity given the proliferation of modes of delivery and consumption of digital content. However, CPE analysis goes beyond a narrow concern with profitability or promotional effectiveness to consider the spectrum of advertising influence. We can begin by asking what is the level of economic dependence by media on advertising finance. We can ask this question historically to trace the development of commercial mass media, and ask it in relation to media sectors, businesses, types of products and specific media vehicles. In broad outline, revenues from advertising represent 50–60 per cent of income for magazines, up to 80 per cent for newspapers and 100 percent for FTA commercial radio and television broadcasters (Bagdikian 2004: 230; Bettig & Hall 2012).

Media dependence on advertising can be exploited by advertisers to secure favourable conditions such as discounted pricing. However advertisers also intervene to influence editorial content, as numerous studies have shown (Soley 2002). Bagdikian (2004) cites testimony from advertisers on setting conditions to control the programme content in which their marketing communications, sponsorship or brands appear. Tobacco companies used their influence as heavy advertisers to curtail media discussion of the health effects of smoking. Procter & Gamble prohibited programmes 'which could in any way further the concept of business as cold, ruthless, and lacking all sentiment or spiritual motivation' (cited in Herman & McChesney 1997: 7).

Instrumental and structural explanations

There have been two main alternative explanations of advertiser influence. *Instrumentalist* explanations focus on the intentional actions and behaviour of actors (people owning, working for or in some other way involved in promoting advertising interests) in seeking to control communications. These may range from efforts to affect specific communications, actions to influence the editorial environment, efforts to influence the broader orientation of media vehicles and their allocation of resources to tell stories and reach particular audiences. However, other critical scholars argue that the influence of advertising on media is better understood as an impersonal force. These offer a *structural* explanation. Curran describes how advertisers in nineteenth-century Britain refused to place advertisements in radical newspapers on political grounds. But his argument is that the main way in which advertising influenced British media from the early twentieth century was not through such deliberate acts of control or political censorship. Advertising operates as an 'impersonal force'; the cumulative decisions of advertisers seeking the most cost-effective vehicles to reach target consumers creates a source of finance that is unevenly distributed across media. Market censorship arises less from deliberate acts of media control than as the outcome of innumerable decisions on ad-placement based on cost-effectiveness. The influence of advertising 'is essentially an impersonal one that is inherent in the system of advertising finance of the press rather than an "abuse" that can be attributed to "rogue" advertisers' (Curran 1978: 232).

Increased professionalism and sophistication in market and media analysis meant media planners relied more heavily on quantitative data over subjective judgements. Second, the 'licensing' effect arises from the innumerable decisions of individual advertisers. Baker (1994) highlights another aspect of this impersonal process; the outcome of ad-placement decision can lead to outcomes which are not intended by advertisers and are even detrimental to their interests. For instance, shifts of advertising spending to media that can reach the largest number of the target market at low cost may force competitor media out of business, but then advertisers face a monopolist who can raise advertising rates, as occurred when the distribution of ad-finance contributed to monopolization in US local newspapers from the late nineteenth century. Baker argues:

> Advertiser influence is so built in to the market context that not only is it often difficult to prove, but advertiser influence frequently occurs without the advertiser's inducing it by any specific act, sometimes even without the advertiser's wanting it.
>
> (Baker 1994: 103)

Advertising subsidy functions as a de facto licensing system, determining which ad-dependent media have the resources to survive and thrive. Oscar Gandy (1982, 2000, 2004) explores the effects of uneven distribution of commercial subsidy and their implications for media serving poorer, ethnic minority audiences in the US, concluding '[t]o the extent that advertisers place a lower value on gaining access to particular minority audiences, those who would produce content for that segment will be punished by the market' (Gandy 2000: 48).

Consideration of rival instrumentalist and structuralist explanations invites us to assess how relationships between marketers, agencies and media vary across different media arrangements and market conditions. The structuralist analysis is helpful in highlighting theoretical deficiencies in instrumentalist explanations, but historical analyses show that the forms of influence change under different conditions and that advertising influence can take a complex combination of forms. We may then ask: Under what conditions can marketers or agencies successfully intervene to influence editorial decisions? If media firms position a media vehicle to attract advertising finance, how do the various influences operate and interact, from more 'impersonal' market signals to the interactions with agencies and marketers themselves?

One of the most famous CPE analyses is Herman and Chomsky's propaganda model. They describe advertising finance as among the five 'filters' that shape what news content is published in elite media, leaving 'the cleansed residue fit to print' (Herman & Chomsky 2008 [1988]: 2). News media systems filter out oppositional and alternative views, limit the range of debate and restrict people's ready access to fundamental criticisms of both private and state power. Their account combines structuralist and instrumentalist explanations of advertiser influence. Working-class media attract less advertising interest and subsidy, disadvantaging them against better-funded rivals; media compete for advertiser patronage and must accommodate to their 'requirements and demands ... if they are to succeed'; 'political discrimination is structured into advertising allocations by the stress on people with money to buy', but firms also discriminate in what media they will fund ('Large corporate advertisers on television will rarely sponsor programs that engage in serious criticism of corporate activities'); 'Advertisers will want, more generally, to avoid programs with serious complexities and disturbing controversies that interfere with the "buying mood"' (Herman & Chomsky 2008: 15). As Fenton (2007: 13) puts it: '[Advertiser] influence commonly functions pre-emptively: the sensibilities of the advertiser are taken into consideration by the media company prior to the screening of contentious material'. TV programming is required, under financial pressures and inducements by marketers, to provide a suitably positive selling environment by 'privileging genres that employ the same capitalist realist aesthetic as the advertising that surrounds them' (Murdock 2011: 29).

Previous studies have suggested that advertising influence is largely internalized by media management, influencing strategies designed to maximize revenue (Curran 1978, 1986). Baker summarizes how ad-dependence encourages the media to shape and adapt media content:

> (1) to treat advertisers' products and their broader interests charitably in both news reports and editorials;
> (2) to create a buying mood that will induce readers or viewers to react favourably to advertisements;
> (3) to reduce partisanship and often reduce controversial elements in order to avoid offending advertisers' potential customers and to increase the media's potential reach;
> (4) to favour the middle- to higher-income audiences whose greater purchasing power advertisers value most.
>
> (Baker 1994: 44)

The level of economic dependence on advertising revenue has always been a key factor shaping the content and structure of different media (Mattelart 1991; Bagdikian 2004; Baker 1994; Curran 1978; Curran 1986; Wernick 1990). Advertising influence though depends on such factors as the proportion of income derived from advertising, reliance on particular advertisers and wider market conditions. Another factor is the acceptability of advertising influence on content decisions (and the 'cost' of consumer, or public, disapproval arising from advertiser influence), which varies according to the media format, type of enterprise and user expectations. In addition, 'accepted industry practice' in the sector can in turn influence the behaviour and demands of advertisers. Major factors affecting advertising influence on media therefore include:

(1) levels of dependence on advertising finance and support;
(2) institutional traditions of specific parts of media and media-advertiser relations;
(3) behaviour and influence of owners;
(4) professional norms of media workers and managers;
(5) formal regulations;
(6) self-regulation influenced by users (including anticipated consumer responses).

A common theme from research is that with increasing commercial pressures across media comes increasing dependence on advertising and accommodation of advertiser interests (McAllister 2000). However, this is always a dynamic process since there are various countervailing forces to counter advertiser influence. For instance, institutionalized professional practices can limit advertiser influence. The 'firewall' separating 'Church' and 'State' – that is, separating editorial from advertiser or corporate interests – is a central trope structuring debate about US journalism (Bagdikian 2004; McChesney 2008: 25–66). The firewall concept provides a normative standard for critique while spotlighting profound economic, structural and behavioural changes in journalistic media, especially news journalism. In his extensive participant observation in the 1970s, Gans (1980) noted the strength of US news journalists' resentment of advertiser influence and their partial, institutionalized insulation from such pressure. While journalists identified and criticized the influence of commercial considerations on senior producers and editors, Gans also argued that national news firms could control advertiser interference by their ability to attract and substitute other advertisers (1980: 257). All these conditions have been significantly eroded since the 1980s as US newspapers have plunged into crisis (McChesney 2013).[2]

The results of surveys, interviews with practitioners, commentary and analysis of corporate data (Pew Research Centre Project for Excellence in Journalism 2013) indicate how pressures have increased on ad-dependent media to secure advertising by complying with advertiser demands and by offering a host of added benefits. Advertisers have been able to exact more and more 'editorial support' beyond paid advertising (McAllister 1996; Hardy 2010a). Studies show increased integration of advertising into content through plugs in news programmes (McAllister 2002; Compton 2004), entertainment marketing and cross-promotion. Herman and McChesney (1997: 140) describe how:

> major TV networks offer their 'stars' to sell commercials and appear at advertiser gatherings; they enter into joint promotional arrangements with advertisers, each pushing the other's offerings; they show 'infomercials' produced entirely by or for advertisers and displaying their products; and they co-produce programs with advertisers and gear others to advertiser requests and needs.

Confirmation of the adage 'who plays the piper calls the tune' is arguably most pernicious in regard to the way commercially funded media covers capitalism in news journalism. Mainstream US journalism is accused by critics of cheerleading for capitalism, failing to sound the alarms on corporate scandals and debt bubbles and neglecting to cover rising poverty, disadvantage and inequality. McChesney *et al.* (2011: 37) conclude 'a privately owned and advertising-supported media system is structurally incapable of providing an honest picture of the economy and is therefore inadequate and unresponsive to the needs of a democratic society'.

Accounts of advertiser power by Bagdikian (2004) and others are critiqued by Richards and Murphy (2009 [1996]). They concede that 'economic censorship' takes insidious forms and can be detrimental, but argue that a 'top-down', linear account which locates all power with advertisers should be replaced by a circular one of mutual influence between advertisers, media and consumers. They are right to highlight mutual interaction but in doing so they exaggerate the independent power of media consumers. Their motivation is to oppose calls for public regulation of advertisers. In doing so they argue that the effects of economic censorship can be minimized by the availability of information: 'it is hard to imagine that a newspaper or broadcast station decision to avoid a topic will severely handicap an audience member's ability to obtain that information' (Richards and Murphy 2009: 106). Is the availability of alternative sources, however, sufficient to justify tolerating economic censorship when it occurs? The expansion of digital media enables consumers to be more active in exercising power to switch media, block ads or even take part in activism such as boycotting advertisers. Whether such activities are or can be a sufficient remedy for the cumulative effects of advertising finance on informational content are matters for debate.

Advertiser pressure to integrate promotional content into ostensibly 'independent' public media content is a complex matter for analysis, but three main considerations are pertinent. First, strategies of 'embedded persuasion' (advertising in media content) increase the promotional content of media discourse. Second, such promotions influence the commercial orientation of media communications; and third, they influence norms and professional behaviour as increased reliance on and accommodation to advertiser interests shape a more commercial and promotional orientation. Yet traditional patterns of advertising influence are also disrupted across digital networks. Widespread participation in the co-creation of promotional content in social media challenges presumptions of audience resistance to content imposed by advertisers. Digital interactivity also enables an increasing variety of communications about brands to circulate outside of marketers' control or their traditional means of influencing media. In place of either the 'circle of mutual influence' model or the linear 'top down' account of advertiser power, I outline in the final section below a more dynamic framework for assessing instances of advertiser influence.

Media and advertising integration and disaggregation

The characteristic relationship between media and advertising in mid-twentieth-century media was one of *integration with separation.* Advertising was integrated in the sense that it was physically combined with the media product. In newspapers and magazines, adverts appeared alongside editorial; in linear television, spot (or block) advertising appeared in designated breaks within or between programmes. While advertisers controlled their commercial communications, media businesses controlled their content and controlled the packaging and distribution of the ad-carrying media. It can be argued that this was in fact a short-lived period, between the advertiser-sponsored and produced radio and TV shows of the early twentieth century and the growth of advertiser-produced content from the 1990s. Yet integration with separation reflected the norm that 'advertising – as the major funding system of the mass media – should not unduly influence the non-advertising content' (McAllister 2000: 101). There have always been pressures and opportunities to integrate but the principles of separation were generally upheld by journalists, and by creative professionals in television, supported by managers, underpinned by self-regulatory codes of conduct in both media and advertising and subject to stronger statutory regulation in some sectors, such as UK broadcasting (Hardy 2010a).

In both ad-dependent print media and television, there was an institutionalized effort to capture the benefits of ad finance while protecting the quality, integrity and independence of media speech. This drew on a combination of values derived from democratic, consumer-welfare, artistic and cultural concerns. Media and advertising should be separated to ensure that consumers know when they are in a selling environment and to ensure that advertisers should not be the principal arbiters of media content and provision. The emergent relationship is *integration without separation.* Media and advertising integration is by no means a new phenomenon and has a long history across all media forms. Product placement, branded entertainment, advergames and infomercials are among the most familiar outcomes (Lehu 2009; Hardy 2010a, 2013; McAllister and West 2013). However, the opportunities and challenges of convergence and digitalization, not least the struggles to finance an enormous expansion of media, have brought increased pressures from marketers, met with increased accommodation by media. Global spending on product placement rose 11.7 per cent to $8.25 billion in 2012, with annual growth of more than 20 per cent in China, Russia and India, according to PQ Media (Warc 2013). Television was the main channel ($5.37bn) but online and mobile was up 31.4 per cent ($247m), while product integration in music (videos, lyrics, etc.) increased by 22.7 per cent. The emergent forms are *integration without separation*, but this coexists with trends towards *disaggregation* of media and advertising.

Like integration, disaggregation of media and advertising takes various forms with different consequences. The most challenging feature is that advertising is much less dependent on media vehicles than in traditional models. Media content matters, since it attracts the consumers that advertisers seek to reach. However, marketers have much greater opportunity to reach consumers without subsidizing or accommodating media content providers. The intermediary role of media, creating an audience to sell to advertisers, is being undermined, in part because the production and distribution of physical goods are expensive ways to reach audiences, and in part because of the advantages of new ways to reach target consumers. Content is becoming less important than the person being tracked. Advertisers can link advertising to search and users' activity online so that advertising follows people's profiles rather than being bundled with media content for aggregate audiences. The greater range of opportunities to reach target consumers also diminishes value and exclusivity of mass-media vehicles. There is still a value in content that attracts prospects desired by advertisers, but the affordances of digital communications and targeting are driving marketers to demand that they pay only the actual costs of delivering an advert onto a selected platform (Turow 2011). Consequently the traditional subsidy supporting the news, information or entertainment surrounding advertisements is diminishing, with truly profound consequences for democratic communication resources, public media and cultural pluralism.

Advertising integration and disaggregation trends are obviously contrary tendencies: the embedding of advertising within content, and the disembedding of advertising from content publishing and packaging online. Yet both tendencies spring from the same underlying dynamic. Both trends reflect a new shift towards marketer power in an era of increased competition for advertising finance. Taking advantage of the competition among web creators and distributors, 'media buyers are eroding the power of Web publishers and causing them to play by advertisers' new rules to survive' (Turow 2011: 112).

Marketing professionals identify three main kinds of media: paid, earned and owned. Traditional advertising is 'paid', inserting advertisements into media vehicles or other advertising spaces. Earned media describes public relations activities to generate editorial coverage. The third area, owned, has been transformed by the opportunities for marketers to reach consumers directly via the Internet. Industry bodies like the Internet Advertising Bureau chart the ever-increasing proliferation and hybridization of promotional forms including native advertising, content farms and social-media ad-integration. Owned media has taken various forms such as contract publishing that pre-date digitalization. But the commercial expansion of the Internet has been a game-changer: the increasing accessibility and reach of owned media increases pressures on media for accommodation in paid and earned media.

Advertising, regulation and democracy

Product placement, corporate consolidation and invasive advertising have arisen not from technology, innovation or market forces alone, but from the ways in which these practices have been regulated. UK advertising, for instance, is subject to supranational regulation (notably European Union), statutory regulation (notably the Office of Communications), a self-regulatory system (Advertising Standards Authority), laws and other arrangements. Changes in regulation have generally created a more permissive environment for advertisers, responsive to their lobbying demands, but governments and regulators have also responded to civil society pressures on issues such as 'junk food' advertising to children. The significance of regulation and the struggles between state, market and civil society actors to shape governance are neglected in some culturalist accounts, which treat promotional culture as the outcome of sociocultural change and market evolution. The political economy tradition, by contrast, identifies regulation as a site of struggle between private and public interests and examines how policies that favour market actors over citizens' interests have arisen.

Advertising regulation is a dynamic and contested area. On the whole, marketers and agencies advocate the 'right to advertise', seek to minimize imposed controls and promote industry self-regulation. Global marketers seek to avoid local regulatory impediments to transnational campaigns. Advertisers have been powerful lobbyists at national and supranational levels advocating liberalization, and have often been joined by commercial media interests, in efforts to extend the place, duration and form of advertising. For instance, advertising and commercial television interests pushed hard to relax European Union rules to allow product placement (Hardy 2010a; McAllister & West 2013). Lobbyists for Google and other digital media are seeking to prevent privacy safeguards from diminishing the scope to monetize user data. However, public regulation in democratic systems is susceptible to other pressures ranging from public health interests, charities, consumer welfare organizations and critics who can influence both formal regulation and the environments in which firms operate.

No other group in democratic societies commands the same power as marketers to exercise speech. Marketers pay to communicate directly though advertisements and to insert promotional messages into other kinds of content. Supporters of advertising argue that it is preferable to have a media system that relies on advertising rather than on government funding and control. Writers such as Jhally challenge this, arguing that the relationship between advertisers and media firms hinders democracy (Turow 2010: 618). Advertising generates selectivity for the reasons explored above. It is selective in advancing the interests of those paying for communication and, where commercial interests dominate, there is resulting selectivity in the messages and through the influence of advertising on the communication vehicles, channels and environment. In his famous formulation of advertising as capitalist realism, Schudson (1984) finds affinities with Soviet realism, the selective, typified, affirmative art hailing Stalinism.

The critical tradition explores the relationship between advertising and systems of domination that restrict capacities for human emancipation and for democratic rule. The relationship between corporate media and advertising narrows the range of information, ideas and imagery in media. Advertisers tend to reinforce politically conservative content and values and tend to be hostile to criticisms of the status quo in which they are major beneficiaries (Herman & McChesney 1997: 6–7). In these ways advertising reinforces corporate media tendencies to filter content. Herman and McChesney describe a media/advertiser complex that prefers entertainment over cultivation of the public sphere. 'Advertisers have ideological – and practical – biases that have nothing to do with viewer demand', argues Lewis (2010: 343). Messages that contradict the consumerist ideology – which most advertising depends upon and promotes – are unlikely to please advertisers, regardless of the interests of the viewer.

The CPE tradition has strong affinities with organized efforts to challenge excessive and invasive advertising, commercialization and consumer culture, exploring the histories of activism (Stole 2006; McChesney 2008) and engaging with the work of campaigning organizations, critical-artistic interventions such as Adbusters (Lasn 2000), consumer groups, charities and other civil society organizations, links which help to amplify, nourish and sustain critical work.

Renewing the critical tradition

Critical political economy has insisted on examining the economic, political and cultural aspects of media and advertising relationships. Yet the radical tradition needs to be revised and renewed to take account of changes in convergent media and to offer a suitably rich and compelling analysis and theorization of media–advertising relationships. Radical perspectives lost ground in the 1980s subject to revisionist attacks from media and cultural studies. Culturalist approaches to advertising have emphasized, and often celebrated, people's immersion in branding and brand culture. In doing so they turned away from what they regarded as crude, Marxian domination theories. Critical accounts of advertiser power have been critiqued as misplaced and displaced. They are misplaced because they focus on selective visible aspects (advertising texts) to the detriment of analysing production, labour and consumption (Nava 1997). They are displaced because they are rooted in a critique of consumer capitalism but focus their ire on advertising. 'Sociological critiques of advertising are, in any event, really critiques of market society', says McFall (2011: 193), echoing Leiss *et al.* (1997: 33).

This culturalist critique makes valid points but the attack is lopsided. Critical scholarship is not wedded to presumptions of strong ideological effects or manipulation associated with mass-media domination paradigms. Instead, it is distinguished by the concern to identify and address problems arising from the manner in which resources, including communication resources, are organized in social life. A central argument of contemporary critical scholars is that the potentialities of modern communications cannot be fully realized by a privately owned and financed media system. However, rather than replacing a celebratory account with a sceptical one, critical analysis is strengthened by addressing the tensions and contradictions in capitalist cultural production. The radical tradition can be renewed by addressing both the ways in which advertiser power is bolstered across contemporary communications systems and the ways in which such power can be contested and undermined.

Marketers can now track, measure, profile and target users more (cost-)effectively across converged media. Such 'economic surveillance' combined with social segmentation presents profound challenges for democracy, social inclusion and cultural exchange (Turow 2011). At the same time, the marketing communications industries are adapting to challenging new conditions and volatility across markets. US consumers are spending nearly 30 per cent of their time online with media but while part of that time is spent with ad-supported destinations, such as branded websites, most is spent on communications including email and social media. 'As a result, only eight per cent of total ad spending is going to online media', 'social media … have exploded in terms of consumer usage, but Madison Avenue still hasn't figured out how to tap into that consumer behaviour in anything resembling conventional advertising and marketing' (Mandese 2010: 13). The challenges for advertising, and the work of creative professionals to achieve advertising effectiveness, must be fully addressed and incorporated into analysis. CPE attention to advertising as a support mechanism for media remains of central importance but needs updating, not least as 'possibilities for the direct influence of content keep changing' (Leiss *et al.* 2005: 120).

The radical tradition highlights key problems arising from media dependence on advertising finance – but to investigate and challenge this persuasively we need to examine the configuration of influences in a more dynamic and open manner. In Table 4.1, I offer a revised mapping that attempts to identify the main factors that tend to strengthen marketers' influence on media and communications content and services and countervailing forces (see Hardy 2014). This mapping is designed to invite more open investigation of advertising influence by suggesting key factors to consider when assessing the power of marketers to influence editorial, operational or strategic decisions by communication providers.

Table 4.1 Assessing the influence of marketers on media communications

Factors that tend to enhance advertiser influence on (non-advertising) media content and services	*Countervailing influences*
1. *Media dependence on advertising finance.* The dependence of media on advertising revenue tends to influence media decisions at various levels, from corporate-strategic to operational and editorial. Factors include the proportion of total revenue made up from advertising; reliance on particular advertisers, etc.	1. *Governance and regulations.* Marketing communications remain subject to public controls based on a variety of purposes that include consumer protection and regard for communications content and cultural expression. Politicians and regulators can respond to societal pressures to place limits on marketers' 'freedom to advertise'.
2. *Market conditions and structural influence of ad finance.* Advertising finance also has a structural influence on media markets (and content) by granting more resources to media serving wealthy consumers.	2. *Public service media.* Another type of regulatory intervention, public service media, can provide a countervailing force to advertiser influence by sustaining non-commercial media and values in media systems.
3. *Advertiser-media placement behaviour.* Ad influence on non-advertising content (affecting both what is promoted or suppressed), arises also from the instrumental interactions between marketers, marketing agencies, media firms and content makers.	3. *Market conditions: firms' behaviour, competition and consumer acceptability.* Powerful inhibitors on marketers' integration into media content can arise from the actual/anticipated responses of users/consumers, and also from the behaviour and norms of other market actors.
4. *Technical capabilities and marketing effectiveness.* Digital media capabilities for tracking and targeting consumers provide enhanced opportunities for marketer-controlled content, and contribute to pressures on media to accommodate marketers in media-controlled content.	4. *Content producers: professional cultures and values.* Staff power, influenced by professional (or pro-am) codes and values, can counter pressures to accommodate advertising in non-advertising content and also, through journalism, expose marketers' efforts to public scrutiny.
5. *Corporate ownership and interests.* Corporate integration, joint ventures and common corporate interests between marketers, marketing communications and media firms strengthen ad influence.	5. *Civil society action.* Consumer and citizens' activism can counter marketers' power by influencing policy-makers and groups in society.
6. *User involvement.* Various kinds of user interactivity and (co-)creation can promote ad-integration into media content and communications.	6. *Users.* User activities, both individual and collective, can serve as a countervailing force to marketers/marketing, such as fostering non-commercial (gift) exchanges, taking part in online campaigning or joining boycotts.

Table 4.1 (continued)

Factors that tend to enhance advertiser influence on (non-advertising) media content and services	*Countervailing influences*
7. *Professional (and pro-am – professional–amateur) values and behaviour.* Advertising influence is enhanced when marketing goals and promotional cultural values are accepted and normalised by media providers and content creators.	
8. *Marketers influence as media content providers.* Marketers engage in communications across their own media channels (owned), advertising (paid) and through public relations (earned). There is increasing convergence and blurring of forms as marketers invest in owned media content (websites; native advertising), commissioned content (paid bloggers, content farms), co-owned media content and public relations activities with media firms.	
9. *Governance and regulations.* Liberalization of regulations concerning corporate consolidation, media ownership, marketing behaviour, advertising placement, advertising content, and media content, can all enhance marketers' power and influence.	

Conclusion

The critical political economy tradition is guided by critical social theory to identify and address problems. Critical scholarship from the 1970s established studies of advertising finance but tended to provide an aerial view, with limited close observation of advertising practices and processes. The rise of sociological and culturalist studies of advertising fills this gap but tends towards an uncritical, descriptive account of marketing, partly in its effort to distinguish itself from earlier critical discourses. The extension of advertiser power in the digital age, as well as its limits, cries out for further analysis and public debate. What is needed is critical scholarship that is informed by the theoretical sophistication of new media studies, gives close attention to material practices, but which continues to ask and address larger, critical questions about the ways in which advertising shapes the communication environments in which we learn how to live.

Notes

1 In the UK between 2000 and 2008, the Internet's share of classified advertising grew from 2 per cent to 45 per cent, while the local and regional press share fell from 47 to 26 per cent, and national newspapers' share fell from 14 to 6 per cent (Office of Fair Trading 2009: 13).

2 Between 2008 and 2012 global advertising expenditure on newspapers fell 5.7 per cent to £54 billion. Internet advertising grew fastest at a compound annual rate of 16.4 per cent, reaching £63.6 billion in 2012, behind television at £103.8 billion (Ofcom 2013b: 19; on advertising spending across media platforms, see Hardy 2013).

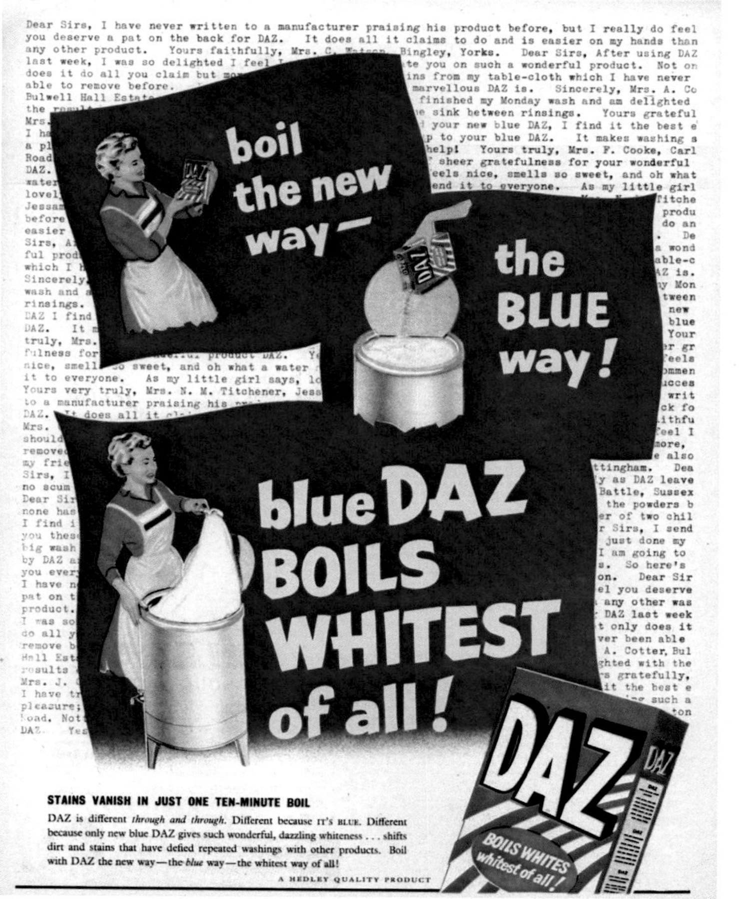

Plate 1 'Daz boils whitest of all', mid-twentieth century. Reproduced courtesy of The Advertising Archives.

Plate 2 'Omo makes whites bright', mid-twentieth century. Reproduced courtesy of The Advertising Archives.

Plate 3 Wall painting, House of Julia Felix, Pompeii, pre-79 AD. Reproduced courtesy of the Bridgeman Art Library.

Plate 4 Pear's soap advertising postcard, dated 1907. Based on J. E. Millais's 'Bubbles', 1886. Author's own collection.

Plate 5 Edouard Manet, 'A Bar at the Folies-Bergère', 1882, oil on canvas. Reproduced by permission of the Samuel Courtauld Trust, the Courtauld Gallery, London.

Plate 6 L'Oreal New Elvive featuring Cheryl Cole, 2009. Reproduced courtesy of The Advertising Archives.

Plate 7 Perugino, 'Christ Handing the Keys to St Peter', Sistine Chapel, Vatican, 1481 (fresco). Reproduced courtesy of the Bridgeman Art Library.

Plate 8 John Lewis Christmas newsprint advertisement, 2007. Reproduced courtesy of John Lewis.

5 Cultural and critical approaches

Introduction

This chapter outlines approaches to media and advertising in the twentieth and twenty-first centuries from a cultural perspective. The late nineteenth and twentieth centuries are referred to as the period of modernity, characterized by the establishment of a modern industrial society and market economy. *Modernism* is the term given to trends of thought associated with this. The latter part of the twentieth century is often referred to by writers in a wide range of areas from the arts to sociology as late modernity or postmodernity. *Postmodernism* is the term used to refer to a set of theories and ways of thinking about recent developments in society, its culture and advertising. The chapter begins with an exploration of the 'culture and civilization' tradition of thought that dismissed advertising as a 'debased' form of culture. This is followed by an analysis of the Frankfurt School, whose work is of major significance to an understanding of culture and advertising, emphasizing the political role that advertising has in a capitalist economy. The chapter explores some elaborations and challenges to this line of thinking in the latter part of the twentieth century. The work of the Birmingham Centre for Cultural Studies was important to this and ideas and forms of analyses associated with postmodern thinkers are then explored. The chapter concludes with a consideration of media and advertising based on Stuart Hall's encoding/decoding model, which is introduced as a framework for approaches to advertising studies.

By the beginning of the twentieth century the economic and cultural effects of a market society were clearly visible in Britain. It was rapidly becoming an urban culture connected by transport systems and served by a mass media in which advertising played an increasingly important part. The mass production of goods was accompanied by forms of consumption previously unknown. Indeed the 1920s – frequently referred to in popular history as the 'roaring twenties' – is often recognized as the first real consumer decade (Slater 2008: 13). It was also the decade that came to a close with the Wall Street crash in 1929. The collapse of the US stock market contributed to the economic depression of the 1930s. The 1920s and 1930s were characterized by mass unemployment, painfully experienced in places such as Jarrow in the north of England. The period is also marked by important changes in production, which in turn created new forms of employment. Heavy industry such as ship building, coal and steel was joined by lighter industry such as automobile manufacturing. By 1924 Oxford car makers Morris were the largest British car manufacturer, providing new kinds of work. For those in work, weekly wages almost doubled between the end of the First World War in 1918 and the beginning of the Second in 1939, by which time half of manual workers were receiving paid holidays.

The First World War was in part the outcome of competition and conflict between the great empires that colonized both land and people; and the Second World War largely put paid to Fascism as a state ideology. The 1920s saw the creation of a worker's state in the Soviet Union as Lenin and the Bolsheviks attempted to build a progressive alternative to Western capitalism. By the close of the decade Socialist optimism was being replaced by Stalinism as a political force. In the same decade in Britain and the US, women, following in the wake of their New Zealand sisters who won the vote in the 1890s, finally secured the right to participate in elections. Across the 1920s and 1930s the relatively new forms of mass communication, telephony and photography, continued to take hold, with radio and cinema becoming increasingly popular forms of mass media. Cinema had become one of the foremost popular culture activities with audiences steadily increasing across the 1920s. In 1939 there were 990 million cinema admissions by a British population of 46 million people. Mass communication was important to the consolidation of advertising, which by this time was operating across numerous media through full-service agencies providing a range of facilities from copywriting to systematic research.

As we have seen the study of advertising in the modern and late modern period is informed by many different areas of enquiry: from political economy to art and design history. Cultural studies, an important element of this eclectic approach, views advertising as both part of the economy and an increasingly important aspect of culture. Today, cultural studies often begins its enquiry with an account of attitudes to 'high' and 'low' culture. Jim McGuigan makes the distinction between what he terms '"Culture" with a capital C' and 'lower-case culture as the medium of social communication' (2010: 2). In everyday use, 'capital C culture' is often thought of in the way Raymond Williams referred to it as the 'works and practices of intellectual especially artistic activity' (Williams 1983: 90). Williams also considered these to be part of a wider aspect of culture that he termed 'a way of life' (Williams 1981). If art can be thought of as an example of high culture because of its visual content and art-gallery setting, then advertising is largely considered low or popular culture. For many it can be included in the category of 'common culture' (Petrie 1996) as objects and activities that are open to and experienced by all people.

Popular culture and civilization

The 'culture and civilization' debate of the twentieth century is in many ways an extension and development of nineteenth-century ideas associated with Matthew Arnold. For Arnold authentic culture was about the best art and thought that humankind had produced and its appreciation was largely limited to a few. The standards of elite culture had to be maintained, and this was accompanied by a distrust of an emerging urban popular culture. This attitude continued into the twentieth century and has become known as 'culture and civilization' thinking, represented by F.R. Leavis, his wife Q.D. Leavis and others. The 'Leavisites' as they became known were literary critics who gained prominence through the journal *Scrutiny* between the 1930s and 1970s. F.R. Leavis was a prominent Cambridge literary critic and academic whose influence over cultural life was exerted through his writing and teaching. He shaped the thinking of an elite group of students in the literary values and criticism associated with 'close reading' of a narrow canon of English literature. The novel was afforded particular regard and the methods of inclusion in the canon and techniques of appreciation of chosen works helped create a distinction between high and low culture (Lury 2011: 93). These values came to permeate education through the teaching of literature in universities and grammar schools and through other cultural institutions (Mullan 2013).

The Leavisites' faith in a high culture which is neither common nor popular was informed by Arnold's conviction that culture belongs to the elite: 'culture has always been in minority keeping' (Leavis and Thompson, quoted in Storey 2009: 23). John Mullan in a recent article quotes from a 1968 lecture where Leavis mocks working-class leisure activities: 'the telly, the car, the bingo hall ... eating fish and chips in Spain' (quoted in Mullan 2013: 10). Leavis, like Arnold, was critical of the effects of nineteenth-century industrialism, but unlike Arnold he was *of* the twentieth century and recognized the power of commodity culture. Denys Thompson was part of the Leavis circle and in conjunction with Leavis wrote *Culture and Environment*, one of three books that formulated the group's position on popular culture. Thompson also wrote directly about advertising and in the article 'Advertising God', published in *Scrutiny*, described it as composed of 'debasing ideas and language ... promoting undesirable attitudes' (Thompson 1932: 241). Many decades later, this time in conjunction with Leavis, he would criticize the effects of advertising as creating a 'debasement of emotional life, and the quality of living' (Leavis and Thompson 1977: 4). Thompson's general critique might be one that many share today. For Leavis and Thompson the malign effects of advertising could be mitigated through education as a means to 'resist rampant commercialism'. Teachers were to be encouraged to expose the 'crude manipulativeness and cheap emotional falsity of popular culture' (Buckingham 1998: 34). Leavis and Thompson went on to create exercises for students to encourage a critical reading of advertising texts. Today we might refer to this as advertising deconstruction in which texts reveal their deep meaning within a wide range of contexts. According to John Storey, the effect was to 'construct membership of a small educated elite' and 'such questions rather than encouraging discrimination and resistance would invite anything other than a critically deliberating and self-confirming snobbery' (2009: 25–6). These critical skills established by an elite were to be impressed on the people rather than encourage the development of innate cultural resistance based on collective cultural identity and experience.

The Frankfurt School

Culture for Mathew Arnold and F.R. Leavis was considered an important element of social experience. However it was divided into two separate categories: on the one hand, 'minority culture', the preserve of an elite, composed of the 'values and standards of the best that has been thought and said'; on the other, 'the mass culture of mass civilisation', represented by commercial and popular culture (Storey 1998: 5). As we have seen advertising was regarded as part of the problem of popular culture. Media and advertising played an important role in the developed capitalist economy according to Marxists Theodor Adorno and Max Horkheimer, German intellectuals associated with the Frankfurt School. To some extent the Frankfurt School of 'critical theory' shared certain concerns with the 'culture and civilization' critics. As John Storey suggests, 'they condemn the same things, but for different reasons' (Storey 2009: 70). Arnold and Leavis were concerned that mass culture undermined cultural standards and threatened the power structure of the social system, whereas Adorno and Horkheimer felt that it worked for the system in the interest of capitalist economics and power.

The Frankfurt School operated in Germany from the early 1920s until 1933 when Hitler was appointed chancellor. Its 'critical theory' was an analysis of culture in which popular culture, such as film, popular music and advertising, worked as social cement helping to maintain the dominant order. Adorno and Horkheimer emphasized that culture was saturated by these kind of standardized commercial products. Providing an undemanding pleasure and easy satisfaction, they helped depoliticize the working class, distancing it from what Marxists believed was its historical role in challenging capitalism. Marx, writing in the 1840s, referred to working people as the 'grave-diggers' of capital – just as the bourgeoisie and capital had transformed feudal, medieval society, the proletariat through organization and association, 'the ever expanding union of the workers', would overturn a society organized around exploitation (Marx 1935a [1848]: 33). Marx suggested in *The Communist Manifesto* that this transformation would be 'helped on by the improved means of communication that are created by modern industry' (Marx 1935a [1848]: 33). The Frankfurt School of Adorno and Horkheimer regarded the twentieth-century mass-communication system not as an aid to emancipation but rather its opposite. The media was characterized as part of the superstructure – other aspects would include the institutions of religion and education – that contained and limited the development of the working class. The media confined the political aspirations of working people within the horizons of capitalist society. There was, however, another side to the Frankfurt School, one that provided a more optimistic reading of the potentially emancipatory nature of media technology. This was associated with Walter Benjamin and his interest in mechanical reproduction, which came to deprive much of culture of its 'aura', its mystique or specialness. But it is the 'pessimistic thesis' of Adorno and Horkheimer that is the side of the Frankfurt School that is most often noted (Benjamin 1973; Schultz 2000; Storey 2009).

The idea of the oppressive relationship between the media and its audience was at the heart of what Adorno called the 'culture industry' (Adorno 1991; Adorno & Horkheimer 1997 [1944]; Murdock & Golding 1977). The industry produced and marketed the cultural goods that occupied free time. Free time was the time spent outside of the work process, necessary for rest, recuperation and leisure. This was also the time allocated for the consumption of the products created by the media and entertainment industries. For the Frankfurt School, the culture industry steeped workers in the values and thinking necessary for the untroubled continuation of the economic and social system. This depoliticized workers and encouraged an acceptance of the inequalities the system was built on. Marcuse referred to this form of thought as 'false consciousness' (1968) and it operated according to Enzenberger, extending Adorno and Horkheimer's term, through the 'consciousness industry' (1974). It produced a combination of acceptance and deference, acquiescence and suppression. Advertising could be seen to be at the heart of this system, creating what a later thinker, Judith Williamson, was to call a 'structure of meaning' in which ideology attached to advertising crucially operated (1978: 12).

Adorno's ideas called attention to the difference between pseudo-individuality and the real individuality of 'pleasure and happiness, consensus and freedom' (Bernstein 1991). Advertising emphasized consumption as the most significant element of social life at the expense of production and people's creativity. The nature and experience of work for many under capitalist relations of production was less about personal or social satisfaction and more about the creation of surplus value. It created an alienated experience, one that was far from the free expression and creativity associated with what William Morris, in the previous century, had termed as 'useful labour'. Pseudo-individuality was based on the passive consumption of standardized products: 'the achievement of standardisation and mass production, sacrificing whatever involved a distinction between the logic of the work and that of the social system' (Adorno & Horkheimer 2013 [1944]). Adorno and Horkheimer referred to these aspects of popular culture when they stated, 'The ossified forms – such as the sketch, short story, problem film, or hit song – are the standardised average of late liberal taste, dictated with threats from above' (2013 [1944]). This provided easy satisfaction in the here and now.

In consumer capitalism, competing social identities – the way people think about themselves and others as citizens with social rights or as workers with shared interests – can become dominated by the single, overarching identity of the consumer, one that reduces a complex set of social identities to a single social category – that of purchasing and using commodities and services. This is in the main ideological, and in many ways it is how people are encouraged to see themselves. The real difference between consumers – that is, their spending power based on an increasingly unequal distribution of income and wealth – is a real difference but one that is seldom acknowledged. If this was how culture under capitalism functioned it left open for the Frankfurt School the possibility of what might be classed as authentic culture. 'Authentic culture is different', according to John Storey, it is a 'utopian space keeping alive the desire for a better world beyond the confines of the present. It embodies both a critique of today and the promise of tomorrow' (1998: 188).

The Birmingham Centre for Contemporary Cultural Studies

The Birmingham Centre for Contemporary Cultural Studies was founded in the early 1960s to further research and study into culture. Richard Hoggart, the author of *Uses of Literacy* (1957) – an account of the shift from traditional popular culture to commercial mass culture – became its first director. He was followed by Stuart Hall in the late 1960s and the Centre instigated a body of work that became known as British Cultural Studies. The approach was interdisciplinary, drawing on history, anthropology and sociology, literary criticism, semiotics, Marxism and feminism. Hall's method was eclectic, blending elements of thought from Bakhtin and Volosinov to Lacan and Derrida in what has been described as a 'multidimensional analysis' (McGuigan 2012). The works of Antonio Gramsci and Louis Althusser were central to Hall's project and have become important to advertising studies.

The Centre was important to promoting ideas and research in the area of media and cultural studies (Curran 2002b; Rojek 2003) and much of this has directly impacted on the study of advertising. In addition it supported a wide range of related research areas: for example, in the work of David Morley and Charlotte Brunsdon on television; Angela McRobbie on feminity and consumption; Dick Hebdige on subcultures and Paul Gilroy on culture and race. The significance of the work of Stuart Hall in the areas of media, culture, politics and race cannot be overstated, nor can the importance of his organization and application of theory (Davis 2004). The impact of the Centre has been wide ranging and its effect on advertising studies substantial.

Crucially Hall brought together two distinct perspectives or paradigms in media and cultural studies, often summarized as 'culturalism and structuralism' (1981a). This juxtaposition has provided the basis for much work in advertising studies. On the 'culture' side Hall aligns the work of Raymond Williams, Richard Hoggart and F.R. Leavis, which had explored the texts and 'lived experience' of culture, as 'a whole way of life' (Williams 1981: 43–52; 1992). On the structuralist side Hall placed the ideas and methods of anthropology represented by Claude Lévi-Strauss, Louis Althusser and his work on ideology, the linguist Ferdinand de Saussure and the semiology of Roland Barthes.

Semiology provided an analysis of signs and signifiers and the potential meanings advertisements have for people. On the one hand, structuralism is about 'determinate conditions', how people are encouraged and constrained by systems of thought (Hall 1981a: 30). On the other hand, culturalism emphasized people's lived experience, and how they interpret and act on these experiences. Together they emphasize the economic and organizational power of the advertising industry and how it structures experience and behaviour and how people respond to this.

Ideology and hegemony

The works of Louis Althusser and Antonio Gramsci were important to Hall's formulation. The concept of ideology and Althusser's general thinking on the subject has had a major effect in media and cultural studies (Stevenson 1996; Fiske 1997; Curran 2002b; Storey 2009). It is important to a critical analysis of advertising (Williamson 1978; Goldman 1992) and Corner (2001) provides a concise overview of the area.

Althusser's exploration of the working of ideology is complex and he identifies different definitions of it. Crucial to advertising studies, ideology 'represents the imaginary relationship of individuals to their real conditions of existence' (1971: 153). In this approach ideology shapes the way people come to see themselves and the world they live in, their relationship to others and to objects such as the things they use in everyday circumstances. Althusser's concept of ideology has proved controversial and seems to suggest that 'misrecognition' and 'false consciousness' are the hallmarks of ideology and that through ideology the individual misrecognizes themselves as self-creating free agents (Stevenson 1996; Corner 2001). An understanding of Marx's base and superstructure is important to this. In rigid interpretations, economic activity in the base creates or determines ideological formulations in the superstructure. In Althusser's understanding there is a relationship of 'relative autonomy' between the two. This is important to advertising studies as advertising is part of the economic base creating work and wealth as an integral part of market mechanisms, and at the same time advertising shapes, in an ideological manner, the way people view goods and the society in which they live.

The superstructure organizes the way people see and understand their world. For Althusser it is in two parts. The ideological state apparatuses (ISAs) create the intellectual order that maintains capitalism over time. Media and advertising alongside religion, education and the culture industries are important components of this. These institutions work ideologicaly – they create ways of seeing, understanding and valuing the world. In times of stability ideology is sufficient to maintain the system. However when this is not the case and order and stability are threatened, what Althusser termed the repressive state apparatuses (RSAs) are deployed. RSAs such as the penal system, police and armed forces are used against social groups often in times of crises when the ISAs are unable to provide order, stability and continuity. In Britain the 1984–85 miners strike or the 2010 suppression of student protest in London against tuition fees might serve as examples.

Althusser's explanation of how ideology works has proved useful to advertising studies in a further way. Ideology works by 'hailing' or 'interpellating' people to itself. Advertisements are particularly adept at this 'calling' people to believe in the world that it presents. An early example of this is the famous Kichener poster deployed during the First World War and intended to encourage people to enlist in the British army. It displays the slogan 'Your country needs you' directly addressing its reader. This is positioned underneath an image in which a pointing finger is prominent. It both singles out the viewer and, in conjunction with the text, calls on them to 'sign up' to take part in the war. A further and more recent example of interpellation can be drawn from the development of Nike's 'Just do it' slogan. It was used in conjunction with the famous swoosh motif and brand advert created in 1988 by advertising agency Wieden + Kennedy. The tick/swoosh image is a sign of approval designed to imply ease and direction. Used alongside the tagline it announces brand presence and at the same time hails the viewer into an imaginary but unspecified future: it offers everything and nothing. It is limited by what the viewer contemplates and can imagine yet is enabled by the brand presence. Like the Kichener advert it speaks to you as an individual. It doesn't directly employ the 'you' word but it implies and interpellates a very special 'you', different from all the others 'yous' it simultaneously addresses. It interpellates and personalizes, creating an imaginary sense of identity and an unstated bond with the brand and the product. This is what Althusser might have identified as 'distortion' and 'misrecognition'.

The Birmingham Centre's analysis of ideology and interpellation of the subject in ideology was accompanied by an interest in Gramsci's idea of hegemony (Rojek 2007; McGuigan 2012). Hegemony is a form of power – such as the power that advertising holds over people and culture – but this is not power that is simply imposed by those people that are 'in power'. Hegemony, as Gramsci explained it, 'presupposes that account be taken of the interests and tendencies of the groups over which hegemony is to be exercised' (Bennett *et al.* 1981: 197). This is power that results from negotiation and incorporates different interests, even those of the people over whom power is exercised. It is less about domination and more about 'intellectual and moral leadership'. This concept and way of thinking about power has been applied to various aspects of advertising. But it is its application to the advertisements that the industry produces, the impact they have and the social influence the industry has over people that is most significant. This power is generally considered hegemonic.

Putting together Althusser's explanation of ideology and Gramsci's concept of hegemony underpins approaches to the study of advertising. This was applied to the media in the 1970s through Stuart Hall's encoding/decoding paper and since utilized by advertising studies. The original encoding/decoding paper, although an important methodological contribution to media and cultural studies enquiry, was neither based upon empirical evidence nor was it intended as a disquisition on the practical applications of research method (Davis 2004). However the findings of Morley and Brundson's Nationwide research project – one of many ethnographic studies launched at the Birmingham Centre – largely confirmed Hall's theory and method (Morley 1980, 1981; Tudor 1999). The encoding/decoding model that emerged from the Centre provides the basic 'picture' of how advertising works as an element both of the economy and of culture. It helps analysis of advertising in its widest, generic sense as a specific sector of an economy or as a significant part of visual culture and of the lived cultural experience of society. Similarly the model enables an analysis of specific information and meanings that advertising campaigns impart. It encourages consideration of the production of adverts, corresponding to the encoding element in Hall's model. It also enables an analysis of the meanings of individual advertising texts, and it explores how these are understood by people in the circumstances and contexts they inhabit.

Between modernism and postmodernism

The Birmingham Centre's exploration of contemporary popular and mass culture and Hall's use of the encoding/decoding media model to explore this occurred at a moment of profound social, media and cultural change. Since the 1970s, political change – too vast in scope to adequately summarize here – has been marked by the demise of the Communist bloc and the rise of radical Islam. Major attacks on sovereign states and civilian populations such as Iraq and New York, the weakening of working-class movements, the rise of anti-capitalist protest and the spread and intensification of markets and globalization mark this period. The production and reception of advertising media messages have also undergone significant realignments with the introduction of and further developments in new technologies such as the mobile and the Internet. Economic, technological, political and social change has been accompanied by developments in ideas and in theory. The encoding/decoding approach to advertising studies is best thought of as a framework to which further ideas can be attached (see Figure 5.1). It is explored more fully and in greater detail in subsequent chapters.

The latter period of the twentieth century is often described as postmodern. Postmodernity has been articulated as the most recent period in history which started with the demise of modernity. Christopher Norris writing in the 1990s suggested that the ideas associated with postmodernism corresponded to 'the perceived self-image of the times' (1993: 3). Some of the major themes and ideas that have arisen in the period are briefly outlined in the subsequent discussion. Jean Baudrillard (2003) and Jean-Francois Lyotard (1979) suggest that the period of modernity came to a close in the latter half of the twentieth century. But David Harvey (1992) and Frederic Jameson (1984, 1991) also refer to this period of postmodernity as 'late modernity' and 'late capitalism'. Others, such as Anthony Giddens (1990), although recognizing that important changes in culture, society and economics had taken place towards the close of the century, characterized these as continuing developments of modernity. This ambiguity is well captured in the title of Zygmunt Bauman's book on the period *Liquid Modernity* (2000).

Lyotard's condition

A good starting point for a summary of recent ideas that impact on this area of study is the publication of Jean-François Lyotard's book *The Postmodern Condition* in 1979. For Lyotard, postmodernism challenged what became known as 'metanarratives'. A metanarrative in literary theory is a narrative about a narrative. In cultural theory more generally it suggests a theory or explanation, a set of ideas, beliefs or an intellectual system that claims to tell overarching universal stories and lays claim to universal truth. It offers an all encompassing explanation about people, the world they live in and how that world works. Examples of metanarratives might include the religious certainties and explanations of life associated with fundamental Christianity. Marxism has been considered an influential twentieth-century metanarrative. As a philosophy and form of analysis – some aspects of Marxism claimed scientific status – it came to be criticized for what was perceived as an all-encompassing explanation of history, economics, society and culture. In 1992 Francis Fukuyama published *The End of History*, a book that suggested that free-market capitalism had won out over other forms of economic, social and cultural organization. This was interpreted not only as a commentary on the end of the Cold War and

→ encoding → advertising texts → decoding →

Figure 5.1 Diagram illustrating the framework of encoding–decoding

the collapse of the Soviet Union, and with it Communist and Socialist economies, but as an end to effective political challenges to the capitalist system and way of life. In 1979, the year that Lyotard's book was published, the Conservative government of Margaret Thatcher was elected in Britain. The following year Reagan won the US presidential election and in a similar vein to Thatcher inaugurated a programme of tax reduction, money supply control, government-spending cuts and the curtailing of trades union rights and activities. For many thinkers on the left this challenged a progressive postwar consensus. In Britain many public services were transferred into the for-profit sector and in 1984–85 a major confrontation between government and the trades union movement represented by the National Union of Mineworkers ensued.

Foucault – genealogy and contingency

Postmodernism posed numerous challenges to orthodox ways of thinking about society and culture and even about the nature of the historical past. For instance, Michel Foucault's genealogical model of historical analysis has had an important impact on historical enquiry and the writing of historical accounts such as the history of advertising. A series of related and historically contingent occurrences rather than a grand metanarrative sweep make up advertising history in Foucault's model. In early approaches the history of advertising was presented as a series of inevitable chronological developments, a set of building blocks on which contemporary advertising is based. The present moment in this kind of account is celebrated through terms like the 'information age' which stress unprecedented communication technology and inventiveness that overwhelms the past with its innovation. This has been called an 'exaggeration of the novelty of the present' when talking of contemporary advertising (McFall 2004: 189). A genealogical approach disparages a history of advertising that moves inevitably from early advertisements for slaves posted in the ancient Athenian agora to digi-ads on mobile handheld screens in the present. Rather, the history of advertising in the genealogical approach is composed of 'a diverse, haphazard and uneven array of institutions, practices and products adapted to fit specific contextual circumstances at different historical moments' (McFall 2004: 5).

Contingency is important in the work of Foucault as historical context and as discourse. Structuralist accounts such as those of Saussure and Barthes locate meaning in objects such as advertisements. However, discourse theory suggests that the meaning advertisements come to have is to be found in the way they are interpreted, understood, discussed and become part of everyday experience. This becomes apparent in an understanding of the factors involved in decoding advertisements. Discourse involves the contextual features and knowledge that support and make sense of objects and social actions. A discourse of advertising therefore might be said to range from the kind of visual, spoken or written language, including music, art and graphic styles, through which the advert is drawn and presented to interpretations and decodings that involve cultural aspects that are part of the wider experience. The encoding-decoding advertising framework enables these considerations.

Simulations

Jean Baudrillard's portrayal of the world as being 'hyperreal', one increasingly marked by simulation and simulacra, can be related directly to advertising and in particular to its visual aspects (Baudrillard 1981, 1983). In his postmodern account of the contemporary world, the authenticity of image-saturated social experience is brought into doubt. In this approach, simulacra – the signs and symbols that represent reality – come to overwhelm the real. The quest to uncover the real is unfulfilled as, according to Baudrillard, the simulation is without an original: it is a copy of something that never existed. Ridley Scott's film *Blade Runner*, in which synthetic humans known as 'replicants' are barely discernible from real human beings, is a good illustration of this.

The concepts of hyperreality and simulation are highly significant to film and television production generally and to advertising in particular. Screen advertisements are an assembly of clips and takes, scripts, visual devices, musical passages and sounds – the finished product that is seen and heard by the advertising viewer hasn't taken place, doesn't exist outside of its digital assembly. Yet the vibrancy of the advertisement's surface appearance seems to correspond to authentic real experience. For the viewer it exists only in the moment of its transmission. In addition the television advertisement exists in multiple copies and can be received simultaneously by numerous viewers in different places at different times.

Postmodern advertising for Baudrillard is 'absolute advertising'. But as advertising increasingly becomes disconnected from the product it is promoting, its role in providing information about commodities diminishes. It ceases to refer to the signified to which symbolic meaning can be attached (Baudrillard 1994). Consequently the advertising sign system becomes increasingly detached from products and use values. We can see this as a feature of much brand advertising as distinguished from product advertising. Nevertheless this does not reduce advertising as a potent prescence in the contemporary world. Indeed Odih (2010: 117) describes postmodern advertisements 'that saturate our daily lives' as being 'splendid; indeed spectacular.'

Spectacle of culture

The idea and image of the spectacle associated with advertising is a reminder of the work of the Situationists who coined the phrase 'the society of the spectacle' (Barnard 2004; Stallabrass 2006). The term was part of the group's critical analysis of a capitalist, consumer-orientated society (Debord 1992 [1977], 1991; Watts & Orbe 2009). The concept of the spectacle was originally developed by Guy Debord in the late 1950s and has more recently been characterized as 'the submission of more and more facets of human sociability – areas of everyday life, forms of recreation, patterns of speech, idioms of local solidarity … to the deadly solicitations (the lifeless bright sameness) of the market' (Boal, Clark, Matthews, & Watts 2005: 19). Furthermore the spectacle of culture is about 'an unstoppable barrage of … image-motifs … aimed at sewing the citizen back (unobtrusively), individually into a deadly simulacrum of community' (Boal *et al.* 2005: 21). Debord talked about two forms that the spectacle could take: the 'concentrated' spectacle that characterized totalitarian societies such as the USSR or Nazi Germany or the 'diffuse' spectacle that is a characteristic of the intense capitalist economies and accompanies the abundance of commodities (Debord 1992 [1977]; Crary 2009). Modern-day Situationists view life as increasingly commodified. This is aided by the spread of new technologies, information and communication systems and flows and extended frames of representation in which increasingly 'all of life presents itself as an immense accumulation of spectacles' (Seltzer 2010: 125). Consequently the spectacle promotes mass consumption as a way of life. This is particularly evident in the exploration of outdoor urban advertising.

Speed up

David Harvey's response to many of these general trends and ideas associated with postmodern thinking is to emphasize these phenomena as a result of a 'speed up' in the economy. This has, for Harvey, resulted in an acceleration in the production and circulation of commodities. More things are produced and more quickly. This acceleration of production is set against, and contributes to, rapidly changing fashions, styles and tastes. Commodities have a built-in obsolescence which assists in creating demand for new products. Consequently speed up becomes an aspect of the culture in general. This occurs in conjunction with what he terms the 'space-time compression', where both time – the duration of life, experience and objects – and space – the distance between things – appears to compact.

Globalization

In addition globalization is an increasingly identifiable aspect of contemporary society. Its economic and political underpinning has become manifest in the social and cultural experiences of many people (Giddens 1991; Held *et al.* 1999). Advertising has long been an important element of the global economy, accumulating profit, directing production and providing employment. Major advertising agencies operate on a global scale, representing companies and marketing products, many of which are no longer being sold only on domestic markets. They create advertising campaigns that are international in their visual and marketing impact. The development of the Internet and subsequent Internet marketing has been a significant feature of this. In the late nineteenth century advertising was already starting to be pitched across national boundaries; and in the early part of the twentieth century US agencies began to expand. For instance McCann Erickson, now a global advertising agency, moved into Europe in the late 1920s and into Australia in 1959 (Faulconbridge, Beaverstock, Nativel & Taylor 2011). Campaigns for products like Coca-Cola, Shell and other globally marketed goods were designed for worldwide consumption (Mattelart 1991).

The representation of local cultures and experiences has proved difficult in a globalized world. For instance the differences in local language, dress codes and forms of behaviour, in addition to the cultural contingencies of advertising expectations and reception, have made this a complex area. McCann Erickson's L'Oréal advertising, which started in 1973 and famously included the 'Because I'm worth it' line spoken by actresses and models such as Cybill Shepherd and Jennifer Aniston, is a good example of a global campaign that sought national-local validity. Throughout the 1980s and 1990s the adverts featured a series of female actresses or models who demonstrated the benefits of the L'Oréal product with exaggerated 'hair' movements, overly stylized poses and a general fetishization of the body and physical appearance. British actress Cheryl Cole fronted the UK 2009 version of the L'Oréal New Elvive advertisement (see Plate 6). A textual analysis of this adverting campaign suggests an assembly of visual, verbal and textual signifiers of celebrity and glamour mixed with specific local features represented by Cole's north-east English, working-class accent, her on-screen persona and celebrity history. The advert used a significant colour combination of red, white and blue: the components of the national flag. Similar L'Oréal adverts for the same product aimed at other national audiences were broadcast in the same year. Different colours dominated the adverts, with blue and grey used for Brazil and grey and red for France. Similarly, different celebrities have been chosen by L'Oréal to star in the New Elvive adverts, with soap opera and film actress Ana Serradilla featuring in the South American version and middle-class English- and French-speaking Canadian Evangeline Lilly for the French. Market strategy is global – but tailored to the specifics of regional and national characteristics familiar to the audience.

Active audiences

According to postmodern thinking, audiences are also thought of as being active as well as being global. In both the advertising industry and in the academic world, the idea of the unidirectional advertising message that secures its univalent message through a preferred reading has fallen out of favour. The importance and variety of circumstances in which reception occurs, and how these impact on the reception and construction of meaning, are enabled through the encoding-decoding advertising framework. Extreme 'active audience' theory underplays or even disavows the part played by the encoder of the message, suggesting that audiences are totally free to create their own meanings around advertisements without recourse to any intentionality on the part of the message sender. This has recently been termed an 'uncritical populist strand of Cultural Studies to an absurd extreme' (McGuigan 2012). It developed from late 1980s postmodernist 'active audience', 'resistance', and 'semiotic democracy' theories (Fiske 1986, 1987, 1989; Grossberg 1984; Ang 1996). However, linked to this is what some commentators have called 'second wave' and 'third wave advertising' (Leslie 1997), which involves an appreciation of more creative and ambiguous campaigns and greater knowledge of audiences through research. Audiences are conceived as sophisticated consumers with a high level of self and market awareness. In addition saturation advertising and emersion of advertising within the general culture has led to consumers becoming 'cognitively and aesthetically reflexive' (Faulconbridge *et al.* 2011: 13). The decoding aspect of the encoding-decoding advertising framework enables consideration of the complexity of audience response and participation in the creation of advertising meaning.

Deconstruction

Jacques Derrida's theory of *deconstruction* – of taking apart or stripping down a text and exploring interpretations and conflicts that might be apparent in it or arise from it – has had a particular resonance in the study of advertising. Derrida's deconstruction technique identifies not only what is there in the text as a presence but also what is unstated or unseen as an absence. It highlights the inconsistencies and contradiction in a text. *Différance* is another of Derrida's concepts, suggesting that words and images don't have absolute, unchanging meanings but draw their significance from being different from other things around them. The idea of the 'decentring of the subject' in which advertising meanings shift according to the identity of the viewer was also important to his thinking. Derrida's work on the framing of cultural images is also important to an understanding of the presentation and reception of advertisements (1987). All adverts need 'frames' if only to mark them out from other aspects of the world. This is of particular significance when considering the flow and circulation of screen-based advertising such as television, cinema, Internet and handheld. This helps in an understanding of the significance and meanings that advertisements might have as part of a flow of images and ideas which are part of the contemporary world (Appadurai 1996; Lash & Lury 2007).

These ideas inform an understanding of the decoding aspects of the encoding-decoding advertising framework.

Pomo style

In art and cultural production, postmodernism, as we have seen so far, is considered a series of underlying ideas, themes and approaches. It is also considered a visual style (Foster 1983; Heartney 2001). Many highly stylized advertisements in the 1980s and 1990s that concentrated on visual effect came to be labelled postmodern (Gee 2013). This was particularly noticeable in television advertising and to a lesser extent in newsprint and outdoor advertising. Guinness and Benetton advertising were, in different ways, part of this trend. With a detachment from product and lavish visual display in the former and shock-ad product disengagement in the latter, narrative became disjointed and fragmentary. Stylistic postmodernism, including nostalgia as a cultural form and referencing of the past often as an ironic allusion to previous advertising styles, became familiar. Gibbs SR toothpaste advertising in the 1990s imitated the content, characters and discourse of its own 1950s advertisements. Self-referencing became a well-used feature of the pomo style in advertising and culture generally. In an ironic manner one such toothpaste advert made reference both to young women as 'sweeties', an old-fashioned but common sexist term, and to the authority of white-coated scientific experts endorsing the product. Both were features of an earlier age of advertising. Frederic Jameson distinguished between pastiche and parody in postmodern culture noting the critical edge of the latter (1984). Advertising pastiche is a pale copy of previous advertising styles and forms, and became prominent itself as a style of advertising in the early 1990s.

Conclusion

This chapter began with an account of 'culture and civilization' thinking, which followed in the tradition of Matthew Arnold's work of the nineteenth century. Associated with F.R. Leavis, high culture was perceived as an elite preserve and popular culture an inferior form of expression. Advertising as part of this latter category was frowned upon as having little cultural merit. It gave rise to genuine, if condescending, concern about advertising effects 'promoting undesirable attitudes' in a mass society (Thompson 1932: 241). In many ways these concerns were also those of the Frankfurt School, who considered the political effects of manipulation and false consciousness in a capitalist economy and society where mass culture was fuelled by the mass media, of which advertising was an important part. Ideology and hegemony were seen to be essential features of social stability through time, and advertising played an important part in this. Postmodern and late-modern ideas added to and enhanced many of these considerations and in some cases came to challenge the premise on which they were founded. Considerations of metanarratives and historical genealogy, the nature of global society and the society of the spectacle and consequence of simulation enhanced an analysis of culture and advertising.

In the 1970s the Birmingham Centre for Contemporary Cultural Studies inaugurated groundbreaking research and analysis into popular and mass culture: the study of culture was interdisciplinary and required a broad remit encompassing an exploration of both its production and reception. Advertising studies benefitted immensely from this, and Stuart Hall's encoding/decoding paper provided the framework for an approach to advertising. One of the main qualities of the encoding/decoding model is that it offers a model of *communication exchange* which enables the whole process to be conceptualized. It also provides a clear framework in which the production of advertising can be imagined, how advertising campaigns come to appear as they do, and the kind of economic, social and cultural work they do. Finally the framework enables and encourages a serious exploration of the role of media audiences and potential consumers in the reception of advertising meaning. This and the three elements of the framework (encoding–text–decoding) are explored in subsequent chapters.

Part II

Frameworks

6 Advertising framework and encoding

Introduction

This chapter outlines the advertising framework, identifying stages of advertising production and reception. The framework classifies and isolates for the purpose of analysis three areas of advertising study – encoding, texts and decoding. The framework can be used in the widest sense, to conceptualize or paint a general picture of the process of contemporary advertising, or in a narrower sense, enabling an analysis of a specific advertisement. The encoding element of the framework is that part of the advertising process where the advertising idea is selected and formed from economic, social and cultural knowledge and research and then shaped into a text. Advertising encoding is about the making of advertising. The textual element of the framework refers to the advertisement that has been created. It can also refer to an advertising campaign or to a form or genre of advertising. The decoding part of the framework refers to advertising reception and is primarily instigated by the first two elements of the framework. It is the place in the advertising process where the public receives and interprets advertisements. One of the main qualities of the advertising framework is that it offers a model of *communication exchange* which enables the whole process to be conceptualized. On the basis of this introduction to the advertising framework this chapter proceeds to explore advertising encoding and the role of 'cultural intermediaries' in this process. It offers an analysis of the encoding of an advertising campaign for Pantene, a hair product that was widely promoted before and during the London Olympics of 2012. The chapter concludes with an exploration of certain cultural strands concerning celebrity, cycling and in particular women encoded in the Pantene advertising campaign.

Encoding/decoding model

The advertising framework is based on the encoding/decoding model expounded by Stuart Hall in the 1970s and 1980s and further developed through the work of the Birmingham Centre for Contemporary Cultural Studies (Hall 1973, 1981a). Hall wanted to examine the nature and effect of news programmes. He used the model as a means of exploring a media and political consensus against trades union 'militancy' which operated within television news programmes and other media outlets in the 1970s. Hall examined how certain social groups were able to stand outside of this ideological consensus during what became know as the 'winter of discontent'. This was the popular term used to describe the effect of the widespread strikes of 1978 and 1979, which took place while Jim Callaghan was prime minister. The Labour government had imposed a pay freeze. Media news coverage was hostile to working people taking strike action to defend their standard of living against rising prices. Widespread strikes, mainly local authority and public sector, took place. Despite media 'encoding' of a consensus that striking was 'wrong', strikers and militant workers decoded news messages in a different way to that which had been preferred by the broadcasters. The model was an attempt to examine this (Hall 1981a).

The model has subsequently been used to analyse a range of other, often less obviously ideological constructions associated with ordinary, everyday experiences, such as viewing television programmes or television advertisements as part of mundane leisure and recreation activity. These are less overtly ideological in creating a social consensus but may well be where, to paraphrase Louis Althusser, 'ideology is working behind your back'. The model was the basis of much study into television (Morley 1992) and a wide range of theoretical and empirical work, for instance the production and reception of press reporting (Deacon *et al.* 1999) and the interpretations of news editorials (Torrenen 2001). It has been used explicitly to examine advertising production (Soar 2000), advertising texts (Kelly, Lawlor & O'Donohoe 2009; Wharton 2013) and occurs implicitly in many accounts of advertising production and reception (Leiss *et al.* 2005: 501).

An initial outline of the process can be explained like this. From the wide range of material available to them, broadcasters select and then form particular meanings or values. These are then translated through specific words, images or sounds into the form and nature of the particular medium. The message is then in place to be decoded by an audience. At this explanatory level, the Morse code system provides a suitable analogy. However, in the encoding/decoding formulation different decodings can occur according to a range of factors. Hall refers to the mass communication process that the model seeks to represent as 'the articulation of linked but distinctive moments – production, circulation, distribution/consumption, reproduction' (Hall 2006 [1973]: 163).

Advertising framework

The encoding/decoding model has been extended and applied to advertising and operates primarily as a conceptual framework. The advertising framework is first composed of encoding, usually carried out in advertising agencies, which bring together a range of technical and creative abilities and is informed by research and economic considerations. Advertising texts form the middle element of the framework, presented in different media which enable and constrain the scope and impact of the advertising message. The advertising framework encourages an 'image' of the totality of advertising from message production, presentation through radio, television, billboard, Internet or other advertising forms, to the decoding of the advert by an audience. The decoding takes place within a range of contexts and environments in which a variety of factors can be important. These stages form what Hall has described as 'the articulation of connected practices, each of which retains its distinctiveness and has its own specific modality, its own forms and conditions of existence' (Hall 2006 [1973]: 163). In 1989 Hall suggested that 'if you are going to work with the model, you have to change the model and develop it' (Cruz & Lewis 1994: 272).

encoding → text → decoding → preferred reading
negotiated reading
oppositional reading

Figure 6.1 Advertising framework

Therefore, inserting 'advertising texts' between the encoding and decoding aspects of the model gives emphasis to its necessary but unstated element and in the process strengthens the model as a conceptual framework for both theoretical and empirical research. This addition, although already implicit in the encoding/decoding model, gives a greater weight of emphasis to the text – the actual advertisement or products – as an element of the communication process *in its own right* (Jordin & Brunt 1988; Poster 1990; Cruz & Lewis 1994). Consequently, while exploring any of the three stages of the message exchange – encoding/production, text in momentary isolation and reception/decoding – this analysis will draw attention to the whole process or totality of the chain of production and exchange. This is what Hall refers to as 'the circuit as a whole' (Hall 2006 [1973]: 164), in which is situated the specific area to which analysis is to be applied.

It is in the area of reception that the advertising framework enables an account of the breadth of culture and social experience of the advertising audience to be imagined as part of the advertising process. There are according to Hall three potential positions associated with decoding: the preferred or dominant reading of advertising, a negotiated reading and an oppositional one. The preferred reading is where the meaning intended by the producer is accepted by the reader, listener or viewer of the advert. In the preferred reading there will be a close match between the set of codes, values and assumptions about the world from which the message is encoded and the codes with which the reader or viewer brings to the advertisement and makes sense of the message. In other words it requires a close cultural match between producer and receiver and agreement about a range of issues – from social values to design preferences. The negotiated reading does not fully accept the preferred meaning of the advert. The viewer, reader or listener accepts the main features of the message in the widest sense, but will locate its meaning in a personal, local sense associated with that individual's experience and place in the world. This produces a negotiated reading – one of partial acceptance but negotiated to suit the circumstances of the receiver of the advertisement. Third, according to Hall, the message may be decoded in a totally oppositional way in which the preferred meaning is rejected. In this scenario the advertising message is received within an oppositional code – a set of values, understandings, experiences – that are based upon an alternative framework or way of seeing the world. This may be based on a variety of factors, but for Hall the ideological content of the message is made visible in the oppositional reading.

Advertising loop

Descriptions of the original model tend to create an image of linearity with the process starting with encoding and terminating with a decoding outcome. Indeed when the model was first applied to advertisements the tendency was to identify a series of decodings/reading outcomes produced in different circumstances and environments by a wide range of decoders. These readings appeared to stand alone as outcomes. However, Hall had referred to the model as 'the circuit as a whole' (Hall 2006 [1973]: 164) which contained the three stages of the message exchange: encoding, text and decoding. This draws attention to the whole process or totality of the chain of production and exchange.

The advertising framework when considered as a loop creates an image of a continuous or continual process over time. This process is often referred to as the feedback loop (Couldry 2012: 23). This emphasizes decodings of advertisements entering the

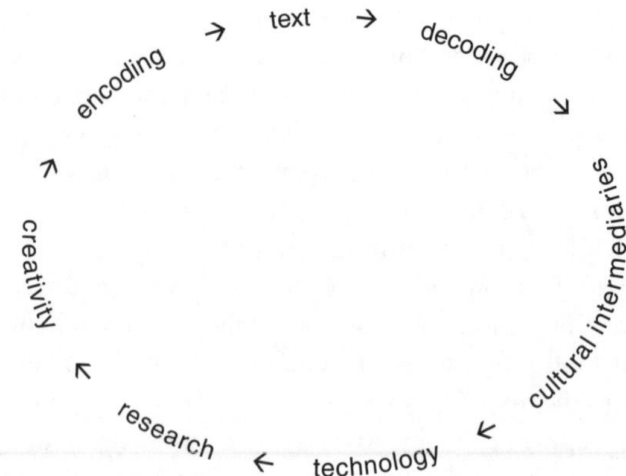

Figure 6.2 Advertising framework loop

general culture – the store of references, images and phrases. Advertising decodings, even oppositional decodings, are identified often through research carried out by agencies into advertising appreciation or by the informal observational research carried out by creatives in the process of identifying trends, styles and popular interests which become the basis for advertising ideas (Fenwick & Wharton 2013). These are then fed back into the advertising process. Indeed Odih goes so far as to identify this process in which 'advertisers rummage through everyday culture in the relentless search for symbolic meanings to augment the utility value of commodities' (2010: 96). Consequently this creates an **advertising loop** as culture is tapped for ideas, images and representations that can be incorporated into advertising campaigns (see Figure 6.2).

Trends in the diffusion and dissemination of advertising through Internet technology encourage an element of creativity on the part of decoders, who are encouraged to post-on, sometimes in an abridged form, advertising messages. This is a form of word of mouth advertising and is often labelled electronic word of mouth (EWOM). This activity is often referred to in discussions about 'prosumption'. The term 'prosumer' is formed from bringing together the words *producer* and *consumer* and is intended to describe ways in which consumers take part in the process of production (Toffler 1980). For example, Jeremy Rifkin describes how prosumers use Internet and network culture in 'producing and sharing music, videos, news and knowledge' (Rifkin 2014; Ritzer & Jurgenson 2010). If 'advertising prosumer' is a useful description of people 'working on' and transmitting advertisements to friends and colleagues through electronic networks, it indicates how they become part of the advertising communication process creating value for advertising campaigns but without receiving wages in return (Davies 2014).

Encoding advertisements

The production or encoding of advertising is by and large organized by advertising agencies. The advertising agents have been a part of the advertising process since the early 1800s. As we have seen they at first performed basic media functions – for instance, securing advertising space for clients in the pages of newspapers. Manufacturers and retailers produced their own copy and the agency made money from buying space cheaply and selling it on at a higher rate. Over time the functions of the agency became more developed and sophisticated.

Advertising agencies of the twentieth century were the outcome of a new type of society based on the development of industrial production. The mass production of goods created mass markets with economies producing commodities and mass consumption on a global scale. Advertising agencies developed across the nineteenth and into the twentieth centuries and came to provide a range of other services in addition to space brokerage. Buying and selling-on media space and time required a level of knowledge about the media, its circulation and audiences who were to be transformed into potential customers for the advertised products. This knowledge became the basis for the encoding of advertising that largely took place in the agencies. Consequently the advertising agency role expanded and became a channel for culture to enter advertising and for advertising to become, in its turn, a key aspect of culture.

Modern agencies

By the 1920s 'full-service' advertising agencies were operating, providing the advertising functions such as media planning, research and account management required to create and direct successful twentieth-century advertising campaigns. As they developed they came to offer the advertiser the necessary means to create an advertisement. At first copywriting – the production of the textual body of the advertisement – was offered as a free service, and served as an inducement and enhancement of the media space the agency offered. The association between art and culture was affirmed as the art, skills and people associated with the production of literature and journalism began to work in advertising production. Agencies also came to offer the services of illustrators and photographers, forming the full 'creative' mechanism of personnel and skills for producing an advertisement. The visual language of art – painting, photography and film – also became part of advertising.

Advertisements are shaped by the art and skill of the people working in agencies who provide the words and images that make up the advertising text. This creative process involves the ideas and knowledge of copywriters, art directors, visualizers and photographers. It also involves a wide range of other people and skills deployed in the agencies: for instance, account planners developing campaigns, writing creative briefs, using and possibly commissioning research. Advertising encoding is increasingly based on a wide range of quantitative and qualitative research (Fenwick & Wharton 2013). Media planners are also important, choosing the appropriate medium to carry the advertising campaign, with media buyers selecting and acquiring media space (Kelly *et al.* 2009). Advertising is also dependent on the enabling technology of the medium chosen to carry the advertisement. From the representation of products and creation of promotional methods to the voice, tone and mode of address, the advertisement is shaped by the formal and representational methods of the medium of which it is a part. Agencies therefore, as part of the encoding process, require a sophisticated knowledge of different media. This can range from an understanding of the organization of media to its technological and creative potential. Some elements of advertising agency activity, such as research and accounting, can be aligned with scientific and economic methodologies. The creative production of words and images has a close relationship with artistic and literary practice (MacRury 2009b: 143).

As the agencies developed towards the close of the twentieth century, cultural production was still seen – not least by the practitioners themselves – as part of the 'charismatic ideology of creation'. This is where the production of ideas in advertising is viewed as akin to the aesthetics of artistic production, which is usually accompanied by a high-minded sense of 'taste' (Bourdieu 1984). Bourdieu offered a sociological theory of cultural production which stressed the cultural *power* attached to production and consumption and where 'taste functions as a marker of class using the word in a double sense to mean both a socio-economic category and the suggestion of a particular level of quality' (Storey 2009: 219). In addition, advertising creatives were seen as being part of a general social group. Florida referred to a 'creative class' and advertising creatives can be seen to be an element of it (Florida 2002: 69).

The creative class in advertising can be viewed as producers and shapers, the 'taste shapers' of culture (Featherstone 1991; Nixon 2003; Powell & Prasad 2010). They are referred to as 'cultural intermediaries' which can suggest a role as 'critic or social commentator' and as a 'producer of symbolic meaning' (Powell & Prasad 2010: 111–24). Advertising creatives also play a part in shaping cultural forms and values into advertisements. As cultural intermediaries they 'shape both use values and exchange values, and seek to manage how these values are connected with people's lives' (Negus 2002: 504).

Nixon and others have discussed the formal knowledge of creatives working in the advertising industry based on market research, sales and other knowledge based on research (Nixon 2003; Kelly, Lawlor & O'Donohoe 2009). This is in addition to their own informal knowledge based on observations of consumer culture often drawn from their own everyday experiences (Nixon 2003: 35). Kelly *et al.* have put this succinctly, referring to the cultural intermediaries' ability to 'know what was out there' (2009: 139). The encoding of an advertisement includes the formal and informal knowledge, creative skills and abilities of advertising creatives/cultural intermediaries working within the milieu of the advertising agency. The agency is itself situated within a context of research, marketing and sales promotion, and in the wider changing cultural patterning of the contemporary world.

Advertising encoding is that part of the advertising framework (see Figure 6.1 above) that precedes the presentation and delivery of the advertisement. The advertising director, creative or designer, working individually or as part of a team, is central to this process of advertising production. It creates what Hall refers to as a 'signifying process', the moment of the presentation of the advertisement (1972, 1997). This has been addressed in both theoretical and empirical work (Shapiro 1981; Schudson 1993; du Gay 1997; Soar 2000). Advertising encoding includes not only the process of advertising production, but the conditions and relations of production, which contribute to, or in part determine, the nature of the message. Encoding as an element of the advertising framework emphasizes the constructed nature of the media message. A list of productive elements and activities that go into advertising encoding is wide ranging. It might include: individual and group conceptual work; production of copy, layouts and sketches; the organization of service functions; technical production of film or printing; and the consideration and organization of outlets within practical, technological, ideological and cultural parameters (Nixon 2003; Soar 2000). In short, the process of advertising encoding includes the selection, shaping, creation and packaging of information and culture into highly structured formats: advertising texts.

Encoding case study – Pendleton and Pantene

The encoding of advertising is explored in this section through an analysis of an advertising campaign for Procter & Gamble's hair-product range Pantene Pro-V.

This was an international, integrated marketing campaign organized through newsprint, television and Internet advertising in the run-up to the 2012 London Olympics. In particular the analysis focuses on a newsprint advertisement appearing in various UK newspapers featuring cyclist Victoria Pendleton. It was accompanied by a related television advertisement (http://www.youtube.com/watch?v=CzOBGaymHfQ). The advertisement was referred to extensively on various Internet sites, including Pendleton's own web page.

The Pantene advertising campaign was part of a wider Procter & Gamble 10-year Olympic sponsorship deal that involved the deployment of 150 athletes as 'brand ambassadors' for Procter & Gamble products. In the UK this included cyclist Chris Hoy promoting Gillette razor blades, runner Paula Radcliffe promoting Fairy washing-up liquid and pairing Pendleton with Pantene. The worldwide Pantene campaign featured highly successful sportswomen due to compete in the 2012 Olympics, including US swimmer Natalie Coughlin, Argentinian tennis player Gisela Dulko and Pendleton representing Great Britain. Procter & Gamble used full-service marketing communications agencies such as Wing in the preparation of the campaigns.

Olympics and advertising

The major media and cultural narrative of 2012 in Great Britain and to a lesser extent other parts of the world was based on the summer London Olympic Games. It provided a range of national and international advertising hooks, and the Games were supported by a variety of sponsorship arrangements with the leading global companies (Poon & Prendergast 2006; Davis 2008). Saturation television coverage attracted a worldwide television audience which increased from 3.6 billion for the Sydney Olympics of 2000 to 4.8 billion for London 2012 (Statista 2012). Although heavily regulated and protected by the International Olympic Committee (IOC), the five-circle Olympic logo became associated with advertising brands such as Visa, Samsung and the ubiquitous McDonald's and Coca Cola.

Since the Second World War, the Olympic Games has undergone major transformations with modifications to funding and sponsorship arrangements and with athletes presented as sports personalities. Until the 1970s Olympic sport was nominally considered amateur. Since then, a widespread commercialization of social experience has occured (Streeck 2012) involving the representation of celebrity as part of culture (Lawrence 2009; Cashmore 2006); the presentation of the physical self as stylized embodiment (Rojek 2007: 76–85); and a development in trends in the representation of women in advertising (Frith, Shaw & Cheng 2009; Goodman 2009). Sport in general and the Olympics in particular have come to offer 'ample opportunity for celebratory self-presentation ... fashion has come to play an essential part in this, for athletes as well as spectators' (Streeck 2012: 34). Streeck offers the rise of sportswear firms like Adidas and Puma, which specialized in a limited number of sports shoes a few years ago and have become 'multi-billion-dollar global companies that essentially make their money from fashion products', as an example of the commercialization and centrality of sport to the global economy (Streeck 2012: 34). The Olympics attracts vast audiences and a strong brand presence through association with sportsmen and women, events and activities and through media and non-media discursive elements (MacRury 2009b).

Golden signs

The encoding of the design elements in the Pantene advertisements featuring Victoria Pendleton brought together several cultural strands. (The campaign image can be viewed online at www.the5thfloor.co.uk/2012/01/30/victoria-pendleton-in-pantene-ad or at http://pantenegold.advertimage.co.uk. You can also scan the QR codes on the left on your mobile or handheld.) Narratives of individual sporting achievement, celebrity presence and glamour and the media's own presentation of the games were combined in the advertising sign (Powell 2009). These came together in the sign of gold as success in which associations and meanings were created and articulated. Gold is denoted through Pendleton's sequined costume, her tanned golden features with eyes upturned, the general abstracted setting and vaguely defined golden horizon and the connotation of gold through value, success and glamour. Olympic gold is affirmed in the strapline: 'It could only be Gold shining from start to finish' (see http://itcouldonlybegold.advertimage.co.uk).

The encoding of the celebrity sign relies on several background narrative elements. First, Pendleton's well publicized private life and relationships function to affirm solidarity with the lives and experiences of ordinary women. Yet at the same time fame and celebrity place her at an exotic distance. Second, as is often the case, the natural good looks of female celebrities are connoted as glamour. The image of Pendleton featured on the covers of magazines such as *FHM*, *Esquire* and *Style*. The third element is Pendleton's sporting achievement – the winning of medals and breaking of records culminating in a final appearance as a professional cyclist at the London Olympics.

Pendleton's achievements based on her remarkable sporting accomplishments are real, and her celebrity status can be distinguished from that of other celebrities whose status relies on media presence alone. Paris Hilton and Jade Goody, for instance, were presented as being famous for being famous, without a referent in affirmative behaviour necessary to sustain celebrity presence in a positive and meaningful manner. In many ways celebrities correspond to Baudrillard's simulations – media constructs without referents. MacRury draws on a distinction made by Ruth Sunderland in 2008, suggesting two distinct categories of celebrity: 'class one celebrities, whose fame is based on real talent or achievement, and class two celebrities whose fame has less admirable provenance' (MacRury 2009b: 142).

Encoding considerations

A series of considerations in advance of the launch of the Pendleton-Pantene advertising campaign would have guided the encoding of the advertisement. One is to do with the technical production of a campaign that included both newsprint and television advertising, involving issues of availability of studio space, technical equipment and personnel including that of the main player. The coordination of production deadlines for internal and external teams of creative and technical staff would have been important. Considerations based on available time and space are followed by issues of the general cost of production matched against its likely pecuniary gain. The second set of considerations are to do with the content of the advertisement. How would the signification of celebrity and glamour and the costume-gold of Pantene cycling sustain itself as a serious image and successful advertisement over time? This would have involved research, testing the advertising idea in its formative and final stages of production. This may well have involved feedback from client representatives and through potential consumer surveys designed to gather reflexive accounts from focus groups and individuals using a variety of research methods and techniques.

The question of advertising content can be divided into two main areas. First: how does the idea measure against the real-life experiences that the likely viewers of the advertisement and potential consumers of the product encounter in their own lives? This is emphatically not to ask the question: does the advertisement *reflect* the lived experience of ordinary women? The advertisement is not intended as a 'realist' image but as a symbolic representation. However, the tropes 'women', 'activity' and 'sport' are grounded in women's experience of home, work and as users of public space. The advertisement's attraction and to some extent its success is based on an engagement with a range of female roles and perceptions of how people behave for others and how they feel and behave for themselves. It might even – if it is based on keen cultural observation – consider how woman negotiate real public space as cyclists. How does the image of overtly stylized hair, golden bicycle and party kit relate to a reality not just of cycling but of being a women in everyday space?

As has been acknowledged the advertisement is not a realist image. Nevertheless how authentic or desirable is the distance between lived reality and the depiction of a fantasy of golden accomplishment? What sort of realizable achievement, in addition to or comparable with Olympic success, is being intimated here? Or is the image intended to shine as a celebration of detachment from the real – as a gratifying image of an aesthetic–glamour spectacle, but without credibility or validity. The stylized hair – which is after all the central point of the advertisement's promotional technique and the referent that binds the protagonist, product and its potential users together – is depicted as a form in which shape, colour and implied texture are prominent. It is not unlike the depictions of female hair in modernist paintings such as those of Ferdinand Leger where the female form is accompanied by hair 'shapes' seemingly unattached to the women's bodies. The depiction of hair as display item is central to the overall connotation of the image, and other depicted items and activities are subsumed into this. So in a real but roundabout way, the encoding of the advertisement is to do with the distance between women's real-life experiences and the stylized and ethereal imagery of the advertisement.

A further consideration guiding the encoding process of the Pendleton-Pantene advertisement is: how might it compare to other advertisements for similar products? An advertisement needs to stand out enough to be noticed but operate within audience expectations of an advertising genre. The constant question becomes: how does it compare with advertisements featuring women as glamour subjects or with advertisements featuring cycling as an activity? For example L'Oréal and other similar forms of advertising have deployed celebrities and comparable styles for some considerable time. Cycling as a reference to fitness, leisure and transport in advertising is less usual. However, it is interesting to compare

Pantene cycling with Persil's cycling advertisements featuring the strapline 'blood sweat and tears' from 2004. These were the large-scale outdoor advertising campaign posters positioned in fast-flowing, car-dominated cities in which cycling was a marginal and dangerous activity (Wharton 2013: 70).[1] In addition the encoding process had to account for how the completed Pantene image would compare with the saturation of cycling imagery in coverage of the Games and not least with Pendleton's own performances in the velodrome and media coverage of the event.

Several more general issues and questions relating to the encoding of the Pendleton-Pantene advertisement remain. Similar questions might be posed of other high-profile advertising campaigns. First, what are the gains that Procter & Gamble make from an advertising campaign encoded in this way? Does it merely maintain its product market share or increase sales because of this design? Does it encourage a wider audience for the product creating a more diffuse profile? Does the product become connected or attached to new aspects of social activity? Second, what does the encoding of this marketing message in this way do for women: for their social status as athletes; as everyday participants in sporting and other social and cultural activities; for female identity, self-image and self-esteem? Does the accentuated style and glamour trend in advertising appear as one type of representation of women among many or the overriding image of modern women? Third, what does it do for cycling and in particular the image of cycling? Cycling as an activity is not only part of Olympic and other high-profile sporting events. It is also an everyday activity and important to debates about sustainable transport, the use of public and especially urban space and healthy living. Cycling goes to the heart of social, cultural and economic debates about the human presence amidst an accelerating techno-culture.

Despite the track success of the Olympic cyclists, the Pantene image lingers on even after the closure of the Games. The everyday bodily experience of cycling is dependent on movement and direction. This is reinforced through observation of elite athletes, the fastest in the world, competing in the Olympic velodrome. Dromology is the study of speed and is in the words of Paul Virilio 'the science of the ride, the journey, the drive, the way' (Armitage 1999: 35; Virilio 1986 [1977]). It suggests that the speed at which something travels is part of its being and part of our perception of it. The Futurists, painters of movement and speed, in the early part of the twentieth century depicted people and objects in motion in their paintings in a vital and convincing manner. Pantene's advertisement presents cycling as a spectacle of petrifaction. The implied passage of the cycle is from left to right in front of an ill-defined and unreal backdrop not unlike the backdrop to many car advertisements. It creates a semi-abstract setting unsupportive of even the illusion of movement. A reading of the advertisement starts with a recognition of vibrant human activity (speed generated by the body) and finishes not with the warm glow of gold as the advertisement wishes to suggest, but in a suspended frozen moment. In addition to the concept of dromology, Virilio has introduced to the world the idea of 'polar inertia' (2000), which 'complicates the association between speed, movement, time and duration' (Shuner 2013). Polar inertia as the term suggests is about the lack of movement. The human body becomes overwhelmed by technologies of representation and telecommunications and movement comes to a halt. Movement, driven by human effort, appears suspended, going nowhere: turning to stone.

Conclusion

This chapter has established an advertising framework built on the work of Stuart Hall's model of encoding/decoding of media messages but incorporating elements from other traditions. The advertising framework is composed of three parts: encoding, text and decoding. It enables an image of the production of advertising as a general activity and the analysis of specific advertising campaigns. The encoding element of the framework is that part of the advertising process, largely carried out through advertising agencies, where concepts based on considerable cultural, social and economic knowledge and research are loaded into advertising form. The text refers to the advertisement or advertising campaign; and the decoding element of the framework is where the public receives and interprets the advertisement in their own cultural lives. People's cultural experiences are often the basis for ideas and concepts built into advertisements, suggesting that the advertising framework operates more as a loop than in a linear pattern.

The chapter explored encoding through a discussion of Pantene's 2012 Olympic advertisement. The cultural threads that led to the advertising looking as it did have been unpicked and the advert was compared both to other similar advertisements and to the life experiences it references. The next two chapters deal with advertising texts as they appear in media outlets and as they may be interpreted by audiences.

Note

1 This was written in the week that Bradley Wiggins, celebrity cyclist and winner of the 2012 Tour de France, was knocked from his bike by a motorist on an open road and taken to hospital with suspected broken ribs.

7 Texts

Introduction

This chapter examines advertising texts, as the central part of the advertising framework, and the different approaches that can be taken to them. Sociological, media and cultural studies perspectives of quantitative, content analysis explore the prevalence and frequency of advertisements in different media and cultural environments. This approach is contrasted with qualitative, textual analysis, including formal and iconographic methods of exploration involving icons and symbols from the art-historical tradition. This is followed by an introduction to a study of signs as elucidated by Barthes, Peirce and others in the semiotic manner. Advertising context and intertextual relations are important, as is technology, to a recognition of advertising meaning and ideology. This chapter offers an analysis of newsprint car advertising as an illustration of content and textual approaches to advertising.

Texts

Advertisements are often referred to as texts. This highlights their affinity with other items of culture. The term *text* describes written documents, computer files or messages sent on mobile phones. Television, radio and other media outputs are referred to as *media texts*. The term refers to a wide range of cultural products and activities that may include imagery, words, sounds or other signifying elements that produce a meaningful message (Danesi 2006: 69). What these different things have in common is a series of patterns, shapes and narrative that bring them together as an experience for a reader, viewer or listener. Advertising texts also have specific qualities related to sales and promotion and are the product of the advertising encoding process. The related term *textuality* refers to the particular way an advertisement speaks to its audience.

Most twentieth-century studies of advertising have focused on advertising texts (Barthes 1977; Williamson 1978; Goldman 1992). This has according to Liz McFall led to a 'fascination not with advertising but with advertisements' (2004: 2) to the detriment of an understanding of other aspects of interest such as advertising institutions and practices. However, the significance of advertising cannot be separated from its place in contemporary culture and the widespread familiarity of advertising texts to people's lives and experiences (Wharton 2013). It is, today, usual to discuss advertising as a form of culture and also, as Tony Purvis has argued, 'culture … continues to be shaped in relation to advertising and advertisements' (2013: 16). Studying advertising texts helps to understand the world and how it appears.

Advertisements as texts

Advertising texts are the product of different forms of media (Corner 2002) and share similarities with elements of the host media output. For instance, a television advertisement might appear to have more in common with other forms of television than advertisements for the same product appearing elsewhere. The way in which an advertisement relates to other cultural items, including media texts and advertisements, is important and referred to as *intertextuality*. Analysis of advertising texts usually takes two forms: the qualitative, interpretivist tradition of textual analysis and the quantitative and positivist approach of content analysis (Deacon *et al.* 1999).

Textual analysis involves a close scrutiny of advertisements posing questions about meaning, whereas content analysis is about the frequency of advertisements or of elements that appear in them. The term *content analysis* is sometimes used to describe a general approach to the analysis of texts (Holsti 1969), but can also refer to a specific method of enquiry that involves some form of measurement of textual phenomena. Content analysis tends towards the *enumerative* approach, adopting statistical techniques in order to quantify and measure the frequency of occurrences of key advertising elements. These can include words, sentences, paragraphs, references, images, image types, aspects of images and other elements that form the unit of analysis within or between a volume of texts (Deacon *et al.* 1999; Hansen *et al.* 1998; Leiss *et al.* 2005: 163; Scott 2006a: 40). Content analysis as a quantitative method in the positivist and empiricist tradition is primarily concerned with establishing the frequency of certain phenomena in media output; whereas textual analysis falls within the qualitative tradition of research and is concerned to investigate the meaning and signification of texts (Scott 2006b: 297).

Content analysis

Content analysis as a method was developed in the early twentieth century. It was intended to deploy the objectivity and rigour of the natural sciences in the study of human and social phenomena. Berelson described content analysis as a 'research technique for the objective, systematic and quantitative description of the manifest content of communication' (1952: 18). In 1910, Max Weber advocated perhaps the earliest form of the method, 'to measure the quantitative changes of newspaper contents during the last generation' (quoted in Hart 1979: 181–2). Early work included the quantification of political propaganda in media outputs (Laswell 1936; Laswell & Leites 1949). At first confined to print and radio, content analysis was extended to a scrutiny of American television by George Gerbner in the 1960s (Gerbner *et al.* 1980; Gerbner 1995). It has since been used across a wide range of contemporary media forms from cartoons to music videos (Deacon *et al.* 1999) and in advertising studies exploring children and magazine advertising (Viser 1997), gender roles in radio commercials (Hurtz & Durkin 1997) and norms of female beauty in women's magazine advertising (Frith, Shaw & Cheng 2009).

Content analysis has been criticized for its claim to 'objectivity' and 'value free' research, which can lead to a masking of research choice, values, interests and ideologies that underpin the research process and contribute to its findings. However, Hansen *et al.* (1998) summarize the quantitative elements of content analysis as systematic and replicable, suggesting that research projects can be repeated at a later date. A further strength is that the method can easily deal with a large volume of media output and can create an overview or 'map' (Winston 1990: 62) or 'big picture' (Deacon *et al.* 1999: 117) of the area being studied. It is also important in identifying frequency and pattern to 'provide some indication of relative prominences and absence of key characteristics in media texts' (Hansen *et al.* 1998: 95). Content analysis rarely ascribes value, depth or significance to a text or to the signs and symbols that constitute it. For some commentators (Holsti 1969; Leiss *et al.* 1997) this is a strength, as content analysis deliberately restricts itself to measuring the manifest or surface content of the message 'expressed in quantitative measurements' (Leiss *et al.* 2005: 163). But as Sumner has succinctly put it: 'It is not the significance of repetition that is important but rather the repetition of significance' (Sumner 1979: 69).

Most commentators agree on the limited use of content analysis when deployed as a singular method of enquiry. As Lewis argues, 'cultural studies has, from its inception, surpassed the notion that the world is a value-free, objective, experiential realm that can be reduced to neat rows and columns of numbers' (1997: 86). However, when used in conjunction with other analytical techniques, quantitative content analysis has its place (Deacon *et al.* 1999; Hansen *et al.* 1998). Content analysis allows the student of advertising to gain a picture of the kinds of advertising that are prevalent at any given time or the amount of media time allotted to advertising on television or on the Internet. As a research method it is applied to the car advertising case study at the close of this chapter.

Textual analysis

In contrast, the term *textual analysis* refers to a qualitative method of enquiry 'for assessing the significance of particular ideas or meanings in the document' (Scott 2006b: 297). Textual analysis has different strands. Deacon *et al.* (1999: 135, 144) refer to textual analysis as 'semiotic and structural analysis' and 'critical linguistics', the latter emphasizing the language element of this approach. Hansen *et al.* (1998: 129) suggest something similar referring to 'discourse analysis'. The discourse studies approach to advertising texts is well represented by Guy Cook, who takes a systematic approach to texts and written language (2001). Textual analysis of advertisements also includes an analysis of imagery as well as language. Therefore, textual analysis is best thought of as an approach that looks at the details of advertising as texts in the use of both written and spoken language and of imagery. It is a qualitative rather than quantitative method. It is also interpretative, emphasizing both the researcher's and audience's involvement in interpreting and understanding advertisements.

As an analysis of imagery, textual analysis can be compared with art historical enquiry. Paintings and other art objects are the subject of art historical enquiry, looking at the conditions in which art is commissioned and produced. Art history locates art objects within prevailing stylistic circumstances and conventions through analysis and comparison with other art works over time and is keen to locate art as an aspect of the society in which it was produced. It is particularly interested in the changes that occur in art over time. The textual analysis of advertisements utilizes some of these art historical insights and skills.

Iconography

Art history predates the study of advertising and the ascendancy of semiology. Iconology or iconography is an aspect of it and is the study of the content of paintings and the interpretation of symbols. It was pioneered by the art historian Erwin Panofsky (1993 [1955]) and developed in the work of Warburg, Gombrich and others (Woo 2001;

Gombrich 1979). It is the 'branch of the History of Art which concerns itself with the subject matter or meaning of art' as distinct from a more formalist approach (Panofsky quoted in Doro & Greenhalgh 1992: 55). This involves knowledge of the meanings attached to pictures and to the people and things depicted there.

For instance, in Christian art, St Peter is usually depicted in paintings and in sculpture as holding a key or set of keys. These were understood as attributes of the saint; through possession of this symbol he would be recognized as the first of the apostles and an important figure in Christian stories. In Perugino's Sistine Chapel painting *Christ Handing the Keys to St Peter* (1481–2), the standing Christ passes the set of keys to the kneeling St Peter (see Plate 7). Either side of them are groups of disciples and other spectators framing the event on the horizontal. The keys are given prominence against the foreshortened rectangular stones that form the open square. The eye of the viewer is led across the square to the backdrop formed by Solomon's temple and two Roman triumphal arches that flank it.

In Renaissance paintings of the Annunciation, the angel Gabriel is often shown holding a lily as he visits the Virgin Mary to announce that she will give birth to Christ. The lily was a symbol of purity and represented an important idea in the narrative. The lily was also, in conjunction with other symbolic elements in the paintings, an identifier of a particular scene from the Bible. Colour was also symbolic. Ultramarine, a vivid blue, was after gold and silver the most expensive colour and often used to represent the figure of Mary in Renaissance painting. Different blues were available and contracts for paintings were known to state the quality of blue to be used to depict the Virgin (Baxandall 1972). This was the case, for example, in the contract Piero della Franscesca received in 1465 as part of his commission to paint the Madonna della Misericordia in Sansepolcro, Tuscany. The Virgin's mantle, depicted in ultramarine blue, is drawn around the kneeling figures and is positioned against the flat gilded background of the painting. This is a symbolism that helps identify people and ideas as well as ascribe value.

Formal analysis

Art historians consider an image not just in terms of its content – what it has to say through the use of symbols, motifs and other visual elements – but also through its form (Pooke & Whitham 2003; Csikszentmihalyi 2009). If the content of the image refers to what it says, form refers to how it says it. An exploration of the form that an image takes is often referred to as pre-iconographic analysis. A pre-iconographic or formal analysis involves taking into account all the visual aspects that make up the image. These might include the use of form or shape and colour, perspective and composition. A formal analysis will identify and explore the use of certain formal elements. This approach is also of benefit in an appreciation and analysis of advertising texts.

In visual advertisements, these **formal elements** might include the use of **shape** – how the advertisement is arranged and how shapes fit together and connect to create the overall image. You can see how this works in the Perugino painting, by looking at the image not so much in terms of what it depicts, but how it is made up of shapes and other formal elements. The use of **line** is also important and is used in different ways, for instance in distinguishing the edges of shapes and especially in hand-drawn images to create **tone**, the variations of **light and shade** which can create an illusion of depth. These elements make up the photographic images used in advertising which are often reworked to create a stronger visual effect. **Colour** is important. It can be naturalistic, making a reference to something in the real world being represented. Colour might also be used in an unrealistic and more abstract way as part of an overall colour scheme creating an effect that sets the advertisement apart from others. **Perspective** creates the sense of depth on a two-dimensional surface in which objects are represented in spatial recession. The illusion might be of deep or of shallow space. **Light sources** are important to this illusion and are along with other aspects of the image part of the overall composition.

The **composition** is the arrangement of all the elements within the frame, and this may well include written language. The use of different fonts and sizes should be taken into account in the overall formal analysis. These and other formal elements can be understood as contributing to the balance of the image or to its sense of movement and rhythm, and enhance the advertisement's effect. Some advertisements lend themselves to a formal analysis where others are more difficult to explore. The John Lewis Christmas advertisement of 2007 is a good example of an advertisement where shape, perspective, line and light source are important features of the image (see Plate 8). Once identified they can be considered as contributing to the overall effect of the advert before an attempt is made to explore the significance of different objects to an overall scheme and to the meaning of the advertisement.

Advertisements as signs

In everyday use the terms *symbol* and *sign* are used interchangeably. In textual analysis, symbols aid recognition and represent ideas. As we have seen, the study and recognition of symbols is an important aspect of art history. Symbols such as the keys of St Peter in the Perugino painting or the Madonna's cloak in the Piero della Francesca painting have largely fixed meanings. They represent the idea of salvation and protection respectively and their associations can be recognized as such in other works of art. The symbol has a relatively stable relationship with a preexisting idea that it represents. Symbols in paintings are similar to the sign in advertising. However, the sign is a less rigid representation, more open to interpretation. The study of signs is important to advertising studies and this is either referred to as semiology or semiotics.

The term semiotics refers primarily to the American tradition instigated by Charles Sanders Peirce (Gottdiener 1995; Merrell 2001; Short 2007; MacRury 2009a). Semiology refers to the European tradition emanating from Saussure and popularized by Barthes which relies more on a linguistic foundation for the development of its method (Cook 2001; Bignell 2002). However, the terms are often used interchangeably referring to either aspect of the study of signs (Deacon *et al.* 1999), although it appears that *semiotic* is now becoming the more commonly used term (Silverstein 2012).

Peirce and semiotics

Charles Sanders Peirce's nineteenth-century theory of 'semiotics' was an important development in an understanding of how signs work. (MacRury 2009a; Merrell 2001). Peirce's sign system was based on a highly detailed and complex taxonomy of signs and formulated as part of his wider scientific and philosophical enquiries. Peirce's categorization of signs outlined three main types – indices, icons and symbols – which have become important to an understanding of the natural and cultural world including advertising (Peirce 1958; Short 2007). **Indices** allude to natural occurrences such as the presence of dark clouds in a landscape suggesting rain, or animal or human footprints in the natural environment indicating the prior presence of a living creature. In both of these examples there is a direct causal link between the thing and its sign. In other words, they provide links between phenomena and the signs of those phenomena. The **iconic** sign refers to a visual similarity between the sign and the natural or social object it stands for. For instance, the stylized image of a male, for instance on a lavatory door to indicate a male domain, is an example of a contemporary iconic sign. The third categorization of a sign in Peirce's semiotic system is the **symbol.** The symbol counts as a sign because of its use and familiarity – it has come to have a certain familiar meaning over time. For instance, an image of keys – such as those being handed to St Peter in Perugino's painting – suggesting the unlocking of the future, had become a familiar feature in art by the fifteenth century. A further example might be the use of an image of a window in an advertisement to imply future possibilities. The contemporary English phrase 'window of opportunity' has a metaphorical meaning in language but its current overuse dampens the creativity of its image.[1] But the general point here is that for Peirce, symbols are formed through familiarity and use. As Gottdiener points out, in Peirce's model of the sign 'truth claims, or meaning, arise through language only when an idea or concept can be related to by something else already existing in the mind of the interpreter' (Gottdiener 1995: 9).

Knowledge and appreciation of the meaning of signs is formed as part of everyday thought, and signs constantly circulate in everyday contexts. This is particularly true of the concentration and flow of advertising signs through cultural life. The term *semiosis* was used by Peirce to describe this circulation and exchange of information, which occurs through social interaction. Semiosis requires a recognition of the factors and conditions that prevail to make the transmission and reception of a text both possible and part of the lived experience of people through decoding factors and environments. Semiosis can be applied to the idea of flow, of the movement of advertising signs through time and space and to the accumulation and connected development of advertisements as part of the cultural fabric and social experience. The image of a seamless flow of advertising through contemporary life is one that increasingly fits with modern lived experience.

Barthes and semiology

Most explanations of and operating guidelines for semiological analysis of texts including advertisements begin with the various works of Roland Barthes (1968, 1973, 1977, 1981). *Mythologies*, first published in 1957, is perhaps one of the most important books on semiology and myth. In the section 'Myth Today', Barthes famously offers an analysis of a 1955 *Paris Match* cover in which a black soldier is seen to salute the French flag. Barthes analyses the image using a semiological process and shows how it created a positive image of France and its imperial politics (Storey 2009). This was for Barthes myth. Myth is Barthes's term for ideology, and ideology is the common-sense understanding of the world through which particular views of the world are naturalized. It obscures the real conditions of being in the social world. This works in the interests of social groups that benefit the most from existing distributions of power and resources. As Dick Hebdige suggests, Barthes examines 'the normally hidden set of rules and codes and conventions through which meanings particular to specific social groups (i.e. those in power) are rendered universal and "given" for the whole of society' (Hebdige 1979: 9). Barthes specifically addressed advertising and advertising imagery in works such as 'The Rhetoric of the Image' (2002); and in *Elements of Semiology* (1968) he makes the distinction between denotative meaning and connotative meaning. The denotative level identifies and labels elements that appear in advertisements, and the connotative – which is where myth becomes associated with the process of advertising – is 'the range of associated meanings that it triggers in the mind of the reader or audience' (Scott 2006b: 297).

Saussure

The basis for Barthes's semiological work is to be found in the work of the Swiss linguist Ferdinand de Saussure and his highly influential *Course in General Linguistics* (Saussure 1974). The course, delivered at the University of Geneva in the first decade of the twentieth century, was a series of lectures about language, its structure and how it works. Emanating from the study of written and spoken language, semiology has developed into a general science of signs. It encompasses the idea that human actions (things people do) and human productions (things people make) have and convey meaning and therefore function as signs. As Leonard Bloomfield, a structural linguist working in the 1930s, was to put it: 'When anything apparently unimportant turns out to be closely connected with more important things we say that it has, after all, a "meaning"; namely it "means" these more important things' (quoted in Kempson, Fernando & Asher 2012: 14). Semiology/semiotics is applied not just to written and spoken language but to all aspects of culture.

There are four important elements to Saussure's thinking about the nature of language which are applicable to an understanding of signs and their use in advertising. First, speech and writing are based on language as a system which can be broken down into two elements: **langue** and **parole**. Langue refers to language as a formal system composed of certain words and phrases organized through norms and rules. Parole is the utterance, the actual speech or writing produced as part of the communication. Three important conditions arise from this: parole does not exist without langue; parole is formed from langue; and langue has to be shared between communicators. The structural requirements necessary for language to take place have often led to Saussure being called a 'structuralist'. A structure is necessary to provide the codes from which communication takes place.

The second element uses parole – the act of creating written communication or the discursive act of speech – and involves an organization of language and its delivery or transmission. In written forms this is clearly identified as phrases, sentences and paragraphs. At the heart of these are words, and the word functions as a linguistic sign. For example, the word *cat* functions in language as a signifier and the concept of 'cat' is termed the signified. Together the **signifier** (word *cat*) and **signified** (concept of cat) equal the sign. There is nothing in the letters or the ordering of letters that automatically means cat. So the word can be thought of as the primary sign.

Third, according to Saussure's understanding, the relation between words as elements of language is important to speech. In the construction of the linguistic sign there are two relations, the **syntagmatic** and the **paradigmatic**. The syntagmatic relation is between a linguistic sign and other items in a sequence. For instance, in a sentence this is the relation between a word and another word in the same sentence. So, to continue with our example, the sign 'cat' is put into a combination with other signs in the sentence 'The cat sat on the mat'. The paradigmatic element is the relation between the word and what it might be contrasted with. In the example of our sentence the contrast is between 'cat' and other words that might replace it such as 'dog'.

The fourth of Saussure's elements of semiology is that of time. As with the previous elements it has two characteristics, **synchronicity** and **diachronicity**. Language is shared by its users in any given moment of time. This horizontal aspect of language use occurs in synchronic time. So, for example, we might conduct a synchronic study of the speech of a particular age group within a generation, such as the forms of speech used by the 'cool' generation of late capitalism (Pountain & Robins 2000; McGuigan 2010). Or we might be interested in the use of the English language in which Shakespeare penned his sonnets in the first Elizabethan period. The synchronic relationship is between elements in the same horizontal historical moment. In contrast, diachronic time refers to the relation of elements through time and how language changes over time, for example from the seventeenth century to the present day.

Advertising and semiology

These binary pairs – langue and parole, signifier and signified, syntagmatic and paradigmatic, and synchronic and diachronic – can be applied to advertising as a general category and to individual advertisements and campaigns. The visual and textual language of advertising, its stock of ideas and references, are drawn from a general 'language' of advertising – an advertising langue. Advertising parole can be thought of as the themes and ideas, references and images which are selected for use. The design and organization of the advertisement is based on a combination of words and images combined in sytagmatic relationships and each might be replaced paradigmatically by alternative elements. Advertising content and style can be tracked through time diachronically and shared themes, styles and modes of address explored synchronically in any given moment.

For Barthes and others (Barthes 1973; Williamson 1978) an advertising text is to be read as a series of signs that are meaningful, 'everything has a meaning, or nothing has' (Barthes 1981: 170). Barthes' starting point is to explain how a sign is constructed in its relation to reality. In an advertising image an object or person is signified by formal elements of line, shape, colour and other aspects that form a signifier. The advertising sign is a combination of signifier and signified, the means of expression and the thing referred to. These two elements in combination – sometimes they are called the referent and reference – become the sign. In a complex process of layering, the sign, now acting as a signifier, reenters the process and becomes a component part of a new sign which is perceived to be operating at the level of myth. Crucially for Barthes, this is when ideology enters the field in the distinction between what is **denotative meaning** and what is **connotative meaning**. At the denotative level, a sign placed at the side of the road depicting two walking children suggests the shapes that can be read as two children walking, but at the level of connotation it will mean something like 'drive carefully – you may be approaching a school – children may be crossing the road you are now driving down'. The Stars and Stripes, the national flag of the United States, primarily denotes geographical and legal discourses, but it may connote an idealized, certainly ideological and perhaps mythological notion of 'the American way of life'.

The semiological approach to identifying significance in the social and cultural world is prevalent in a range of disciplines and a breadth of objects and phenomena. The approach has continued to be applied to the critical content of advertising in the academic world (Williamson 1978; Dyer 1982; Goldman 1992; Myers 1999; Cook 2001; Bignell 2002; Leiss *et al.* 2005; Odih 2010) and by the advertising industry in the creation and scrutiny of its own products (Wernick 1997; Lury & Ward 1997). Critical appraisals of semiology and semiotics have continued to accompany these various applications (Lash & Urry 1994; Gottdiener 1995; Deacon *et al.* 1999; McFall 2004).

Texts and ideology

In addition to Barthes and the tradition of semiology, Louis Althusser (1971) and his understanding of ideology has had an immense impact on the understanding of the textual aspect of the advertising framework. Althusser allows us to imagine the procedures of a text where ideology – identified by Barthes as myth operating as connotation – engages a viewer in the advertisement. Althusser's **interpellation theory** suggests that ideology interpellates or hails the subject of an advertisement to itself. As Judith Williamson (1978) has pointed out the subject of an advertisement is not only the product it is attempting to sell, it is also the beholder, the one who is being persuaded and consequently drawn to the advertising text. The **mode of address**, the way the advertisement addresses the viewer, is important in this. The ideological work of advertising is multi-layered. At one level it draws us into an imaginary relationship with the product where use value is converted by the sign representing the commodity into increasingly complex relations often grounded in fantasy. For instance, the car as a sign is equated with numerous attributes and social relations such as power, wealth, status, sexual attractiveness, family and child friendliness, and social estrangement. It is perhaps worth recalling Raymond Williams, an early critic of contemporary advertising, who suggested that '[i]f we were sensibly materialist … we should find most advertising to be an insane irrelevance. Beer would be enough for us, without the additional promise that in drinking it we show ourselves to be manly, young in heart, or neighbourly' (1980: 85).

Advertising technologies

A criticism of Althusser's concept of ideology as applied to advertising is that it fails to fully recognize the importance of different technologies in shaping the appearance and content of advertising texts. This is often referred to as 'technological difference', the specific forms and methods of any given advertising technology and how different forms produce different kinds of advertisement. Newsprint advertising is obviously different to television advertising. Through the technology of print it creates a static setting for its associations and fits within the format and layout of newsprint media form. The moving imagery and duration time of television advertising is the product of television technology and this produces different kinds of advertising. For instance, a car advertisement in a magazine may use a depiction of the countryside in which to situate an image of the car, creating social or cultural connotations; but a television advertisement with a moving car speeding through an open landscape is a more powerful image. Freedom associated with travel, choice and open spaces are favourite connotations of car advertisers, and they are often equated with a broader sense of political and economic freedom. In both the newsprint and television advertisement the viewer is 'drawn into' the perspective – the illusion of real space. The relationship between the viewer and the represented countryside, the commodity and the ideological value ascribed to it through connotation will not be exactly the same in television car advertising as newsprint car advertising. 'Freedom' implied in words and still imagery is different to the freedom inferred in the movement of objects across the television screen and through televisual space.

Difference in advertising technology and the form of advertising language that arises from it is overlooked in the application of Althusser's formulations of ideology and intepellation to advertising texts. Advertising texts may well distort the *relationship* of the individual to the real conditions of existence (Althusser 1971: 155), but, as Mark Poster notes, Althusser's formulation fails to 'specify the mechanisms at play in each such apparatus' (Poster 1990: 56). Stuart Hall, reflecting on television production, makes a similar point and identifies two levels of signification: the first 'what Althusser would call "signification in general", like ideology in general'; and the second a more specific technology-related ideological production associated with 'the activity of producing a television programme' (quoted in Cruz & Lewis 1994: 259). The plurality of technologies producing advertisements and the difference in formal presentation that arises from this is a significant factor to an understanding of how connotation and ideology work in advertising.

Context and intertext

Advertising texts, in whichever technological form they are presented, do not appear in isolation. The immediate context is the media form in which they appear, for instance television, radio and billboard, and the wider context of the environment they are found in, such as the home or the outdoors. An advertisement speaks for itself but it does so in the company of other advertisements and media content. A television advert appears among television programmes and normally within a string of other advertisements. A newspaper advertisement is juxtaposed with other advertisements and with news articles and photographs. This may reinforce, inflect or contradict the meaning the advertisement is intended to achieve and the readings it generates. Advertising posters are often placed side by side with other advertising posters. An advertising text is rarely in isolation and consequently enters into a relationship with other texts.

Advertisements are intertextual, sharing ideas, themes, production qualities, styles of presentation and so forth with the medium in which they are embedded. They play on the language and visual forms of the media of which they are a part. In the case of television, cinema and radio this extends to narrative forms, concepts taken from programmes, actors and celebrities and even scripts (O'Donohoe 1997). For example, a chocolate bar advertised on television in the 1970s featured Eric Idle in an advertisement based on a Monty Python scene and reworked elements of the original script. This involves advertisements in what (Rojek 2007: 52) has called 'a field of texts' or, as Fiske (1987) puts it, 'horizontal intertextuality'. The relationship may be parasitic, where advertising draws directly from other media and cultural works such as popular music (Stephenson 2013) or art (Gee 2013). It might also be a symbiotic relationship where media and culture also benefit from the relationship with advertising, drawing on its ideas, techniques and funding (Wharton 2013).

Advertisements also play on and borrow from the language and visual forms of other advertisements. Advertisements for product categories such as household goods, food and drink or holidays often share similar themes and language. Before the UK ban on cigarette advertising two leading cigarette brands, Silk Cut and Benson & Hedges, produced similar Surrealist-style advertisements drawing on each others' interpretations of the method and style of the twentieth-century avant-garde art movement, Surrealism. The purple-themed advertisements of Silk Cut and the gold-themed advertising of Benson & Hedges borrowed ideas both from art and from each other.

Case study – car advertising texts

The final section of this chapter is a survey of the extent and nature of car advertising based on both content and textual analysis. The methods of enquiry include themes and ideas explored previously in this chapter and are applied to a variety of car advertisements. Car advertising is an important component of a culture in which car ownership and use continues to increase. Currently in the UK there is a car for each person who holds a driving license (Leibling 2008). This has had a negative effect on the environment and shared public space. Social, cultural and economic contexts in which car culture operates and a consideration of some of the findings of the car-advertising survey are discussed below.

Research method

This research project into car advertising was conducted in two parts. The first, a wide-ranging survey conducted in 2004, included a breadth of advertising forms and advertising media such as billboards and outdoor, television and print media advertising. A second, smaller survey was conducted in 2012 and focused on newsprint advertising involving newspapers, supplements and magazines. The sample frame of car-related advertisements included in the survey and the subsequent sample of car-specific advertisements drawn from it as a selection for analysis was of greater quantity and breadth in the first part of the survey than in the second. In both parts, time periods and volume limits for data collection were set and car advertising was analysed synchronically, exploring representations across a range of similar advertisements within the two time periods. The survey also had a diachronic element comparing samples and findings from two distinct research periods from different decades. A uniformity of research design and similar methods of enquiry were maintained from one period to the next. Advertising texts were observed and recorded using a variety of methods from photography to video and Internet recording to sketches and scratch notes produced at the time of observation. Contextual and intertextual circumstances and environments were documented from the arrangement of street billboards to the juxtaposition of advertisements alongside other newsprint advertisements and feature articles. The research question 'How are motorcars and motoring environments represented in advertising forms?' was addressed using content and textual analysis outlined in this chapter.[2] Content analysis was used to establish the quantity of car adverts as a percentage of advertising overall and the number of particular types and formats of car adverts within this category. Textual analysis, in particular semiological enquiry, identified potential readings of the advertisements and these were subsequently placed into categories. Textual analysis in conjunction with content analysis established three major themes in the advertisements which emerged from the findings: aestheticization of the car; aestheticization of speed; and reliance on mythologized settings. The differences in medium were found to be significant to the content, tone and 'feel' of the advertisements. The representation of cars within mythologized settings is explored in the following section.

Newsprint advertising

Advertisements in the sample of newsprint media car advertisements featured an illustration of the whole or part of the advertised car. The advertisements differed greatly in style and in the use of written text and imagery. Findings from the study suggested that car adverts usually depict the car in isolation from other forms of road transport including other cars. Depicted settings and environments included representations of the open road and landscape, scenes of natural beauty, seascapes and abstract or ill-defined backdrops. When a road was shown, it was nearly always an open thoroughfare without indication of other traffic. The advertised cars were typically placed within uncongested and unpolluted environments. This was explored in the findings as related to a mythologized aspect of UK car culture in which the car is presented as special and in isolation, yet in reality exists within a crowded, congested often polluted environment.

Newsprint advertising in the 2004 study was organized into three categories according to the context of representation. This was confirmed in the 2012 study with some minor variations. Consequently the combined findings of the survey suggest that certain attributes of car advertising have persisted over a period of two decades. The first contextual category to be identified was labelled as one of **'non-space'**, in which the car is depicted without a definable background; the second, **'semi-abstracted'** space, where recognizable elements or landscape or other background referents were indicated but in a non-realistic manner; and the third category was identified as featuring a car depicted within a specific and recognizable **'natural' setting.** The representation of space was nearly always that of public space.

Figure 7.1 Toyota Yaris, 'There's more to a Toyota', newsprint advertisement, 2012. Reproduced courtesy of Toyota (GB) plc.

The first category of car advertisement features an image of the car against a neutral or non-space background (Figure 7.1). This advertising effect was created by using the natural colour of the paper upon which was printed an image of the advertised car. This produced an advertisement that blended with the overall look of the news-sheet, a black-and-white or colour advertisement set on a white newspaper page. Many of the advertisements within this category were framed by a functional or decorative border isolating but giving prominence to the advertisement. In some advertisements cars were depicted against a lighter non-space background, a shadow often in a non-naturalistic style is added below the body of the car to create the sense of the car in a deeper space. Although the use of text in this category is important, it is used more simply in a less connotative manner than in adverts in the other categories. The overall effect of advertisements in this category is to impart information about performance, price and purchase arrangements, focusing on the commodity status of the product. However, a small number of advertisements in this category presented the car as an aestheticized object with light falling on the body of the car, creating a sensuous contrast between highly polished surface and dark background or with light forming a sensuous contour. In these adverts the cars were described, for example, as having 'never looked better' and 'graceful'. The car's movement and speed did not feature as part of the advertisement. This category of advertisement represented 25 per cent of the sample of advertisements in the survey.

Figure 7.2 Lexus CT, 'Advanced economics', newsprint advertisement, 2012. Reproduced courtesy of Toyota (GB) plc.

The second category of adverts (28 per cent of the sample), that of 'semi-abstracted space', involved the depiction of the car within a more tangible and 'realistic' space that offered a more acute sense of perspective than that of the first category (Figures 7.2 and 7.3). These, however, fell short of the illusionistic representations in the third category. Naturalistic aspects, for example landscape or rural settings, were stylized elements forming grounds, backdrops and horizons that created indefinite space in which the car was presented. Some of these adverts tended towards the semi-abstract, featuring a strong stylistic element. In one advert, there was a clear link between the car colour and the upper horizon. Abstract design elements formed 'horizons' in a wide range of adverts in this category. This 'horizon' aspect of this category linked it to the 'aestheticized' aspect of car advertising noted earlier.

Aestheticization was more pronounced in this second category than in the first, promoting the car as an object of beauty and contemplation, as part of a visual appeal (Featherstone 1991; Bayley 1986). Overhead and side lighting, creating sharp contrasts, highlighted the car's curves. Light was reflected from polished surfaces in conjunction with a sensual descriptive language. The use of text was far removed from the technical language noted in the first category and created a more connotative type of advert. Some advertisements in this category used a stylized and often abstracted rendition of landscape as backdrop against which the car was

Figure 7.3 Peugeot 308, 'Driving sensations', newsprint advertisement, 2012. Reproduced courtesy of Peugeot Motor Company.

Figure 7.4 Volvo, 'It's you', newsprint advertisement, 2012. Reproduced courtesy of Volvo Car UK Limited.

depicted as a moving vehicle, combining an aestheticization of the car as object with an aestheticization of speed.

The third category of car adverts, 47 per cent of the sample, involved a recognizable urban, rural or other naturalistic setting (Figures 7.4 and 7.5). Urban settings involved the advertised car parked on roads or in empty car parks or shown travelling in isolation through the city. The advertised car is nearly always the only vehicle on the road. There were two exceptions to this in the 2004 survey. However, in the 2012 survey there was a greater likelihood that more than one car would be depicted, but this was usually a double offering of the same make of car. Rural settings of open countryside, picturesque landscapes, uncongested country roads and idealized seascape backdrops featuring beaches or sea provided the setting for a large number of cars in this category. Many advertisements that use landscape and open roads as symbols of an ideology of personal freedom and liberty also show depictions of speed. As in the other categories the car is shown in isolation, unhindered in its passage along deserted roads and through wild and untamed landscapes. Exceptions to this are multiple car adverts. In a Toyota multiple advert four cars from the same range are shown travelling in single file. No other car is present. In each of these advertisements the advertised car is the only

Figure 7.5 Porsche Boxster, 'Legacy defined', newsprint advertisement, 2012. Reproduced courtesy of Porsche Cars Great Britain Limited.

vehicle. All of the ads in this third category are aestheticized and often this occurred in conjunction with an aestheticization of speed.

In summary, almost all of the advertisements in the category of 'natural settings' involved a representation of roads, tracks or car parks; and in the second category of 'abstracted space' these were implied rather than shown explicitly. Representation of the product tended in most cases to involve an aestheticization of the car depicted as a solitary object. In very few cases was more than one car shown in the same space, and with two exceptions these were confined to multiple car ads as part of a manufacturers' multiple-range advert. Representations of space as context to the car were nearly always those of public space, but the constant representation of the car across the range of advertisements as a singular and isolated object tends to encourage a reading of public space as private space that contextualizes the private mobility of the car. Williams's concept of 'mobile privatisation' and Sheller and Urry's 'private-in-public' space (2003: 18) are useful references here. The aestheticization of the single car within its own space was often assisted by idealized and romanticized natural settings. Advertisements based on the movement of the vehicle through space and aestheticization of speed were further elements of these advertisements. The survey suggested an idealization and mythology of the car and car culture closely aligned to an ideology of liberty and freedom.

Car advertisements largely depict the car in isolation from other cars and generally from other forms of road transport. The advertised car is depicted in a splendid but mythical isolation, able to flow freely and unhindered through an uncongested and unpolluted environment. This is not how the world dominated by cars appears in reality. Ideologies of freedom and liberty, what Steve Graham refers to as 'the fantasy of complete individual control and total libertarian secession from the social and public spaces of city life' (2010), associated with the extremes of car culture can be balanced by an account of the social effects of the car in the works of a wide range of academic writers. The 'mass diffusion of the automobile and the increasing dominance of car culture' in the modern world has been noted as a general trend across the twentieth century (Graham & Marvin 2001: 6). More specifically, John Howe lists the numerous negative aspects of car proliferation as 'dirt, waste, pollution, clamour and inconvenience; the much anticipated but apparently still remote exhaustion of oil; the dire effects on urban and rural architecture and planning' (2002: 111). Kerry Hamilton and Susan Hoyle (2005: 86) note that the concept of the social and its associated public spaces are in constant threat from the car:

> society's notion of what the street is for has been profoundly altered by car culture. One of the first effects of the car's take-over of the city street is to denude it of people. This creates a physical as well as a conceptual space on the street, a space which is filled (or is perceived to be filled) by crime, insanity, and other social deviation – and by more cars.

The 2012 census suggests that the volume of cars on the roads is on the increase in England and Wales with the average number of vehicles per household rising from 1.1 to 1.2 over a 10-year period (Nairn 2013: 11). However, at the same time the volume of traffic through central London is on the decrease and has been since before the introduction of the congestion charge. A 2007 report prepared for Transport for London suggests that traffic flow in central London had fallen from a peak of around 1.8 million vehicles in the late 1980s to a total of around 1.5 million in 2002 (Evans 2007).

The representations and connotations associated with car advertising are at odds with academic accounts, empirical evidence and everyday experience of increasing urban and rural traffic congestion, environmental pollution and the intensity of car culture that forms the reality for all users of roads and outdoor spaces.

Conclusion

This chapter explored the textual aspect of advertisements and different analytical approaches that can be taken to them. Art historical, sociological and cultural perspectives have been applied to them, including content analysis as an approach to understanding the prevalence, potency and frequency of advertising texts in different media and in different social and cultural environments. This was contrasted with textual analysis – approaches that include formal analysis and the recognition and interpretation of icons and symbols in the art-historical tradition and the use of signs elucidated by Barthes, Peirce and others through semiotic practice. Textual and content analysis were shown as combined methods in a survey of car advertisements over the last two decades. The following chapter explores reception – the decoding of advertising texts.

Notes

1 Metaphor and metonymy as elements of language are similar to the use of the symbol in art and advertising. In essence, a metaphor is a figure of speech which is used to stand in for something else. For instance 'life' in Macbeth's speech on hearing of the death of his wife is analogous to a candle – 'Out out brief candle!'. A metonym is a word or phrase that is commonly put in place for another: for instance, the word *pint* as in 'going for a pint' stands in for the word *beer* or for going to the pub.

2 The initial advertising survey was carried out over a two-month period with the intention to gather the widest manageable sample within the period. The television sample frame included the television channels ITV1, Channel 4 and Channel 5, and involved 18 hours of recorded television, producing almost 340 advertisement slots of which 17 single car adverts were repeated across the days and channels included in the sample. The newsprint media were represented by the daily and weekend newspapers and supplements across the period, which involved a selection of different daily papers covering about 11,000 advertisement slots. The advertising sample frame included all blocked advertisements, but excluding 'personal' and occupation ads. This resulted in the retention of 200 newsprint car advertisements, some of which appear more than once in the sample, representing the breadth of publications they were drawn from and some slight differences in presentational format. In total the newsprint sample consisted of 115 different car advertisements. The billboard survey was conducted in the same period in the centre of Newcastle upon Tyne with billboard, adshell and scrolling backlit advertisements recorded on four different occasions, which resulted in a sample of some fifty outdoor advertisements of which four car-advertising campaigns were selected and analysed and the remainder, car and non-car, are used as comparative material.

8 Reception

Introduction

This chapter explores advertising reception from three different perspectives: effects studies; uses and gratifications; and the 'decoding' aspect of the advertising framework. Effects studies and uses and gratifications approaches are a good starting point for considering audience reception of advertising. Drawn from opposite ends of twentieth-century media reception theory, effects and uses and gratifications are considered in themselves inadequate explanations of an audience's relationship to advertising messages. However features of both are captured in the decoding aspect of the advertising framework. This chapter outlines the range of decodings, and these are explored in conjunction with a jewellery advertisement from 2012. Decoding is understood as an outcome not only of an advertising discourse but of a wider set of economic, social and cultural discourses. Class, gender, ethnicity, religion and sexuality are part of the lived experiences that advertising both draws on and speaks to, and through which people respond. This is important to a cultural and sociological critique of advertising and to the advertising and marketing industry, helping guide its operations. Political and social contexts are explored as background to advertising reception.

Effects studies approaches

The two dominant views of the media and reception of its outputs before and after the Second World War can be summarized on the one hand as 'effects studies' and on the other as 'uses and gratifications' approaches (McQuail 1969, 2002; Morley 1992; Dickinson *et al.* 1998; Curran 2002a). The effects studies approach to understanding audience reception, associated with the work of Paul Lazerfeld and James Klapper, has been described as 'the search for specific, measurable, short-term, individual, attitudinal and behavioural effects' (Gitlin quoted in Zelizer 2004: 49). Effects studies are predominantly behaviourist in conception, assuming audience reception and responses to media messages which result in a particular form of behaviour. For example, a direct response to an advertisement may create, reinforce or alter consumer behaviour. Quantitative analysis of content generally supports effects studies and is largely based on the assumption that the message is unambiguous and univalent (Berelson 1952).

Media effects theory as applied to advertising emphasizes the strength of the 'effect' that the advertisement, or the process of advertising, has on people and how people respond to the messages. It implies that advertising has an important influence over people's lives, providing knowledge and information about products and lifestyles and encouraging consumption. Research along effects studies lines is deployed in investigating the success of particular advertising campaigns in selling or promoting products. This kind of research is important to the marketing sectors of advertising agencies and to a variety of private organizations and public institutions involved in planning and managing economies. Effects studies assists in an understanding of the practical success of advertising and individual advertising campaigns in achieving ends. Effects studies might also be used to offer insight into the negative aspects of advertising, for instance in the promotion of products deemed harmful such as alcohol or tobacco.

Thinking associated with the Frankfurt School can be considered as a form of effects studies when applied to advertising and media output. Critical approaches to advertising have, as we have seen, been influenced by the Frankfurt School and in particular its critique of mass society. Mass society is primarily identified by the large-scale creation of standardized consumer items through the factory system of mass production. Mass production required mass consumption, and advertising had a crucial role in creating this. In the Frankfurt School way of thinking, it concealed real social relations and experiences and privileged consumption over production. It contributed to the ideological context within which capitalism with all of its inequalities could operate (Williamson 1978). Advertising was seen as being part of an ideological system operating through information and persuasion and as a form of standardized entertainment – a part of what Adorno called the culture industry. It promoted specific consumer goods but also consumption more generally as a form of behaviour, a way of life. The advertising effect, in its literal form, suggests a complete compliance and acceptance of the advertising message. According to Bernstein, there is no necessity to 'regard strict belief or naiveté as a condition for the culture industry to succeed' (1991: 10). On the contrary, as Adorno and Horkheimer suggest, 'the triumph of advertising in the culture industry is that consumers feel compelled to buy and use its products even thought they see through them' (Adorno & Horkheimer 1973: 63). The advertising effect is created by saturating the media and therefore modern thought with ideas and images based on a particular form of individualism – possessive individualism. This characterizes individuals according to what they own and by what they might aspire to acquire (MacPherson 1962; Balibar 2002). This depiction of advertising has been contentious not only in terms of its social effect but in the way that it operates.

Effects studies approaches are usually considered under the following headings. The message is depicted as being **univalent** in that it is constituted of a text with a singular and unchanging meaning demanding a specific reading. Quantitative analysis of content generally supports effects studies and is largely based on the assumption that the message is **unambiguous** (Berelson 1952). In advertising, the lack of ambiguity is seen to aid the promotion of the product or service in such a way that the visual and textual language chosen ensures that the advertisement is understood in a singular manner. This is not to suggest that the advertisement is necessarily successful in selling the product but that its message is received in a positive fashion. Furthermore, emphasis is placed on the **unidirectional** nature of the process in which there is a one-way flow of meaning from source to reception. This approach gives weight to the meanings that the message takes to the receiver rather than what the receiver brings to the advertising moment. Consequently, in the early days of effects studies, the receiver of the advertising message tended to be depicted as a **passive recipient** of the advertising message. This tended to limit an understanding of advertising recognition and reception to the specific transfer of information from an advertisement to its viewer. The exchange of meaning was limited to a single moment in which an advertisement is encountered; and it excluded or at least underplayed the experiences of receivers and wider contexts. It underplayed both the complexity of advertising messages and the potential of audiences to discriminate and resist the persuasive power of the message (Gauntlet 1998; Bryant & Oliver 2008). 'Effects studies' assumes that audience reception and response to media messages will result in particular behavioural form. For example, a direct response to the media message might be to alter or reinforce patterns of consumption created by the direct influence of an advertisement on an audience. Advertising naturalizes the process of consumption and claims a significance for it beyond that of other social and cultural activities. Research into advertising effects has featured in a wide range of areas such as the effects of television advertisements on children (Fox 2000) and the deployment of gender stereotypes in magazine advertising (Napoli, Murgolo-Poore & Boudville 2003).

To summarize, in the effects studies approaches to advertising reception, the audience is portrayed as passive, bombarded by advertising images, which are ubiquitous in nature and difficult to resist. The message is not perceived to be polyvalent, open to different interpretations, but is a singular message about consumption. Its behavioural effects might be to stimulate consumer desire or needs and to steer this towards choosing one particular brand rather than another. In both the Frankfurt School version and more marketing orientated versions, effects studies have been perceived as providing a limited explanation of advertising reception.

Uses and gratifications approaches

The second formulation for approaching reception theory in media and cultural studies, and one which has had an important impact on understanding advertising reception, is the uses and gratifications approach (Herzog 1944; McQuail 1998, 2010). This set of ideas came to provide an alternative to the effects studies approach. Uses and gratifications pointed to the active nature of audiences – that the audience was not a passive recipient of advertising media but was aware and discerning in its approach (Levy & Windahl 1985). The audience was perceived as being composed of individuals with their own outlooks and attitudes to media messages rather than the homogeneous group often depicted by effects studies. This and the use they made of advertisements were based on individual judgements and psychologies.

This signalled a shift in thinking about the relationship between media and audiences. Whereas effects studies emphasized the reading of the advertisement as something imposed on an audience and in which the message was understood to be univalent, uses and gratifications approaches tended to emphasize what an audience might want to do with the advertising message. It proposed the audience has an active role in the creation of advertising meaning and that individuals not only choose which advertisements to focus on but how much attention and interpretive time to apportion to them (West & Turner 2010). This emphasizes the choice exercised in advertising interpretation rather than passive reception and inert absorption. It also suggests that advertising might also be actively incorporated into lifestyles and ways of thinking. The relation between media and audience has often been described by effects studies as something akin to blotting paper absorbing ink drops from a fountain pen. In uses and gratifications thinking the audience is deemed to be active and to make choices about which advertisements to give attention to and what to do with the information. This was understood to be based on individual psychologies and decisions informed by media and consumer knowledge. Pleasure, satisfaction and gratification were considered to be the motivation for decision making. Benefits might include an increase in information and knowledge about products at the same time as being entertained and accruing cultural capital – an essential feature of modern identity.

Uses and gratifications approaches and methods of enquiry involve an understanding of how media audiences are formulated and behave. It recognized a new kind of consumer whose needs and wants could be channelled through mass production and consumption (Ewen 2001; Odih 2010). The new consumer had to be imagined and understood not just as part of a general class based on socio-economic categorizations, but as a more clearly defined and specific individual.

Across the twentieth century, advertising psychologists began to typify character traits and ally these to forms of consumer behaviour. The psychology of advertising developed an interest in individuals and how they receive and process marketing information (Fennis & Sroebe 2010). This can involve understanding of such things as 'attitude' to products and campaigns (Rucker, Petty & Priester 2007; Fennis & Sroebe 2010); the nature of 'memory' related to consumer information (Montgomery & Unnava 2007); or 'emotional attitude' in response to advertising (Stewart, Morris & Grover 2007). This more specific knowledge of individual characteristics of people as consumers was supplemented by more general consumer information, often the outcome of complex research projects. This was used to match products to potential consumers, stimulating and creating consumer wants and preferences.

Research

Uses and gratifications approaches have been central to advertising research, creating predictive and increasingly detailed models of consumer preference. These are based on individual demographic profiles such as age, gender, place of abode, etc. and previous purchase history. This is supplemented by information on 'shopping behaviour, travel patterns, mobile usage, social activity and media responsiveness' (Papadatos 2012). In addition, 'customer types' are identified by a range of variables such as a person's use of different types of social media (McElhatton 2012). Psychological approaches are often the basis for refining what can be understood as broad sociological categories such as class, gender, age, ethnicity, race or other social groupings. This is often referred to as *lifestyle categorization* and explores socio-cultural currents, tracking, measuring, forecasting and shaping the form and quantity of people as consumers. Mattelart suggests that in the advertising world 'the project of "lifestyle" studies is to define the coherent profiles and homogeneous typologies of consumers-viewers-listeners which are brought together in individuals' (1991: 164). The VALS system of psychographic market segmentation is a good example of this. Created in the 1970s and developed by Stanford Research Institute it creates a series of 'lifestyle types': a hierarchy against which consumption can be understood (VALS 2012). The consumer types range from 'innovators', who are described as at the leading edge of social change with high incomes and high esteem, down to the 'survivors' on the lowest incomes and few resources but who are described as 'brand loyal'. A recent example of this approach from the advertising industry attempts to categorize people in the age group of 40–50 into types (Smith 2012). Referring to people as 'brands' and 'labels' the research identifies 'six metaphysical categories' in which the class of 'service brands' describe people who are close to family, friends and communities. 'Private labels' are described as private people with childhood interests who tend to imitate rather than innovate. In addition, research material composed of consumer profiles can be used to support a psychoanalytic approach that attempts to uncover unconscious mental processes involved in consumer behaviour (Odih 2010: 28–33). Using the language of Freud, Lacan, Jung and others the advertising industry has explored the human psyche in terms of marketing. The concepts of desire, the pleasure and reality principle, attitude, cognitive dissonance and chains of association have been added to marketing research tools.

In summary: the uses and gratifications approach applied to advertising reception has historically been pitched against the effects studies approach. Effects studies present the advertising audience as a homogeneous mass receiving the same message in identical fashion. Uses and gratifications on the contrary envisages the audience as individuals, and these individuals engage with specific advertisements, enjoying different gratifications while rejecting others. They invest time and concentration on specific advertisements and in return may receive product information, adding this to a store of consumer and other forms of knowledge. Advertising is perceived, among other things, as being entertaining, and receivers derive pleasure from viewing certain adverts – it is part of shared social experience. People invest varying levels of time and intensity in different advertising forms, genres and individual advertisements and campaigns. People's choices are based on individual psychologies, interests and social difference. In essence, people will choose to be receivers of advertising texts or at least will select those which they consider to be worthy of their time and interpretive skill and will use these texts in a variety of ways, eliciting different gratifications from them. Uses and gratifications theories of audiences from the mid twentieth century overlap with more recent conceptualizations of audiences. For instance, postmodern ideas about 'active audiences' have tended to underplay the power of the advertising media and agencies to set the limits on how an audience engages with and interprets an advertisement. Active audience theories have stressed the idea of textual 'resistance' and 'semiotic democracy'(Fiske 1986, 1987, 1989; Grossberg 1984; Ang 1996) but this has not been without its critics. For example McGuigan has dismissed this as 'an uncritical populist strand of Cultural Studies to an extreme' (2012: 427; Morley 1990; Seaman 1992; Cobley 1994).

When taken to extremes, uses and gratifications' emphasis on individual responses to an advertising campaign suggests the number of interpretations and readings of advertisements are infinite. Each viewer's interpretation is potentially different to those of other people and they may produce more than one interpretation according to changing circumstances. Interpretive openness may be as a result of the polysemic nature of the advertising sign, which encourages different readings, but it might also be due to difference in psychologies and social and environmental circumstances. It could therefore be due to a property of the text or an attribute of the audience segment or environment. It might be a combination of the two. Individuals when they are involved in interpreting advertisements draw on codes and ways of thinking which are social and cultural. The similarities in advertising interpretations as well as differences are of interest to critical approaches to advertising. It is also in the interest of advertisers to be in a position to understand optimum readings and interpretations of advertising texts. Being able to generalize, to predict different *types* of response and how they are generated is part of the advertising planning process.

Decoding case study – Ernest Jones

This chapter now turns to the third way of exploring advertising reception – decoding. This element of the advertising framework of encoding-texts-decoding enables an understanding of reception and cultural and social experiences of advertising audiences. This improves upon both effects and uses and gratifications approaches by profiling general potential decodings of individual advertisements, advertising campaigns and the advertising process generally. There are, according to Stuart Hall, three potential media decodings – the preferred or dominant reading, a negotiated reading and an oppositional one. These are outlined with reference to a 2012 newsprint jewellery advertisement.

Preferred

The preferred reading of an advertisement refers to the meaning or reading of the advertisement that is intended by the producer and is accepted by the reader, listener or viewer of the advert. In the preferred reading there will be a close match between the set of codes, values and assumptions about the world from which the message is encoded and the codes which the reader or viewer brings to the advertisement and with which they make sense of the message. In other words it requires a close cultural match between producer and receiver and agreement about a range of issues – from social values to the appropriateness of its design. In an acceptance of the preferred reading, the reader or viewer is likely to feel at ease with the message and the form it takes, the suitability of product references and representations, and the choice of media and position.

Ernest Jones jewellery was marketed extensively across 2012. Two examples discussed below are available online at http://celebratechristmasone.advertimage.co.uk and http://celebratechristmastwo.advertimage.co.uk (or you can scan the QR codes on the right on your mobile or handheld). It is a conventional advertisement – traditional, even old-fashioned in its design, layout and theme. This advertisement appeared in the *Independent* magazine supplement and the *Guardian* Saturday supplement, and formed part of a larger advertising campaign which featured across the spectrum of UK newspapers in the autumn and winter of 2012. The diamond cluster ring at the centre of the advertising sales pitch dominates the lower part of the full-page newsprint advertisement. It is accompanied by price and credit purchase information. The image of the ring is positioned both in the textual information section of the advert and overlaps with the upper part of the advert, which portrays a couple in a romantic encounter. The warm colours and soft-focus image of the pair in warm winter clothing is overlaid with falling snow and the line 'Celebrate Christmas 2012'. The preferred reading of this advertisement involves an implied sense of ease with the representation of romance, a celebration of 'love and life' and a sense of comfort, even identification with, its outlook and seasonal expectations. It is an unremarkable advertisement but its outlook is nevertheless ideological – it has a certain view of the world and its values which we might recognize and accept as comfortable and unchallenging. To say that this advertisement is ideological is not to suggest that it fosters a particular class view or overtly functions to naturalize or legitimize capitalist relations of production. However, the preferred reading embodies a particular way of seeing that implies a way of feeling, of being comfortable with the world. It might be perceived as 'rose tinted' but at the same time successfully drawing the viewer to its worldview. This may or may not be

a true view. In outlining other possible readings, negotiated and oppositional decodings of the advertisement, its ideological outline comes more closely into focus.

Negotiated

In the second possible decoding scenario the viewer accepts the dominant tenets of the message in the widest, global sense, but will locate the meaning in a more personal, local sense. This is usually referred to as a 'situated reading', which includes a situated logic associated with the subject's position in the social structure and thereby produces a negotiated reading. The 'negotiated code' according to Hall contains 'a mixture of adaptive and oppositional elements' and is therefore 'shot through with contradictions, though these are only on certain occasions brought to full visibility' (2006 [1973]: 172). A reading of the Ernest Jones advertisement along these lines would probably involve a sense of unease, discomfort or lack of empathy with the *way* people are represented or the context in which they are depicted. However, the advertisement might at the same time evoke a sense of agreement with its overall theme of celebration, affection and romance. The negotiated reading is described in Hall's initial paper as a negotiated version of the dominant ideology. The preferred and negotiated readings are to a greater and lesser extent respectively hegemonic readings, yet the negotiated code 'might be said to constitute a reflexive engagement with the media' (Rojek 2003: 99).

Oppositional

Third, according to Hall, the message may be decoded in a totally oppositional way, in which the preferred meaning is rejected. In this scenario the message is received within an oppositional code, one that is based upon 'some alternative framework' (Hall 2006 [1973]: 173). In this scenario, the ideological content of the message is made visible and acknowledged as ideological. Hall explains this according to 'class interest' (Hall 1981a). Indeed the advertisement might well be decoded according to price and affordability of the product, evaluated according to income and the financial means of the viewer based on social class. We might want to broaden this oppositional framework to include other social and cultural factors. Oppositional readings of the advertisement might reject its representations and implied values for a variety of reasons, for instance on sexual grounds because of its invocation of heterosexuality or on religious grounds because of its identification with the celebration of Christmas. Age could be a contentious factor, as represented in the image or as an attribute of its audience. Furthermore the advertisement might be perceived as stylistically uncool in its obvious and overt display of sensuality based on an alternative aesthetic and sense of design appropriateness. These scenarios suggest that the advertising producers have encoded assumptions about the audience that do not necessarily hold true. We might say that the producers do not share or have misread its audience's codes of seeing and evaluating. Social class, sexuality, religion, culture, age and design sensibility might all be factors here, and in a variety of combinations and to different degrees. Oppositional readings are based on disassociation and disidentification with the advertisement's message and ambience and are often as suggested here based on an alternative framework of seeing and thinking.

The advertising framework creates a space in which three clusters of readings – three decodings, the dominant, the negotiated and the oppositional – can be identified. These decoding possibilities should be seen as sketches rather than as clearly defined responses. Stuart Hall described decoding positions – now an important element of the advertising framework – as 'hypothetical decoding positions' or 'ideal-typical' positions. He closely associated these with social class. This was the trend in thinking in humanities and social sciences across the 1970s and into the 1980s which conceived of class as the essentialist identity. Further thinking and research in the area of reception 'embraced factors of age, race, gender and generation as well as class in the viewing context' (Rojek 2003: 100). Other thinkers at the time were suggesting something similar, for instance Laclau and Mouffe's (1985) understanding of people's identity was one of fragmentation, and as Hall was to later suggest 'identities are never unified and, in late modern times, increasingly fragmented and fractured' (Hall 1996: 4). The term 'hyphenated identity' (Hall 1999) seems to capture this and is explored in Chapter 12. Identity then is made up of different factors in which social class is an important if not the first aspect of a person's being to be acknowledged in advertising reception. Identity is not set in stone, circumstances and people change of over time. Identity for Hall, following Antonio Gramsci's thinking, is always in motion 'a process never completed – always "in process"' (Hall 1996: 2).

Other thinkers have identified similar formulations to Stuart Hall's three categories of reading media texts. For instance, Michel Pecheux discusses three mechanisms or 'modalities' in which 'individuals are interpellated' by ideological values (Pecheux 1982: 156; see also Sarup 1996). He refers to a form of 'identification' that is 'freely consented to' (Pecheux 1982: 157), to a 'counter-identification' which 'involves distanciation, doubt, interrogation, challenge, revolt' (1982: 157) and to 'disidentification' (Pecheux 1982: 157–9). These correspond to Hall's preferred, negotiated and oppositional categories. Similarly Manuel Castells offers three types of identity: legitimizing, resistant and project identities (Castells 1997). Castells's third type, 'project identity', coincides with Hall's oppositional code, seeking to 'build a new identity that redefines their position in society and, by so doing, seek the transformation of overall social structure' (Castells 1997:8).

Oppositional decodings of an advertisement may appear as occasional, aberrant and individual outcomes of the decoding process: one person's dislike or dissatisfaction with a product or a particular advertisement. But oppositional decodings are not merely individual responses to advertising stimuli but are drawn from real lived experiences which are likely to be, as we explored in the discussion of the Ernest Jones advertisement, shared and therefore cultural. Pecheux's *disidentification* and Castells's *project identity* are closely aligned to Hall's oppositional decoding and suggest the possibility of a more systematic, shared and widespread response to the social world or to its economic and political dimensions. When looked at in the bigger picture, especially where a number of oppositional decodings are taking place, it may well be that a larger and structured response, a *culture of opposition* is operating which is set against the preferred codes and general values of mainstream advertising. This is likely to include alternative values, ways of thinking and perhaps engagement in social and political activity. A culture of opposition is outlined in the following section and explored against the changing social and economic circumstances in which people find themselves and the responses they make to society and advertising.

Political contexts of decoding

Hall's examples of oppositional codes are drawn from the experience of the industrial working class in the 1970s, and these were primarily used to explore oppositional readings to media messages condemning working-class, trades-union action (Hall 1981a). This was at the time of the 'winter of discontent' and the election of the Thatcher government in 1979. For Pecheux 'disidentification' takes place through 'identification with the political organisations "of a new type"' (Pecheux 1982: 158) and is based on working-class industrial and 'militant' experience. For Castells in the mid-1990s the new social movements are the basis for resistance and project identities. These included the Zapatista and women's movements, emergent national, religious and ethnic identities and an environmentalist political culture. For Hardt and Negri the contemporary proletariat could be defined as 'a broad category that includes all those whose labour is directly exploited by and subjected to capitalist norms of production and reproduction' and 'subject to capitalist discipline and relations of production' (Hardt & Negri 2001: 52–3). These people are referred to as the 'multitude' by Hardt and Negri. They are the largest social group in society, broader than the industrial working class but involving trade union input, community and environmental activism and for a minority anti-capitalist anti-privatization politics (Hardt & Negri 2001: 53).

This may well be an aspect of a culture of dissatisfaction or even opposition that finds itself set against optimistic trends that are at ease and prosper in the comfortable economic, social and cultural worlds in which they find themselves, and may be associated with the preferred reading. Similarly a culture of opposition may well be a direct or indirect response to less favourable or even deteriorating social and economic circumstances – welfare, health, pensions and falling wage levels, cuts to education and increased fees, Eurozone chaos and the imposition of unequal austerity measures and falling standards of living. The global financial crisis that became apparent in 2007 with difficulties in the US subprime mortgage market deepened and widened with a 'wave of bank insolvencies and rescues around the world, and rapidly led to a general collapse of business and consumer credit' (Radice 2010: 21). This created a prolonged crisis, which is part of a 'recurrent pattern of capitalist accumulation in which long booms eventually give way to long downturns' (Shaik 2010: 44). In the UK, the Conservative–Liberal Democrat government has pursued a policy of cuts, closures and redundancies affecting society's poorest and most needy (McKibbin 2010). In Europe 'free market economics, written into the constitution of the European Central Bank' has demanded a policy of 'privatisation, wage cuts, pension cuts: cuts in benefits, the minimum wage and social services' (Mason 2012: 92). Oppositional decoding can be part of a general response to these conditions.

Intense political protests against austerity measures and pro-democratic reform have been evident across Europe, particularly in Spain, Portugal and Greece. The occupation of public space by Spain's young *indignados* was accompanied by similar events in Bahrain and Cairo's Tahrir Square, where youth unemployment had been a significant grievance (Hardt & Negri 2011). The Occupy movement's encampments, set up in London's St Paul's Cathedral precinct and New York's Wall Street, proved a potent symbol of opposition to dominant political values. Other places around the world followed suit (Mason 2012). In Britain, campaigns and occupations against education fees and cuts – instigated by a young generation utilizing social media as a new form of political communication – were joined by protests and strikes against threats to jobs, pensions, services and further privatizations.

UK Uncut's direct action on the high streets highlighted widespread tax avoidance by big corporations and had some success in rectifying this in the case of Starbucks.

In addition, countless 'young, poor and unemployed' youths rioted in English cities in August 2011 (*Guardian* 2011) and were characterized as 'defective and disqualified consumers' by Zygmunt Bauman (quoted in Žižek 2011). Analysis of court data showed that two-thirds of people appearing before magistrates were under 24 years of age. Similarly two-thirds of the accused lived in areas that had got poorer between 2007 and 2010 (*Guardian* 2011). Göran Therborn, referencing an International Monetary Fund study of 2007, suggests that 'on a global scale, the only group which increased its income share in the 1990s was the richest national quintile, in both high and low-income countries' (Therborn 2012: 13). Therborn concludes that class and class conflict are back on the political agenda and imagines this taking two routes, one involving 'the hopes and resentments of the middle class', and the second that of 'the plebeians, rather than the proletariat' in what he elsewhere calls the 'new masses' (2014: 7). To add a further category to these – that of disaffected youth – suggests something like Hardt and Negri's concept of the 'multitude' (2011). However, Žižek (2011) makes the point that these and other similar protests and rebellions 'express an authentic rage which is not able to transform itself into a positive programme of socio-political change. They express a spirit of revolt without revolution.' These questions are for the political philosophers but nevertheless must impact on our understanding of advertising reception and in particular the prevalence of oppositional advertising decoding.

Conclusion

Advertising reception is categorized by decodings that are both generated by advertisements and by the wider social and economic circumstances that people find themselves in. Advertising readings or decodings are grounded in people's life experiences. Oppositional decodings have been explored as individual responses to advertising texts. This discussion has also explored a 'culture of opposition', a shared set of circumstances, sensibilities and responses resulting from shared and recognized experiences which are in many ways the antithesis of the consumer culture which will be explored in Chapter 12. Subsequent chapters suggest that other factors impact on and contextualize advertising reception: for instance, the immediate environment, surroundings and social relations encountered in the home and in outdoor space are significant to advertising reception. In addition, technologies constantly change the delivery and content of advertising and reconfigure sensual perception through new ways of seeing and hearing. This impacts on decoding, which has been examined in this chapter alongside effects studies and uses and gratifications. Aspects of advertising reception, including immediate circumstances and environments, and decoding are further explored in subsequent chapters.

Part III

Applications

9 Advertising in the home

Introduction

This and the following chapter examine the 'spaces and places' where advertising is received and decoded. This chapter looks at the domestic space of the home and how advertising is an important part of that environment. The following chapter explores out-of-home advertising and its relation to an outdoor urban environment.

In the first instance the chapter establishes the difference between public and private spheres and how these are linked to the idea of public and private space. It explores domesticity and the space it occupies. There are three aspects to this, home, household and family, things people quite often take for granted in their everyday lives. The household can be defined as a largely social and economic category involving a range of domestic activities including the purchase and consumption of goods. Home is both a physical and a symbolic space. Family can be defined by kinship, that is, relationships occurring through blood, marital or legal ties (Allan & Crow 2001). Advertisers often depict or make reference to families, homes and households in their campaigns. Analyses of these aspects of domestic space and relationships form an important approach to advertising studies.

Domestic space is explored as the place of reception for media conveying advertising, which includes television, radio, newsprint and the Internet. Significantly domestic space features a variety of screens delivering television and advertising, such as personal computers, laptops, smartphones and tablets. However the television set is still a prominent feature of the home and an important purveyor of screen advertising. This chapter explores advertising diffusion, a term used to describe the spread of advertising messages among populations. Screen-based advertising is important to diffusion in the household, which is characterized as an interpretive community that shares not only a home space but a local culture involving codes and familiarities which give a particular substance to advertising reception. The household can be thought of as a local and specific set of economic and social relations in which advertisements and the products they represent enter households and become *domesticated*, made part of the fabric or currency of the home. Advertisements are explored as part of both television flow – appearing between television programmes – and as part of the wider household flow.

Advertising places

This chapter is concerned with domestic space or place and explores the important difference between the two. 'Place' is included in some advertising studies as part of the four *p*'s used in marketing theory to explain the different aspects of the marketing process (Leiss *et al.* 2005: 8). Product, price, promotion and placement constitute the four *p*'s, also known as the 'marketing mix'. Placement refers to the distribution of the products being marketed and deals with how the retail product gets to the potential customer – to the point of sale. In marketing theory, the term also implies the channel by which a product or a service is sold, for instance being marketed online or through traditional retail outlets. Placement is often referred to more simply as place, and this more strongly implies a reference to geographic or topographical location. To consider location is also to refer to the surroundings in which the product is sold. In this chapter we are concerned with how the surroundings impact on the way in which the advertised product is perceived and how the meanings associated with it are received within that environment. So in this chapter we are concerned with domestic space and how the house and home become an important place for advertising.

Public and private – spheres and spaces

Differences between the public space of the outdoor world and the private space of the domestic interior are important to an understanding of advertising and in particular to advertising reception. Quite often the idea of public space is equated with that of the public sphere and private space with that of the private sphere. Spheres and spaces are connected concepts, but it is worth spending a little time considering the difference between the two. Discussion of the public sphere is framed by the work of Jürgen Habermas and his discussion of the rise of sixteenth-century mercantile capitalism (1992). It is connected to the idea of public discussion and debate associated with the world of letters and newspapers and the exchange of opinions about civil society and the state (Thompson 1995). Habermas's take on the public and private spheres is founded upon an understanding of the historical development of public and private, which starts with public life in the ancient Greek city-state (*polis*) and largely occurred in such places as the public arena of the *agora* (market square). This was separate from the privacy of the oikos (home/household). According to Habermas, the contrast drawn in Roman law between *publicus* and *privatus* can be found in the sixteenth century to have a similar meaning to the 'English *private* and the French *privé*' (1992: 11). He clearly establishes the distinction between the public and private which comes down to us today as the public realm or sphere and the private realm or sphere. The public sphere then is the more expansive shared world of social and public discourse and the private sphere a narrower, more intimate set of relationships. These by and large correspond to space.

The 'public' aspect of public space is often perceived as the realm of the outdoors, of open, freely accessible spaces that enable a relatively wide social interaction between people. The 'public' is where we meet and interact with others. The 'private' on the contrary is represented by domestic space, which is the domain of the familiar and the inclusive. It is, perhaps, less varied in scope and breadth than outdoor urban space. Outdoor urban space can be understood as a place in which a wider variety of encounters and transactions take place. It is one in which 'the other', the strange and unfamiliar, is more likely to be signified and encountered. Private space is the space of home, household and family. It is an intimate, materially formed place. Symbolically bounded, constituting the more familiar, predictable, knowable aspects of the social world, it is perceived as being more within the control of its inhabitants. The relative stillness of the private space can be contrasted with the flux and rapid movement of the modern city environment of public space.

Advertising media – public and private space

In the modern world the media is important in articulating private and public spheres and spaces (Morley 1992). Stuart Hall and others suggested the importance of television in bringing the outside world of news and public affairs into the domestic interior. Using the metaphor of a bridge spanning the boundary between interior and exterior, Hall emphasized a largely one-way flow that conveys media content of a 'public character' into the 'private' home (Hall 1981a; Corner 1995: 11). Hall stressed the unequal distribution of knowledge and power (1981a: 270). More recently, Anna McCarthy has emphasized the 'dynamic and flexible' elements of the public/private division, leading her to conclude that the television should not be aligned simply with one side of the equation: 'The arrival of television in the post-war home did not simply bring public space into the private space of the home; rather it reshaped the ways in which the boundary between public and private was conceived in domestic discourse' (McCarthy 2001: 121). New technologies such as the Internet, mobile phones and handheld devices have created a much expanded media with increased capacity, depth of penetration and spread of social reach. For example, the penetration of the World Wide Web into domestic and other spaces, its propensity for interactive debate and discussion and encouragement of new forms of political contact and involvement provides a route into the public sphere and a line back into domestic space of the home. It also brings with it further layers of advertising.

Sheller and Urry (2003) make a similar, but more general, point about mobility across the boundaries of public and private, using the neologisms of 'public-in-private' and 'private-in-public' to describe this. They suggest these forms are both 'physical (in the form of mobile phones, objects and hybrids of humans–in-machines), and informational (in the form of electronic communication via data, visual images, sounds and texts)' (Sheller & Urry 2003: 108). So, for example, hitherto private discussion between people occurs in public spaces via the use of the mobile phone; and public interest and debate about a range of hitherto distant geographic and social concerns are engaged within the private domain (Bull 2004: 285). The blurring of divisions between public and private space has, for McQuire, created 'a crisis of space' where the 'deterritorialization of domestic space goes hand in hand with the increasing subjection of the public sphere' (McQuire 1999: 149). The distinction between public and private is increasingly fluid.

A developing sense of the public sphere that straddles the traditional public and private boundaries has developed across recent years: the Internet appears everywhere and public communication and discussion through social media is widespread. This is often the bedrock of what has become known as the network society (Castells 1996, 2008). Blogs, emails, Facebook and Twitter have contributed to a new sense of public debate and new forms of communication. These are also the mechanisms that bring a new wave of advertising into the private space of the home. Habermas talks about 'the shrinking of the private sphere into the inner areas of a conjugal family … [where] the quiet bliss of homeyness … provided only the illusion of a perfectly private personal sphere' (Habermas quoted in Silverstone 2004: 66). On the other hand, J.B. Thompson has suggested that 'rather than sounding the death knell of public life, the development of mass communication has created a new kind of publicness and has transformed fundamentally the conditions under which most people are able to experience what is public and participate today in what could be called a public realm' (1990: 246). Indeed Couldry suggests that

Habermas's terms of private and public spheres 'have been transformed' (2012: 125). The distinction, however blurred, between public and private is helpful to our understanding of advertising and in particular its reception.

Domestic space

Domestic space is marked by particular social, cultural and economic activities. These can be seen to be productive: some people do a paid job – 'working from home' – and many others perform unpaid, caring duties such as looking after and providing for families. But the home is also a place of rest and recuperation from paid labour. It has a strong symbolic and emotional value expressed in everyday phrases such as 'hearth and home' or 'no place like home!'. Indeed, when we are away from it we are inclined to turn an unfamiliar space into a 'home from home'. Domestic space, the people who inhabit it and the organization of social life we find there are often referred to as 'home, household or family'. Domestic spaces differ quite widely from culture to culture. Morley suggests that it is important to note 'the similarities and differences between families and households and an understanding of their place in the wider culture and society, where issues of class, ethnicity, ideology and power define (should they be forgotten) the materialities of the every-day life world' (Morley 1992: 203).

Domestic space is by its nature bounded. Boundaries are psychological and symbolic as well as material and physical entities. They are often thought to exclude the broader public arena and are materially protective. But as we have seen the public sphere increasingly crosses the threshold of the private, domestic domain marked out by bricks and mortar. Interior domestic space contains different physical and material experiences and symbolic values to outdoor public spaces and forms a quite different context for advertising reception. The social relations of domestic space also create the immediate social relations of advertising reception within which advertising and significantly television advertising is received and decoded. This is explored further in the next section.

Home, household and family

As Roger Silverstone suggests (2004) the domestic can be imagined as three distinct, but overlapping areas, those of home, household and family. In outline, a household is a social and economic category which shares a range of domestic activities, including the consumption of goods, whereas home is both the physical space and the ideological configuration around which much of domestic life revolves (Allan & Crow 2001). A family can be defined by kinship, that is the relationships that occur through blood, marriage and legal ties (Allan & Crow 2001).

Home

Silverstone emphasizes the importance of the *idea* of home for people: 'Home is a construct. It is a place not a space' (Silverstone 2004: 26). To describe somewhere as a *space* is to apply a descriptive yet neutral term, but when we add a sense of importance and belonging to it we endow it with a sense of *place* (Relph 1976; Buttimere 1980). It becomes transformed from a geographically and topographically demarcated area into a significant locality. Silverstone goes on to suggest that the difference is 'between those areas of the world, large or small, for which we have no feeling and those for which we do' (2004: 27; Blunt & Dowling 2006). Home provides shelter, sustenance and protection, which are real and necessary elements of existence. Home is an essential part of being – it helps provide our 'place in the world' or, as Richard Sennett suggests, 'having a place in the world is what makes the human animal a social being' (Sennett 1999: 23). In summary, home is a space occupied and organized: turned from nature into culture, from the strange into the familiar, it becomes a special *place* with a sense of belonging. Because of this, domestic space has a significantly different set of associations through its material and symbolic values to that of urban, public space (Morley 2000; Bolin 2004). It therefore functions very differently as a context to advertising reception (Spigel 1992). Home as place also has a significance for consumer identity. It is where we view, consider and make choices about many of the consumer items we purchase. Consequently advertising that is delivered directly into the home has a special relevance, not least because many of the products featured are consumed there.

Family

The family is important to the reception of advertising texts in the home. As Silverstone has suggested, 'trying to define what a family is is quite an impossible undertaking' (Silverstone 2004: 32; Wilson and Pahl 1988). The traditional view of the 'modern' family is one of a collection of close and intimate social relations based on commitments and dependencies largely devoted to the exercise of conjugal relationships, parenting and the primary socialization of children. The family functions to provide emotional support and the channeling of resources into the family unit.

The family is a social unit around which boundaries are drawn. From within, family members themselves use conceptual, emotional and social material to create a family identity and define the family unit. From without, families are marked out by a range of state and other institutions and organizations associated with marketing and advertising. For these purposes the social unit can be defined as a small social group of related people sharing a sense of identity and intimacy who bring to advertising reception a local family culture. Family culture is marked by a variety of factors such as shared history, memory and activities. It is likely to be based on shared experience and outlook about the world. This might involve knowledge, values and opinions that can be utilized to interpret the outside world. Advertising reception occurs in the home and within a family setting and is primarily decoded through a cultural framework local to the family unit. It may circulate within an economy of family meanings functioning as a resource and helping to form a shared identity.

The prime functions of television and other advertising targeting the family is to promote and sell commodities. The need and desire for commodities is in many respects located in the family and within domestic space. Among its many other functions the family has a significance in the nurturing and development of consumer activity as well as being based partly on the preferences and activities of shared consumption.

Household

As we have seen, the difference between house, family and household is not easy to make even on paper; in lived reality these distinctions may be even more difficult to draw. Living as part of a household often overlaps with the experience of 'home' and 'family'. Each is important to the way advertising becomes a feature of domestic space and to how people respond to advertising. The household is essentially an economic and organizational category. It involves the maintenance of shared space and the purchase and consumption of household goods and groceries, the organization and provision of services and other household items. Households function as 'resource systems' but they are 'differently bounded in respect of different resources available to them, the resources they choose to deploy, and the kinds of value they vest or invest in them for particular purposes in local or cultural contexts of various kinds' (Wallman quoted in Silverstone 2004: 44). Households vary according to size, space inhabited, income, class and other cultural factors. As households people lead different kinds and qualities of life due to income, health, consumption patterns and other factors. Therefore households provide different material experiences and physical environments in which advertising reception takes place.

Households, like the overall population of Great Britain, have changed dramatically across the twentieth and twenty-first centuries. Britain's population has risen from 37 million people, recorded in the 1891 census, to 54 million in 1991, organized into 21 million households (Wood 1961: 449; Linsey 2003). In 2000, 24 million households were recorded, as against 8 million at the beginning of the twentieth century (Social Trends 2001). This has led to a transformation in the typical household. The average size of the family has changed dramatically, with family numbers in the 1870s at 10 persons per household; across the twentieth century the number of people per household has almost halved, from 4.6 people through to a household size of 3.1 in 1961, falling to 2.35 in 2011 (Office for National Statistics 2011). Households are increasing in number but getting smaller. Projections on household size suggest that this is an enduring and deepening phenomenon with a further decline in household size projected to be 2.2 people in 2021 (Social Trends 2001). This is important to advertising targeted at households, not least because of the changing nature of reception. As more households are defined by single membership, the shared elements of advertising decoding diminish. In 2010 there were 26 million households in the UK and of these 29 per cent consisted of only 1 person and almost 20 per cent consisted of 4 or more people (Office for National Statistics 2011). This has a relevance for the diffusion of advertising in which a household may share and exchange ideas about an advertising campaign. The household, however it is constituted and resourced, is a unit of consumption, setting and managing budgets along with selecting and consuming goods.

In summary, domestic space is important to an understanding of advertising. Conceived of as home, it is both a potent symbol and a real private, intimate physical space in which families and households reside. The family functions as a unit of reproduction and welfare. As an economic unit it functions as a household and as a unit of consumption. A household is not necessarily a family, but like the family and the home it is culturally and historically specific.

Ideal families?

The family as a social and moral unit and as a household emerges from the literature as the ideal representation of the audience; as Ang suggests, 'The audience for a programme may total millions: but people watch and listen in the family circle, in their homes' (Ang 1996: 23). Television viewing has traditionally been assumed to take place in the private homes of isolated nuclear families, in which Wilson suggests, '[t]he family, or familial life-world is assumed to be the predominant context of viewing by media organizations'

(Wilson 1993: 19; Ellis 1992 [1982]). This is still largely true although changes in technology have resulted in integration and convergence with crossovers between television, computing and mobile technology. A wide variety of screens now carry live or recorded television. Digital and other technologies have enabled viewers to have greater control of television viewing. This has resulted in more atomized viewing across more diverse viewing spaces (Morley 2007; MacRury 2009a: 98; Livingstone & Das 2013). However, the family remains important as a media-audience identity.

Families, homes and households are constantly changing as is the depiction of them in the media and in advertising. In the 1980s *The Young Ones*, a British sitcom, featured a group of unruly students sharing a rented house. Although not constituting a family they could be classed as a household, however chaotic relations between themselves and the outside world proved to be. More recently, the popular British sitcom *The Royle Family* features a family and is filmed in a single room dominated by the presence of the television set. Their experience of television is significant to family communication, with a constant stream of programmes conveyed into the home. The family's experience as a kinship group is centred around the TV set; this and their response to television programmes helps define the group as a family. From the American 1960s series *The Beverley Hillbillies* to *The Simpsons*, the nuclear family, even when hugely dysfunctional, remains a popular media representation.

The depiction of the family in television advertising is well represented by the Oxo family, which made its first appearance in the 1950s. In the early advertisements, Katie, a devoted housewife, oversees the making of gravy that 'gives a meal man-appeal'. By 2012 Oxo advertising features a father whose image appears on a laptop screen offering cookery advice to his son who is making a meal for his girlfriend. In addition to charting changes in communication technology, these advertisements provide popular representations both of how society views the family and the changes that have taken place within it. The Bisto kids first appeared in cartoon-style newsprint advertising in 1919. Depicted as street urchins they were shown passing open doors and windows from which the whiff of gravy emerged. The image was accompanied by the legend 'Ah! Bisto' Nearly a century later children featured in Bisto's 'Promise ad', in which they were shown promising to be good in return for 'proper food' (Campaign 2011). More recently Bisto's 2013 television advertising campaign features a symbolically all-purpose, but noticeably white, middle-class family composed of well-fed children including a baby in a high chair with parents serving sausages, mash and presumably Bisto gravy. Family conversation is reduced to the single exclamation 'Ah!' and is accompanied by the strap line 'Aah, now you're talking'.

Television and other advertising in domestic space

Advertising enters domestic space in a wide variety of ways, from postal service to airwave and cable delivery. Radio, Internet, television, telephone and below-the-line leaflet advertising makes its way into the home. Newspapers, magazines and periodicals featuring advertisements are delivered or brought into the home often on a regular basis. Between 1998 and 1999, 60 per cent of the UK male population and 51 per cent of the female population read a daily newspaper, and much of this reading occurred in the home. However, newspaper circulation has generally fallen since then. For instance, in 2013 the *Daily Mirror* circulation declined by 5.1 per cent on the previous year and the *Independent* by 28.56 per cent (*Guardian* 2013a). Television advertising is the principal home advertising form not only because of the volume of input but because of the dominant position

Figure 9.1 Bisto, 'When he's back … ', mid-twentieth century. Reproduced courtesy of The Advertising Archives.

television occupies as a delivery mechanism for advertising in the home. Television – its technologies, apparatus and reception – is a significant element of domestic experience and comes to define and visually dominate domestic space. Furthermore, as Anna McCarthy notes, 'the position of the television set … helps to position people' (2001: 119). As the number of televisions in the household has declined, other screens such as those of personal computers, laptops, smartphones and tablets also delivering television and advertising have increased. Domestic space features a variety of screens delivering television, but household television sets are still a prominent feature – to such an extent that domestic space is considered to be the home for television advertising.[1]

Television

The act of television viewing and the symbolic presence of the television set in domestic space has changed and developed over time since the first regular British television broadcasts in 1936 and the first independent television channel (ITV) began broadcasting advertisements in 1955. In addition to its technical function, the television set has come to have a totemic presence as a meaningful and symbolic domestic object. The organizing and positioning of televisions and accompanying technologies – reception, satellite, cable arrangements and acquisition of subscriptions and licenses – became a significant element of household and family expenditure, time and activity. The

Figure 9.2 Oxo, 'Katie says ... ', mid-twentieth century. Reproduced courtesy of The Advertising Archives.

increased number and spread of televisions in the home was noted by Anne Gray in the late 1980s: 'Many households had more than one television, but second sets were usually small black and white portables in the kitchen or one of the bedrooms, preference was for viewing on the main television set' (1992: 78) The increasing trend in television ownership was reversed in the first decade of the new millennium. By 2013 the average household had 1.83 TV sets, which was down from 2.3 sets in 2003 (TeleScope Study 2013). Yet since this time there has been an increase in screens delivering television and television advertising, with viewing occurring online through smartphones, tablets, laptops and desktop computers. The convergence of old and new media has been important to this (Jenkins 2006; Reid 2013). So, despite a reduction in television sets, there has been an increase in advertising penetration of domestic space by television and television advertising. Although television may well 'remain most people's primary medium for the foreseeable future' (Couldry 2012), the position of the television set as a symbolic centre of joint household or family activity and part of a shared media ritual involving television advertising reception has changed. The set as an object of attention has in many ways become part of a wider arrangement of screen broadcasting and entertainment in the home.

However, television remains a focal feature of domesticity as does broadcast television with its traditional forms of advertising (Marshall 2009). The technologies and spatialities of television, the apparatuses of reception, recording and playback and the required distance for viewing take up a significant amount of available domestic space. The more sets per household, the greater the area of space colonized by the apparatuses of TV. Some of this television space is multi-functional, given over to television reception and other domestic activity in which television talk takes place. Television advertising reception combines with a wide range of other material and symbolic activities and pervades domestic space (van den Oever 2012).

The television set takes two forms as domestic object and as medium or channel. It takes its place among other selected items that transform domestic space into a personalized and meaningful place (Morley 2007; Courtois 2012). It is a domestic item chosen for its aesthetic and functional significance and consumed as a household object. It is also the principal means through which advertising enters the home. Morley refers to television as a 'double articulation', 'both meaningful in itself (in its marketing and in its deployment) and the bearer of meanings' (Morley 1992: 210).

Reach and dailiness

Television is central to the passing of everyday time. It has come to form many of the markers that create the real and symbolic moments of passage. Television news and current affairs content mark global, national and local events, through rituals, patterned action and the passing of time (Couldry 2012). Television programming and advertising scheduling involve and reflect 'assumptions about everyday life' (Ellis 2000: 26). Ellis, for example, suggests that the 'dailiness' of television as 'the rhythm of the evening schedule mimics the rhythm of the evening in an imaginary average household' the nature of 'traditional slots' such as news and soap programming through to the 'annual pattern of seasons, events and special occasions' (Ellis 2000: 27). This scheduling mimics the flow of time and the patterns of work, recuperation and leisure. Advertising slots mark out television time, viewing time and routine domestic time. The home has increasingly become the place of an unprecedented privatized and atomized leisure and consumer lifestyle. At the heart of this modern space is the television although this has in recent years been joined by other digital media forms that create new relations with time and space (McQuire 2008; Couldry 2012). Television's very ordinariness and everydayness render it near invisible as domestic object. As Silverstone has noted, 'we take television for granted, in a way similar to how we take everyday life for granted' (Silverstone 2004). As Scannell has put it, 'This dailiness yields the sense we all have of the ordinariness, the familiarity and obviousness of radio and television' (Scannell 2000: 19).

Volume, intensity and penetration

Television as a material domestic object, its programming and advertising delivery creates domestic audiences, and it is a feature of 98 per cent of United Kingdom households. In 2013 the average television set per household was 1.83, and 39 per cent of adults owned tablets, laptops and smartphones that enabled online viewing (TeleScope Study 2013). The television set functions as a totem at the heart of the territorial domain over which it has jurisdiction. With the increase in the number of portable television-bearing screens in the household, viewed in numerous individual rooms outside of the shared leisure space, a fragmentation of domestic viewing takes place. In the past the unifying aspect of television ownership and television viewing helped create the 'togetherness' of the 'family circle' (Spigel 1992: 37). Hitherto, it had been assumed that as TV was at the heart of modern domestic space it helped to construct that space as a symbolic entity, very much in the way that the hearth had been at the centre of domestic life in earlier times. The trend towards divided family spaces began in America in the 1950s, with television sets being placed in children's playrooms and bedrooms away from the shared family spaces.

In 1952, *House Beautiful*, a popular lifestyle magazine of the time, had even more elaborated plans: 'A fun room built adjacent to the home and equipped with television gave a teenage daughter a place for her friends' (Spigel 1992: 67). The home and household became the place for private media consumption including television and other screen advertising, particularly among the young (Livingstone 2002; Bull 2004).

The average amount of time spent watching television in the UK amounted to around 28 hours per week in 2013, with differences in age and gender (Ofcom 2013b). The amount of time given over to television viewing in 1998 increased across the life cycle for both sexes, from under 20 hours per week in the under 15s to almost 40 hours per week for the over 65s. In 2013 the average daily viewing hours per person amounted to just over 4 hours, which was up by 30 minutes on 2006 figures (TeleScope Study 2013). Television viewing in Europe and the USA has risen across the last decade (Couldry 2012: 18), yet the viewing itself might be more accurately described as exposure to the television set and the message or text. Studies rarely measure the 'experience' of viewing in the sense of actual duration or concentration and quality of viewing. Commercial channels in the UK deduct 9.25 minutes per hour from programme time to include advertisements (Ellis 2000: 25–38), and Ofcom stipulates a maximum of 12 minutes advertising and teleshopping per hour (Ofcom 2013b). The amount of advertising differs across the spread of commercial channels and according to the time and day of broadcast.

In summary: the vast majority of household spaces include at least one television set or main screen, with many households having more. These may function in a totemic manner, uniting the domestic unit around the television set, but the number of other screens that carry television may work in the opposite manner, fragmenting the household or family. The television as object is still of significance to the contemporary home with the traditional living room still dominated by the main television. However, additional viewing of tablets, laptops and smartphones often occurs at the same time as household members follow the main screen. Media 'meshing' using the Internet to enhance the television experience and 'stacking' using more than one media at a time as a form of multitasking has led to watching a combination of programmes and advertisements on different appliances at the same time. This has, according to Ofcom, become widespread with 22 per cent of adults reported as watching different devices while in the same room (Ofcom 2013b). A large amount of time, on average around 25–28 hours per week, is spent viewing and nearly 60 per cent of that time viewing commercial channels, with advertising comprising about 7–8 per cent of viewing time (BARB 2013).

Advertising diffusion

Television advertising is an important feature of households and domestic space. It enters homes on a regular basis, its images and sounds conveyed into a wide range of rooms, many of which are part of shared space, where people watch television often in the company of other family members or friends and where the pictures, words and music that comprise a television advertisement circulate. Advertisements often play during conversation or form a backdrop to other household activities. Advertisements become part of domestic discourse and the cognitive lives of the members of the household. Television and other forms of screen advertising are imbued with the potential for diffusion. Product information, tag lines, descriptions of visual elements are readily passed on from one person to another through conversation. Advertisements, like other cultural forms, are able to move out beyond their own broadcast form, to overcome the limits of their original presentation in space and time. In other words they become diffuse.

In this section we are concerned with the diffusion of advertising meanings and the responses they generate within the home and household. Diffusion then refers to the spread and exchange of readings and reinterpretations of advertising texts at a remove from the original decoding. According to Everett Rogers, the term 'diffusion' is intended to include a description of both the 'spontaneous, unplanned spread of new ideas' and the sense of 'the directed and managed' usually associated with the term 'dissemination' (Rogers 1995: 7). Diffusion in both of these senses can be applied to a variety of advertising forms and environments, to both urban outdoor advertising and to television and other advertising viewed in domestic space.

Word of mouth

Diffusion is often referred to by the advertising industry as 'word of mouth' advertising and is generally considered to be part of the below-the-line category (Leiss *et al.* 2005; MacRury 2009a). Word of mouth is perceived as part of an informal broadening of the advertising campaign in which the advertising message or a reference to the advertisement is passed from person to person. This is usually conceived as consumers recommending products or services to other potential consumers which reinforces the advertising or branding communication message. From the point of view of marketing, this is referred to as positive word of mouth (PWOM) and has been described as the 'circulation of good news by satisfied customers' (MacRury 2009a: 77). However, repetition or reference to an aspect of the advertisement can be conceived as negative word of mouth (NWOM) in which the advertisement or product is perceived unfavourably and 'discourages purchase' (Vazquez-Casielles, Suarez-Alvarez & del Rio-Lanza 2013: 44). Studies have suggested that PWOM is generally considered to outweigh NWOM in a consideration of television advertising (Romaniuk 2007). Word of mouth advertising is often viral, buzz or e-word advertising conducted through online social media such as Facebook, MySpace and YouTube (Rosen 2000). However, face-to-face interaction in which the diffusion of advertising takes place is also considered important. Keller and Fay contend from their research that 75 per cent of consumer conversations about brands occur face to face and may occur in the home; 15 per cent are a result of telephone conversations; and only 10 per cent occur online (2012: 460).

Planned diffusion

The 'directed and managed' aspect of diffusion that Rogers spoke of can be applied to the organized, preplanned nature of the advertising message. Producer-intended diffusion creates a campaign or an element of a campaign that is discussed and applauded or criticized after an initial decoding. This includes the built-in aspects of an advertising campaign that are intended to be commented upon in a positive and non-ironic manner. Frequent repetition by young people of the Budweiser brand name following the pond frogs advertisements in the mid-1990s is a good example of a simple planned diffusion of the brand name beyond the advertising slot. Planned diffusion may also be intended to create contentious material likely to be copied or parodied. This may involve negotiated and oppositional readings of advertisements. Benetton's long-running United Colours campaign launched in the 1980s functioned in this manner and has over the years produced controversial and much-discussed advertisements creating a 'secondary circulation' through the controversy and discussion it engendered in the media (Falk 1997). This is also referred to as an 'amplification effect' and has been well documented.

Unplanned diffusion

The other sense in which the term diffusion is used, the 'spontaneous, unplanned spread of new ideas', refers to the way in which an advertising text is 'used' or 'handled' in different forms by members of the public. This may well be in ways unintended or unforeseen by the advertising producers. Members of the household comment upon, criticize and discuss advertisements. They can be thought of as an interpretive community (Fish 1980; Radway 1987). Interpretive communities such as households or families share certain commonalities, interpretive codes based on ways of thinking, seeing and speaking, specific to the particular group of people. This may create a particular take on viewing television programmes including advertisements. Unplanned diffusion in this sense emphasizes the advertisement coming to be 'diffuse' by 'negotiation' or 'opposition' rather than absorption of the preferred reading as explored in the reception element of the advertising framework. Advertising slogans, strap lines or quotations enter the currency of everyday speech and advertisements are discussed as part of conversation. This may be a short-term currency, with the advertisement talked about in the household for a brief period of time and then forgotten. Or it might endure as a cultural reference over a longer period of time.

The effects of diffusion are more keenly observed in domestic space which includes television and other forms of screen advertising than in the reception of billboard or other outdoor forms of advertising. The shared space, close social arrangements and cultural codes of the domestic unit create potential television-advertising receivers who are homophilous. This suggests that shared cultural or economic attributes are likely to make communication more effective. Rogers defines diffusion in communication as 'the process by which an innovation is communicated through certain channels over time among the members of a social system' (Rogers 1995: 10). The tendency of television advertising to be diffuse is enhanced by the significance of television to domesticity and of the central position of the television set or screen as a household object.

Interpretive communities

The family or household can be thought of as forming an *interpretive community*, which is a helpful term for understanding how screen-based advertising is received within the household. The concept is taken from the study of literature (Fish 1980; Radway 1987)[2] and can be applied in a wider sense to the general relationship between the producers and receivers of advertising texts. As Stanley Fish has put it, 'it is interpretive communities, rather than either the text or the reader, that produce meanings ... [They] are made up of those who share interpretive strategies' (Fish 1980: 14). A *vertical* form of interpretative community emphasizes the relationship between the producer and receiver of advertising messages and a shared set of codes that makes communication possible. It requires a level of homology, of fit between producers and readers of texts, necessary to create what Stuart Hall identified as 'the shared frameworks, shared codes, shared knowledge-in-us, shared interpretive frameworks between communicator and receiver' (Hall 1981a: 277).

Another, *horizontal* form of 'interpretive community' emphasizes the common, shared elements of reception: the material codes, understandings and other forms that enable an advertising text to become meaningful to a community. 'Interpretive community' in this horizontal sense can be applied to members of a household who share familiar codes of language and culture. The household or family culture draws on long-term historical resources such as shared memories, events and experiences which create a sense of identity. This local form of culture functions in many ways and is used to make sense of advertising material. Over time the advertising material becomes absorbed as 'television talk' (Silverstone 2004).

Within domestic space, television advertisements may be given an increased potency through 'incorporation' (Silverstone, Hirsch & Morley 1992; Silverstone 2004). This occurs as a *familiarization* process endowing the advertisements with a comparable value associated with objects, speech forms, utterances and glances that are partial components of the domestic unit that create a 'structure of feeling' of shared domestic life (Williams 1981). At the same time, elements that comprise the domestic structure of feeling, 'actions, gestures and speech acts are formed through television's presence within particular environments' (McCarthy 2001: 11). The dialectical nature of this arrangement enables local and familiar association between media forms and other forms and elements in the domestic unit and facilitates the passage of the former into the latter. Domestic space has been characterized as a particular space of consumption, where circulation of commodity representation, values and ideas associated with commodified form, representation of lifestyle and value, contextualize the preferred advertising meaning. This incorporation takes place and is reinforced as transaction and exchange between household members.

Domestic space and viewing

Domestic space occupied by a household is important to the diffusion of television and other screen advertising. Primary diffusion occurs when the advertisement is viewed in a room where the television or computer screen is dominant, so that direct, largely undistracted contact with the screen takes place. In the case of the television screen, the layout of the room is partly organized around the floor-based television set or wall-mounted screen. This is the area that the television is able to command and operate within as part of what Anna McCarthy calls the 'spatial or sensorial arrangements of its location' (McCarthy 2001: 2). In this arrangement, the television effect is at its most concentrated. Secondary diffusion occurs in rooms of the house where the television screen may be less dominant and often subordinate to other domestic activities and concerns, such as the kitchen, bedroom or study. This kind of space is marked by the daily routines and practices of everyday living, of conversation and discussion and the routines and rituals of domestic consumption. It is here, in this potent, material household space, among the trappings of material domestic existence, that advertising texts become diffuse items of exchange, mingling with and giving resonance to domestic and consumer activity. Family or household sensibilities and activities intermingle with the diffuse reception of advertising texts, giving a local and familiar feel to incoming advertisements. Advertisements become diffuse by entering into household discussion and other forms of communication within the domestic unit. Advertisements received in the home also become diffuse by being carried as thoughts and potential conversation beyond the household into the street, workplace, school and playground or spaces of consumption such as shopping centres and towns.

Viewing scenarios

Television and other forms of screen advertising are experienced in different ways in domestic space, impacting on the reception of advertising. This can be referred to through viewing scenarios, which are contingent on the number of people involved and on their viewing behaviour. Three viewing scenarios can be observed. In the first, the viewer or perhaps several viewers interpret the advertisement individually and without comment. The advertisement is received individually and decoded in a singular and non-conversational manner. The received textual reading is then open to exchange in a close temporal framework – close to the moment of broadcast – and in the same spatial arrangement in which the primary reading was received. 'Television content is used in order to facilitate conversation' according to Morley and it is also the primary means by which ideas and interpretations of advertisements are shared (Morley 1986: 31).

In the second viewing scenario, the text might be received by several viewers simultaneously who are engaged in sporadic or intermittent conversation. This entails the advertising text taking part in a very real sense in the flow of conversation. In this scenario, 'the arrangement affords an opportunity for easy switching between two roles – conversationalist and spectator – often requiring no more than a redirection of the gaze, not even a repositioning of the body' (McCarthy 2001: 124). This may take, as Morley suggests, 'the form of conversation running parallel with the programme, commenting directly on television material as it is presented' (1986: 31). In these circumstances the advertising text is a significant part of social interaction and enters what Silverstone has termed '"communitas"' … the shared experience, however fragile, momentary and synthetic, of community' (Silverstone 2004: 21).

A third viewing scenario can be identified when advertising reception is only peripheral to other activities occurring in the space in which television is showing. These might include domestic labour such as ironing (Morley 1986: 150); eating, reading and doing homework (Petrie 1996); or engaging with other electronic media while watching TV. In these circumstances the television is on but not being attended to in a concentrated manner. A further range of variables such as the number of people present in the space, movements in and out of spaces, conversations, thought patterns and experiences blur the boundaries between television-advertising watching and other domestic activity. Wilson emphasizes this social nature of television watching: 'Variations in level of attention to the screen, for instance, may be due not to qualities of the text, or to the absences of pleasurable engagement with the programme, but to the interaction within the social context of the audience's "looking"' (1993: 24). Ang succinctly summarizes the situation recognizing that it is 'difficult to demarcate when we are and when we are not part of the television audience' (1996: 68).

Advertising and flow

Raymond Williams noted the existence of television flow in the 1970s and this is important to the way that screen-based advertising takes hold in domestic space. In the simplest sense television programmes and advertisements flow across the screen in procession. This is referred to as programme flow.[3] Television is viewed within and from domestic space. 'Turning on the telly' is a voluntary activity but television screens are eminently compelling and the animated flow of images attention-grabbing. The screen's presence easily fills and dominates space. Its sound flows beyond the room, and talk about television is carried beyond the reach of the television set as part of household conversation. The close relationship between television flow and domestic everyday life has been noted by many media analysts, who have emphasized it as a flow within the flow of daily life (Ridell 1996; Silverstone 2004) or television's 'seamless equivalence with social life' (Heath 1990: 267). Altman and others outline the relation between programme flow and the social relations within domestic space which are termed 'household flow' (Altman 1987: 571). The routines of everyday living are interwoven with the flow of television advertising. Television was the only form of domestic-screen delivery when Williams used the term 'programme flow'. It is important to recognize the change in patterns in screen-advertising viewing in recent years. The screens of the mobile media such as tablets, phones and laptops are characterized by largely individual viewing rather than group or collective viewing of the static television set and the opportunity afforded to collective advertising reception (Marshall 2009: 47). This becomes important to the way in which television and other forms of screen advertising seep into and flow through the domestic life of the home, family and household.

Although television flow is important to an understanding of television advertising, Paddy Scannell is keen to emphasize media delivery as being made up of a series of 'nows': the different moments in which the message is produced, delivered and received. As he puts it, 'There is the now of the broadcast event ... and at the same time the now of listening or viewing' (Scannell 2000: 20). In the case of television the 'nows of reception' are repeated: this forms part of its communicative strength. Television and other screen advertisements are repeated and consequently the advertisement is viewed many times over. Each viewing is a 'now' of reception and each one is different – occupying its unique historical moment. Alongside each of these viewings must be placed the 'nows' of reflection, discussion, renegotiation and re-encoding that come to form the flow of 'nowness'. Television advertising becomes interwoven with other texts, reflections and social experiences, and this forms part of the potency of advertising. Through repetition and diffusion it permeates and flows through contemporary life.

Television flow can be seen as part of a wider social formation. The 'fact of flow' is for Williams both the television experience and at the same time an important part of modern social experience (Williams 1974: 95; Gripsrud 1998: 28). Manuel Castells more generally has characterized contemporary life as being involved in a 'space of flows' (1996). Flows are for Castells an essential phenomenon of the contemporary world characterized as 'repetitive, programmable sequences of exchange and interaction between physically disjointed positions held by social actors in the economic, political and symbolic structures of society' (Castells 1996: 411). So, society is organized and experienced as a space of flows: '(S)ociety is constructed around flows: flows of capital, flows of information, flows of technology, flows of organizational interaction, flows of images, sounds and symbols' (Castells 1996: 411, 2008; Odih 2010). The modern media and screen advertising is an important element of this process (Adams 2009; Couldry 2012).

Conclusion

This chapter has explored domestic space and the advertising that is received there. A distinction between public and private space was established with domestic space as part of the latter. Television, radio and more recently the Internet have been characterized as a bridge between the public and private. Although a variety of screens transmit advertisements such as personal computers, laptops, smartphones and tablets, the television set remains an important symbolic and real presence in domestic space. Domesticity can be characterized in three ways, as home, household and family, and each was shown, in its own way, to be important to advertising reception. This gives rise to particular viewing and reception scenarios where individual and interactive viewing occurs. Reception occurs as part of an interpretive community based on specific household circumstances where a local household or family culture is an important element in advertising reception. Television-advertising flow across the screen and through the home is also important. Advertising diffusion takes on particular characteristics in the home but is part of a wider advertising application that also functions outside of the home. Decoding of television advertising largely takes place in the household and gives rise to 'television talk', which can include reference to advertising. This mingles with other discourses and activities in the home and becomes integrated into a general household flow, making television advertising a potent form. The experience of outdoor advertising is explored in the following chapter.

Notes

1 The domination of television technology is not of course only confined to domestic space. Increasing colonization of public space – outdoor public areas, concourses, pubs, cafes and shops – by the television technologies associated with consumer surveillance and broadcast TV has become a significant and increasing aspect of the time–space compression. Dissolving material, spatial boundaries through multiple representations on security screens, banks of entertainment video and broadcast television screens result in a tightening of public space around the increased dominance of the ocular. Large screens have come to dominate much of urban social space (see McCarthy 2001; Bolin 2004).

2 Similar formulations of the producer–receiver relationship of cultural texts – such as Gadamer's hermeneutics, Iser's Constance School of reception theory, and Bennett and Woollacott's reading formulation – provide comparative frameworks to the 'interpretive community' concept (Warnke 1987; Iser 1989; Bennett & Woollacott 1987; Bennett 1990).

3 Jaques Derrida explored the phenomena of images, frames and context in his work *The Truth in Painting* (1987). The ergon of the image is preceded in television-advertising flow by the parergon of the previous programme or advertisement and is superceded in television time by a further parergon adding to the complexity of television-advertising flow.

10 Outdoor advertising

Introduction

This chapter looks at advertising within the urban, outdoor environment of largely public spaces. This is in contrast to the private space of the home where certain kinds of advertising are an aspect of the domestic environment. In the previous chapter domestic life was shown to play an important part in contextualizing advertising which targets potential consumers as part of the family and household. This chapter explores outdoor urban life as the context of outdoor advertising. Outdoor advertising refers to advertising in public spaces such as billboards and adshells positioned alongside roads and pathways or to advertising situated in areas open to the public such as shopping malls or railway stations. This has also been referred to by the advertising industry as the 'outside industry' or 'outdoor media' (Goodwin 1991; Mansell 1997). The term 'out of home advertising', which is also used, refers to all advertising that can be accessed outside of domestic space. So in addition to billboard sites, electronic panels and mobile advertising carried by public transport, out of home includes advertising on personal, mobile and handheld devices. Quite often the terms 'outdoor' and 'out of home' are used interchangeably.

Advertising is an important part of the urban experience and the reception of advertising in outdoor city spaces is different to the advertising experience in the home. This chapter explores the changes that have taken place in the layout and social function of cities, the nature of urban time and space, different urban experiences and how this connects with advertising. Different advertising audiences are recognized as part of city life and interpretive time and measurement of potential advertising effects are related to this. The chapter concludes with a case study of a 2013 UK Border Agency advertising campaign. This took the form of an outdoor, mobile 'advan' campaign targeted at a number of areas of London. Whether parked in the street or travelling through traffic the advertisement mingled with the flow of urban activity. Its political and social message was controversial, its target audience unclear and both its message and its mechanism of delivery became the focus for debate and criticism.

Outdoor advertising

Outdoor advertising is an important visual component of the modern town or city and a significant feature in encouraging and directing consumption (Davila 2004). This involves a broad range of urban advertising forms ranging from the traditional paper poster to the more recent scrolling billboards and latest digital screens. In addition, electronic panels that form Adshel Superlites are steadily replacing older forms of bus shelter advertising.

Mobile-advertising vehicles such as advans, advertising trailers and mobile billboards, designed primarily to promote goods and services, are a common feature of the streets. Buses, trains and trams, as a form of public transport, have a primary function carrying passengers from place to place and a secondary function as a vehicle for interior and exterior advertising display. Outdoor advertising appears on public and private buildings and is a widespread feature of publicly accessed space, from shopping centres to railway stations and airports. It adorns urban objects and utilities such as telephone boxes and appears on pavements and occasionally in the sky. The age-old practice of fly posting on walls and leaflet distribution on the streets continues as a feature of modern cities. In addition, digital technology makes it possible to project advertisements onto a range of outdoor surfaces (McDonald & Scott 2007: 20; MacRury 2009a).

The increase and spread of outdoor advertising in public space has been a cause for concern at least since the early nineteenth century. The introduction of electronic billboards, handheld devices and associated targeting technology has increased these concerns in recent years. As Ian MacRury has suggested, it amounts to the 'colonisation of public spaces and formerly private spaces' and can take the form of a 'stressful dynamism' (2009a: 105). But for others the proliferation of outdoor advertising particularly in urban areas adds to the richness and intensity of urban experience. What can be agreed on is the complex and multifaceted nature of outdoor advertising. The outdoor environment is explored in this chapter as an important setting for advertising and for the meanings it may have for its audiences. The impact on urban life and experience as a component of consumer culture and contemporary social life is explored further in Chapter 12.

Outdoor audiences

Advertising is at some fundamental level a means of engaging and speaking to the public. This raises the question of how we, and indeed the advertising industry, are to understand the public as it appears in the modern outdoor urban environment. It also raises the important question of research: how can we have knowledge of advertising audiences? Since the 1980s changes have taken place in how audiences are conceptualized. The idea of the 'mass' society conceived of as a total audience in which common characteristics are emphasized has fallen out of favour, largely replaced by the notion of markets and market segmentation (Turow 1997; Hesmondhalgh 2013: 388). Sociological and critical cultural studies approaches tend to see audiences as social categories such as class, gender, age, ethnicity, race or other social groupings. Indeed a developed categorization of people living in or visiting an urban environment reveals a diverse urban public from a variety of backgrounds and experiences. It suggests people engaged in a broad range of economic, social and cultural activities. This includes people in different kinds of urban-based work which both enable and limit patterns of behaviour including consumer activity. In addition, different forms of leisure activity draw people to the urban environment as both participants and spectators for sport, art and culture. The complexity of audience make-up, based not only on economic categories but on cultural diversity, is widely acknowledged.

The advertising industry had long been criticized for its representation of society as a series of advertising stereotypes. For instance, women were represented as 'types': 'women as homemaker', 'women as sexual object' or even 'women as seductress'. This failed to represent women in the fullness of their experience as paid and unpaid workers, with a wider individual, social and cultural profile. In response to this the industry attempted to represent social reality more fully by incorporating a wider representation of social diversity into its representational system (Akwue 2012). Benetton advertising from the 1980s was important to this, using images that displayed difference, social complexity and challenging social conventions. They were at the same time both groundbreaking and attention seeking. In 2013, Benetton featured a transsexual Brazilian model in its brand advertising campaign (*Marketing* 2013). A flick through the pages of *Campaign* and *Marketing,* both advertising industry magazines, suggests the industry is not yet satisfied with its attempt to represent diversity and difference. Here is a selection of headlines from these publications: 'Does ad industry value ethnic Britain?' (Darby 2012); 'There are many gay role models on TV – just not in the ads' (Newbery 2012); 'Brands have long been accused of reducing women and particularly mothers to easy stereotypes' (Bashford 2012). Critics of the industry point out that this is not about understanding discrimination against gays or supporting equal rights in law or anti-discrimination procedures. Nor is it concerned about single mothers being employed on zero-hour contracts without a guaranteed wage or 'holiday, sick or redundancy pay' (Milne 2013). The advertising industry interest in social diversity, critics contend, goes no further than the supermarket checkout or the Internet cart. Nevertheless, the advertising industry has come in recent years to recognize and represent difference in some sense. Consequently, audiences for urban advertising are subject to intense market research and much of this is to do with identifying the real profile of audiences, measuring them and understanding how they react to advertising messages.

This tendency in the advertising and media industry is linked to what has been termed the rise of lifestyle categorization, exploring socio-cultural currents, tracking, measuring, forecasting and shaping future publics as consumers. In the advertising world, 'The project of "lifestyle" studies is to define the coherent profiles and homogeneous typologies of consumers–viewers–listeners which are brought together in individuals' (Mattelart 1991: 164). The urban public that we encounter in the outdoor spaces of cities and towns may well consist of urban workers engaged in different intensities of work – in shops, in financial and legal institutions or in street work as vendors, cleaners or attendants. In this sense the advertising industry comes close to the sociologist's view, using the socio-economic group (SEG) classifications from A–E in order to measure income and gauge the purchasing power of the worker as they come and go from their place of employment.[1] This classification is also applicable to an even larger category of people: those visiting the city as consumers.

Cities and consumption

In the latter part of the twentieth century, urban space, like the economy generally, has undergone a process of deindustrialization. Towns and cities in the industrial and manufacturing regions of Britain, once formed around factory and manufacturing workplaces, have largely given up on production and its processes. Various reasons are cited. Saskia Sassen suggests that 'manufacturing activities in large cities are viewed as inefficient' and consequently 'city locations are therefore unfeasible' (1996: 26); John Lovering indicates this is due to 'technological change' and that industry has 'moved to cheaper workforces elsewhere' (1997: 68); and Dave Byrne suggests it is part of the general 'trajectories of urban spaces towards postindustrialism' (2001: 53). If the heart of the nineteenth- and twentieth-century city was associated with production and its accompanying infrastructure, housing, transport, services and way of life, it is now characterized by consumption. What remains of industry has moved out of the centre and to the margins of metropolitan areas.

British cities came to be known as 'edge cities' in the latter part of the twentieth century (Garreau 1992; Angotti 1993; Byrne 2001). Edge city is a form of extended metropolis: 'the new urban world without a centre' (Byrne 2001: 122). It creates a new form of urban life with a different kind of relationship to the core of the old city centre. It is according to Angotti 'larger, more complex and plays a more commanding role – economic, political and cultural – than the industrial city and town that preceded it. It is not just downtown, but more like a collection of towns' (Angotti 1993: 1). Byrne offers Cleveland, Ohio, as an American example and Dublin as a European example of the phenomenon, where the people of the region are employed in 'industrial parks, office parks and mall areas which exist both as a ring around the core city and scattered through new postindustrial edge settlements. There is even substantial commuting out of the core city to work in these peripheral zones' (Byrne 2001: 122).

The modern British city is now given over to leisure, consumption and related services (Zukin 1998) with cities being seen as 'centres of consumption and administration – out with factories, in with offices, shopping malls and clubland' (Lovering 1997: 68). UK legislation has enabled longer shopping hours including Sunday and late-evening opening, and permitted extended alcohol licensing hours. Consequently, the city has become an extensive place and time of consumption, and city centres have become attractive and extensive sites for advertising and branding.

In addition there has been the creation of retail parks and out of town shopping centres on the periphery of city boundaries, often on a huge scale, creating vast sites of consumption. In some cases whole lumps of the consumption infrastructure appear to have broken away and drifted out to previously derelict land or metamorphosed on former industrial sites outside of urban areas. In many cases this has left areas of the cities and towns devoid of either productive or consumer activity. Consumer culture has in many ways become associated with car culture and all the inclusions and exclusions of class, age, gender and other social categories that this involves. As the movement of consumption culture has been inward and outward across space, so the 'look' of the urban centre has been refigured and refashioned, first in the late Modernist or Brutalist style used to fashion shopping centres in the 1960s and 1970s, and more recently in the Postmodern eclectic style, borrowing elements of architectural forms from previous historical periods. To a greater or lesser extent capital investment has been channelled into the creation of more complex centres of consumption and leisure. Though not in itself new, the pace and intensification of the creation of these centres of consumption and leisure has increased.

This has involved a quickening and intensity in consumer activity with an increase in sales activity and velocity in the exchange of commodities. As Jackson and Thrift put it in the mid-1990s, 'production, marketing, distribution and consumption all tend to be more rapid (in the modern world)' (1995: 215) and this has a more general effect, 'very much about speed-up and acceleration in the pace of economic processes and, hence, in social life' (Harvey 1992: 230). Where the pace and intensity of consumption increases, so the spaces of the inner city designated for consumption appear to strain under the pressure of hyper-activity. The spaces of urban consumption become squeezed into confined areas of the inner city, with mall complexes such as Birmingham's Bullring and Pallasades and Newcastle's Eldon Square good examples of this. In these largely interior spaces, the new version of the old city billboards, glass-protected poster sites, which are digital and highly visible, oversee these new cityscapes and public-private spaces. They set the scene not only for outdoor advertising and its reception but for the intense pace of consumer activity.

Consumer activity can be seen to fit into at least two categories: recreational consumption and laborious consumption (Prus & Dawson 1991). Laborious consumption is thought of as being akin to work. It is an ordinary, often everyday task and comparable to the repetitive aspects of the labour process. It is, according to Prus and Dawson (1991: 154), 'frustrating, monotonous and unavoidable' and involves the day-to-day acquisition of those things that are necessary in a market economy to the satisfaction of everyday needs. On the other hand recreational consumption is discussed in the positive register as 'a change of pace from other routines and includes novelty fascination and the display of self to others' (Prus & Dawson 1991: 150). It is likely to be accompanied by various social and cultural activities that accompany consumption in the urban centres: from refreshment – coffee bars, restaurants, pubs, etc. – to entertainment – clubs, galleries and cinemas. Recreational consumption is likely to be a total shopping experience, often described today as 'retail therapy' – a very conspicuous consumption in which display and outdoor advertising are important component parts.

In a wider sense consumer activity has become intensified and entrenched in patterns of social and cultural behaviour since the 1970s and 1980s. Described by Streeck as part of 'the sheer extent of the commercialization of social life', it is founded on economic change (2012: 33). At the same time as changes in the economy have taken place an ideological change has occurred that puts emphasis on consumption rather than production. Emphasis is placed on identity associated with what and how people consume products rather than the labour that goes into their production. This theme is explored further in Chapter 12 where changes to the economy are reflected in changes in the relationship between people, consumer goods, retail outlets and the companies that market the goods.

Cool, neat advertising

Description and analysis of these changes occurs in the work of Chris Rojek (2007) and Jim McGuigan (2006, 2009, 2010, 2012), providing powerful accounts of urban consumer activity which inform an understanding of urban advertising. Rojek uses the term 'neat capitalism' to represent a new, informal and irreverent face of capitalism. The Body Shop, Apple and Virgin are offered as examples of this – all high street names that dominate the new urban centres. These companies, according to Rojek, present themselves as consumer-friendly and globally and socially responsible. The figure of Richard Branson encapsulates these values as 'a punchy street campaigner ready to take on corrupt big business' on behalf of consumers (Rojek 2007: 117). McGuigan's 'cool capitalism' is represented by Nike and Gap, associated with the marketing of 'cool' commodities, and well represented by the figure of the late Steve Jobs, who is described by McGuigan as a 'cool dude' (2012: 10).

In a wider sense cool, neat capitalism has coincided with the neoliberal economics instigated in the Reagan–Thatcher years which shifted the economy from a mixture of public and private provision to an economy driven by private gain. This has, critics contend, given rise to new elements in culture. The consumer culture associated with it involves according to Rojek the youthful attitudes of 'absurdity, humour, informality and a playful disrespect for authority' (2007: 126). For McGuigan 'narcissism, ironic detachment and hedonism' form 'the dominant ethic of late consumer capitalism' (2010: 154).

These appear to be persistent images of youth consumer culture (Leiss *et al.* 2005). For instance, high above Newcastle upon Tyne's premier shopping street, Primark has built into its façade a large video window which displays marketing images of cool, composed young models parading clothing sold in-store (see Figure 10.1). The models confront the consumer in the cool, confident manner of the catwalk. It was instructive to view this display in the week that an eight-storey building housing a factory producing clothing for Primark and other labels sold in Britain collapsed in Dhaka, Bangladesh, killing 1,129 people (*Guardian* 2013c). Garment workers in this part of the world employed to produce Western-label clothing have been described as akin to 'slave labour' by critics including Pope Francis (*Huffington Post* 2013).[2]

Uncut capitalism

Despite the above, the countercultural values generated in the political opposition movements of the sixties and seventies have been incorporated into this new form of cool, neat consumer capitalism (McGuigan 2006: 152). 'At its heart is the presumption that socially responsible market solutions are the most efficient way of dealing not only with economic problems, but also with social and cultural questions' (Rojek 2007: 123). In essence, both neat and cool capitalism are a reworking of the doctrine of consumer sovereignty that presents the consumer as the driving force of economic and social change (Hutt 1940; Spies-Butcher *et al.* 2012: 22). In reality, big business and corporate interests shape the

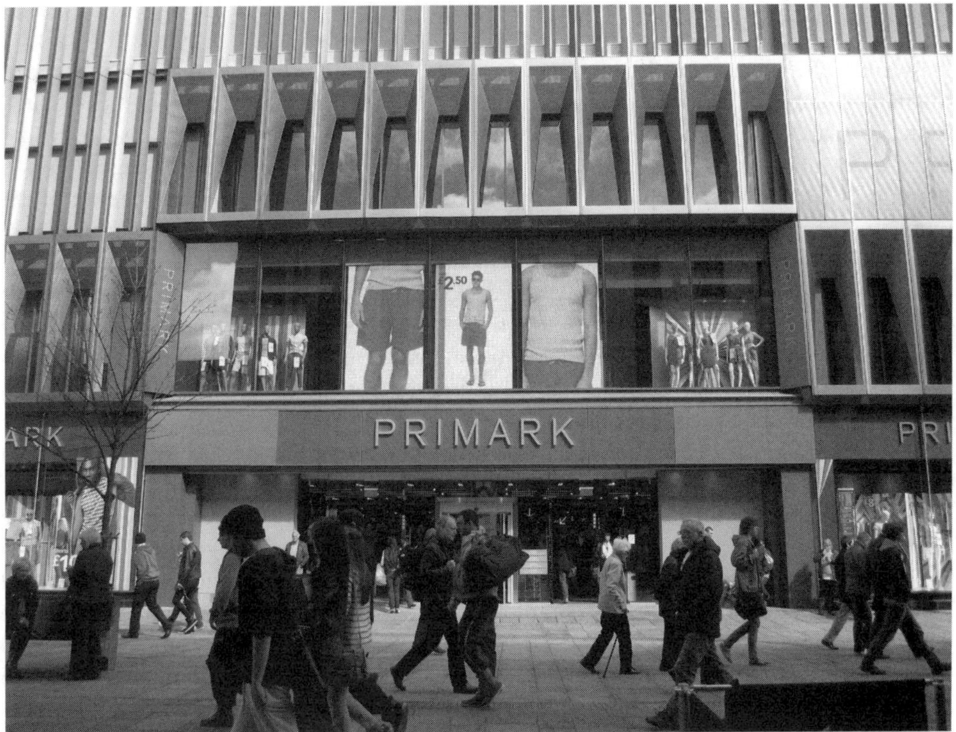

Figure 10.1 Primark store, Newcastle upon Tyne, 2014. Photographed by the author.

economy and much of social life. According to McGuigan, 'neo-liberal capitalism has constructed popular legitimacy of … a resilient kind … in spite of severe and recurrent economic crises' (2012: 7). However, a compliance to consumer capitalism constructed around the ubiquitous cool brands of the high street is not the only form that youthful, urban popular culture can take (Purvis 2013).

UK Uncut is a direct action group that peacefully occupies high-street stores in protest against perceived tax dodging by banks and corporations (Mason 2012). From the invasion of London's famous grocers Fortnum & Mason in 2011 to the flashmob occupation of Apple's flagship store on Regent Street in 2013 the group creates spectacular protests against tax avoidance by the big corporations. UK Uncut is part of a developing series of actions and oppositions to economic and cultural consequences of 'cool' or 'neat' capitalism (Wainwright 2012): from the 2010 UK youth protests against the rise in university fees and scrapping of the Education Maintenance Allowance to the ongoing strikes and protests against unemployment and austerity in Greece (Mason 2012: 46; Spourdalakis 2012). The Occupy movement of Wall Street and London and the Indignados of Spain can also be included in this category (Dean 2012). The large-scale and widespread rioting and looting that occurred on the streets of Britain in 2011 was perhaps not wholly unrelated (Cavanagh & Dennis 2012). In 2013 a wave of strikes by fast-food workers in support of a living wage spread through McDonald's, Wendy's and KFC outlets in the US. These have been supported by large-scale street protests in New York, Chicago and Detroit (Helmore 2013) and suggest a further critical approach to cool, neat capitalism.

Urban time and space

It isn't just the experience of cool or angry youth occupying the streets and walkways of towns and cities that has to be accounted for in approaches to outdoor advertising. Material places and spaces of the contemporary urban landscape give rise to wider experiences and forms of behaviour related to advertising and advertising reception (Cronin 2006). A critical approach to urban time and space needs to take account of the numerous experiences and interactions between people and aspects of the urban landscape. 'Space and time are basic categories of human existence. Yet we rarely debate their meanings; we tend to take them for granted, and give them common-sense or self-evident attributions', according to David Harvey (1992: 201). However, recently these concerns have become more expansive areas of academic enquiry, and the combination of urban time and urban space has become an area of interest for the advertising industry.

Nineteenth- and early-twentieth-century commentators like poet and art critic Charles Baudelaire and the early urban sociologist George Simmel explored the human experience of urban life and its settings. They pictured city life as a constant stream of movement and activity, as we might say today, constantly 'on the go'. These are observations that have endured, although in the first decades of the twenty-first century they might appear in a much intensified and accelerated form. Simmel offered useful insights into understanding the psychological experience of the city. He described the experience of being in the city as an 'intensification of nervous stimulation' which amounts to a 'rapid crowding of changing images, the sharp discontinuity in the grasp of a single glance, and the unexpectedness of onrushing impressions' (Simmel 1950: 48). Denis Cosgrove paints a picture of the late-twentieth-century urban scene as a range of diverse activities taking place and like Simmel places the viewer/consumer at the centre of the experience of 'images', ' glances' and 'impressions' (Cosgrove 1989: 118–19; Simmel, 1950:48).

Charles Baudelaire suggested to the nineteenth-century public that the proper subject of art for realist painters of the time, such as Edouard Manet or Gustave Caillebotte, should be that of modern urban life, which was considered to be 'heroic'. Interestingly for our discussion of advertising viewing in Chapter 11, Baudelaire attached significance to the 'glance' as a way of seeing the world. Perhaps more important is his understanding and commentary on nineteenth-century street life and the value of the minutiae of everyday observations, of the 'ephemeral, the fugitive, the contingent'. The surface form of contemporary urban existence was important to Baudelaire. This is a thread that continues into contemporary critical thinking, where consumer culture is seen to be based on the principle of fashion with its built-in 'systematic obsolescence' (Strasser 2009: 31). Elsewhere, Baudelaire stresses the difference between two elements of social life: 'All forms of beauty, like all possible phenomena, contain an element of the eternal and an element of the transitory – of the absolute and of the particular' (Baudelaire 1982: 17). It is this 'fleeting' and 'transitory' aspect of city life which is in constant competition with concentrated, cognitive processes, both of which are elements of consumer activity and the consumer decision-making processes. The ever-present, often overwhelming sound of the city is also important to our consideration of the urban experience (Bull 2004). This in conjunction with the dynamic visual forms and rhythms help create the flux of city life and provide the context to advertising reception.

Urban movement

People make their way through the streets and spaces of urban environments travelling on foot or by public and private transport. They travel alone or in groups through sparsely populated areas and through spaces occupied by dense crowds, moving through outdoor spaces as focused consumers or as casual wanderers. They might cross an open space unimpeded by other people, moving into close proximity to a billboard site or into a place of 'advertising interpellation' where sustained sightlines and interpretive time are maximized. Or they might move at a pace determined by the movement and speed of the crowd. Crowds in cities have been referred to as 'indefinite collectivities' or as 'the throng as it lives, jostles and consumes in the city of everyday human intercourse' (Thrift & Glennie 1993: 44). Much of this activity is surrounded by advertising and elaborate shop-window displays of consumer items. The lived experience of the city of commodities and advertisements produces what the Situationists considered a spectacular effect. As the leading light of the Situationists, Guy Debord, put it, it is one in which 'the world at once present and absent which the spectacle makes visible is the world of the commodity dominating all that is lived' (Debord 1992 [1977]: 37). The resulting movements of crowds and interpenetration of images, signs and reflections are intensified in the enclosed and covered walkways of the modern shopping development. According to Lash and Lury, 'urban space becomes a space of intensities' (2007: 15) and suggests MacRury's 'stressful dynamism of the modern urban landscape' (2009a: 105).[3] The city experience involves what Steve Graham, following Castells, identifies as flow. The flows of 'water, waste, energy' but also 'information, people, commodities and signs' (Graham 2010: 261). The flow concept is explored more specifically in terms of advertising by Pamela Odih (2010). In many ways this intensity and movement is a disorienting experience.

Enduring and ephemeral

Many urban streets and walkways still follow routes that have been in use since ancient times. Many European towns and cities have been developed as modern postwar urban environments. In Britain some retain open streets of traditional Victorian or Georgian style and width, which may themselves have been fashioned from mediaeval streets and lanes or follow still older Roman ways. Routes may open out into open-air market areas organized around spaces similar to those of the ancient Greek agora or Roman forum. The routes people take through cities might culminate in a modern covered piazza where groups and individuals engage with contemporary outdoor advertising: the neon signs, electric back-lit panels or the flat paper form of billboard advertisements.

Advertising and advertising campaigns are traditionally thought of as short-lived experiences – TV and Internet ads, for example, last mere moments and the page featuring a newspaper advert is often quickly turned. The glance at the billboard is likely to be a short, ephemeral experience. Yet billboard sites endure over time and are often significant visual and cultural features of city spaces. Advertising campaigns come and go but advertising poster sites endure. London's Piccadilly Circus is a good example of a prime advertising site that has an enduring presence over time, playing a part as a symbolic marker of time and identity in the urban environment. The billboard site can be placed in a typology of urban artifacts between ancient monuments, historic buildings and more modern commercial and civic amenities around which urban identity is created and shared.

Advertising site evaluation

The positioning and effectiveness of billboard sites is an important feature of the research aspect of the advertising industry. Roadside billboards have since the 1980s been ascribed performance ratings by research agencies using evaluative systems such as OSCAR and the POSTAR system, renamed Route in February 2013. One of the functions is to enable a market price to be attached to the advertising site, its place and command over potential consumers. Boards and panels are evaluated according to the potential connection they will make with the interpellated subject of the advertising text. The sites are categorized as 'parallel' or running alongside a stretch of road, 'angled' to the road or 'head on' which is in front of the traffic flow (Mansell 1997: 41). The presentation of the advertisement is established and evaluated in relation to sightlines and the 'duration' of potential interpretive time. The notion of 'competition' measures the relationship of the billboard under evaluation to other advertising texts in close proximity or within the same viewer field of vision. 'Visibility adjusted impact' and 'opportunities to see' are mechanisms for 'measuring audiences of roadside poster sites' which account for the place and the positioning of the sites (*Campaign* 1996: 4).

Interpretive time

In many ways, public outdoor advertising can be compared and contrasted to other forms of advertising, such as television, which is mainly received in the private domain, or to cinema advertising, viewed in the public, but entry-restricted domain. For instance, cinema and television advertising have in common the kinetic nature of imagery and text and the narrative possibilities that result from this. These are shared with some digital but not with traditional poster advertising. There is also a qualitative difference in formal presentation to do with duration over time. Presentation time of cinema and television adverts is a few moments in length and considerably shorter than the period of time over which billboard advertisements are presented. In addition, the billboard text endures across time without interruption and the advertisement may be repeated on other sites, thus reinforcing its message(s). This is important in terms of 'interpretive time', which is the time a viewer has to take in and appreciate the message, and is crucial to the nature of the decoding and the creation of an advertisement's meaning and significance for the viewer (Corner 1995: 107). The duration of interpretive time is conditional on a number of factors, many extraneous to the viewers' control. Periods of interpretive time may be qualitatively and quantitatively different: from an extended interpretive time experienced, for instance, from a stationary queued vehicle, to the minimum interpretive time involved in the casual glance of the passerby. All these factors are to be taken into account when attempting to understand the creation of meaning and significance in relation to the urban advertising text and the part that 'interpretive time' plays as an aspect of outdoor advertising.

Case study – 'Go home'

In late July 2013 the UK Border Agency, which is part of the Home Office, launched a pilot scheme that according to the agency's website 'aimed to encourage illegal migrants to leave the UK voluntarily' (UK Border Agency 2013). The campaign launched by the then immigration minister Mark Harper included leaflets and newspaper advertising and targeted six London boroughs in the east and west of the city. The key component of this out of home campaign involved advertisements bearing the slogan 'Go home'. The advertisements took the usual rectangular shape of the outdoor billboard and were mounted on mobile advertising vans that toured through areas of London. The advertisement's message was stark, uncompromising and threatening. It was delivered with a clunkiness of language and a minimum recourse to design, comparable to the unsophisticated, cheaply produced leaflets produced to sell economy goods. A little vague colour hovers in the top right corner and the roundel of a single closed handcuff is held up to the picture surface in the lower left. Three blocks of information – two of which are presented in frames – are set against a dark background. The initial question the advert poses, 'In the UK illegally?', is followed by the threat 'Go home or face arrest' and finally the statement, '106 arrests last week in your area' (see Figure 10.2).

Mobile advertising

To help make sense of this campaign and its effects we need to explore the advertisement as an example of an advertising type. As part of a typology it shares many of the attributes of urban mobile advertising. These take many forms. Advertisements are a prominent feature of a range of public transport vehicles from metro and underground trains to taxis (Leiss *et al.* 2005: 364). Adverts are often positioned inside carriages, above luggage racks and displayed on the inside of windows, and have long been a prominent feature on travel tickets. Buses, trams and taxis primarily transporting passengers across the city have long had a secondary

Figure 10.2 'Go Home', UK Border Agency, London, 2013. Reproduced courtesy of Rick Findler.

function carrying large-scale external advertisements for a range of products and services through residential and commercial urban areas. Interpretive time for external mobile advertising is minimal. In recent years these external advertisements have expanded in size. For example, the rear of double-decker buses convey large-scale advertising images and texts addressing the occupants of other vehicles often held in traffic queues or pedestrians passing by. In addition, there are more unusual mobile advertisements. In the spring of 2013 an East Coast Main Line express train could be seen travelling through cities en route from King's Cross to Edinburgh decked out with the 007 logo, the whole train given over to advertising a recent James Bond film *Skyfall*.[4] Aerial advertisements have been glimpsed on the side of hot-air balloons at least since the nineteenth century. For example, Parisian photographer Nadar painted his name – which was also the name of his studio – across the basket of his hot-air balloon from which he took photographs of things below. Nadar, his camera, balloon and logo are depicted in a famous lithograph by Honoré Daumier, which appeared in the periodical *Le Boulevard* in 1863. Aerial advertising has continued into the modern era co-existing with other forms of mobile advertising: aeroplanes still draw advertising banners across the city skies while below cars, vans and bicycles drag advertising trailers through streets and shopping centres. Trucks and advans like the one bearing the UK Border Agency advert are part of this type of mobile advertising: highly noticeable but with only a short interpretive time.

Political advertising

The UK Border Agency advan carrying the 'Go home' advertisement travelled through London like other mobile adverts, becoming part of the movement and flux of the urban environment. This is not just about the rhythms of traffic flow but the pace of life and the general movement of people in cities. The mobile advertisement creates a sense of immediacy and urgency to its message. In terms of design the 'Go home' advert had something of the tabloid headline about its shrill, sharp mode of address which fits with the sense of immediacy associated with mobile advertising. The phrase 'Go home' created an ambiguity in an outdoor public space. This brings us to the nature of the message itself. It is evidently political and not commercial, negative rather positive, and its design and circulation intended to create amplification, increasing its effect through media coverage (Lilleker & Scullion 2009). Andy Mullen offers three types of political communication associated with advertising: these are 'education, persuasion and propaganda' (2013: 164). There was an element of each of these aspects in the 'Go home' advert. The propaganda aspect was clearly the most controversial. According to Carey, 'propaganda refers to … bringing some target audience to adopt attitudes and beliefs chosen in advance by the sponsors of the communication' (Carey 1995, quoted in Mullen 2013: 166). The propaganda element was accentuated by its appearance in the public sphere and in outdoor public space. When introducing the advertising campaign, the immigration minister Mark Harper clearly placed it as part of a wider political policy and one intended to create ideological support and perhaps win elections: 'The immigration bill being introduced later this year will build on this work by restricting illegal migrants access to benefits and services' (UK Border Agency 2013).

Targeting audiences

Carey's reference to target audiences above begs a further question: who was the target audience for the advertisement? Was the intended audience for the advertisement illegal immigrants who could be educated or persuaded that it is in their interest to 'Go home' without being prosecuted for illegal entry to the country? Or was the message targeted more widely, encouraging decodings and readings by different social and ethnic groups? The variety of potential decodings – preferred, negotiated and oppositional – associated with class, gender, religion and ethnicity that might have been a consequence of this campaign are too numerous to deal with here. But it seems that a series of opposites/pairings was at play in a reading of the advert and its context: home and abroad, insiders and outsiders, residents and migrants, them and us. Some people living in the targeted boroughs of the capital are recent migrants, others long settled. This campaign deals in difference and breeds fear and distrust in the interest of party political gain. At the same time the advertising campaign was running it was reported that police held 'spot and check' procedures based on racial profiling at Tube and train stations around London and elsewhere in the country in which '139 suspected immigration offenders' were detained (Channel 4 News 2013; *Mail* Online 2013). Conservative leader of Redbridge Council, one of the six London boroughs selected for the pilot run, stated that 'whatever effect this campaigning might be intended to have on people who are in the country unlawfully, that message is far outweighed by the negative message to the great majority of people from all backgrounds who live and work together in Redbridge' (*Guardian* 2013b). Other responses to the advertisement included *Observer* columnist Rupa Huq, who called it a 'revolting campaign that smacks of racial profiling' (Huq 2013) and UKIP leader Nigel Farage referred to it as 'nasty' (ITV News – Daybreak 2013).

The campaign was reported to the Advertising Standards Authority by Labour peer Lord Lipsey, who objected to the advert's claim that there had been '106 arrests last week in your area' as being factually incorrect. The ASA upheld this objection and ordered that the advertisement should not appear again in its current form (ASA 2013). But the last word on this sorry example of political advertising goes to Rupa Huq: 'It smacked of a cross between a 70s National Front repatriation drive and an Ealing comedy shot through with cruelty' (Huq 2013). After much criticism and amid reports in late October 2013 that only one illegal immigrant had left the country as a result of the poster campaign, the Home Secretary Teresa May admitted that the campaign had been 'too much of a blunt instrument' and would not be extended nationwide as originally planned (Wintour 2013).

Conclusion

This chapter has explored outdoor advertising as part of the public space of the modern urban environment. Cities and towns are important for the advertising industry and form a very specific context within which advertising reception occurs. Urban time and space is distinctive. The speed and frenetic movement of the modern city is an important feature as a context for outdoor advertising and its reception. Experiences and interactions that distinguish the contemporary form of city life have been explored in this chapter in conjunction with urban advertising such as billboards and mobile advertising. The modern city is often referred to as the 'edge city' in which an intense form of consumption is a very visible and dominating presence. 'Neat' or 'cool' capitalism are terms used to describe an economy and in particular a way of life apparent on the surface of the public spaces of modern cities. However, challenges to this are mounting. The chapter explored features relevant to outdoor public advertising from interpretive time spent on adverts to the nature of mobile advertising. Many of these themes to do with outdoor advertising were explored in conjunction with other more political issues through a case study of a mobile advan campaign deployed in London in 2013.

Notes

1 There are usually six socio-economic groups (SEGs) used by market researchers. They are based on paid occupation. These grades give some idea of a household's income and how it might be spent. They are:

- A higher managerial, administrative, professional, e.g. chief executive, senior civil servant, surgeon
- B intermediate managerial, administrative, professional, e.g. bank manager, teacher
- C1 supervisory, clerical, junior managerial, e.g. shop-floor supervisor, bank clerk, sales person
- C2 skilled manual workers, e.g. electrician, carpenter
- D semi-skilled and unskilled manual workers, e.g. assembly-line worker, refuse collector, messenger
- E casual labourers, pensioners, unemployed, e.g. pensioners without private pensions and anyone living on basic benefits

2 See McDougall (2008) and Odih (2010: 145–8) for a wider discussion.

3 In the early years of the twentieth century, Futurist artists such as Umberto Boccioni and Giacomo Balla, using techniques developed from early Cubist art, attempted to paint the sensual effects of the modern city and its dynamism. They depicted urban crowds and objects at rest and in motion in paintings like 'The City Rises' (1910–11) and 'Speed of a Motorcycle' (1913).

4 Image available at http://www.youtube.com/watch?v=KMBA3a1wk_w.

11 Sound and vision

Introduction

This chapter explores the way advertisements are projected through sound and vision, and how people engage with this. It examines different modes of viewing the visual elements of advertising and the effects of sound created by radio, television and Internet advertisements. The organization of sound and vision are important elements in encoding and delivering the advertising message and significant features of advertising reception.

This chapter deals with the viewing of television and other screen-based advertising, and this is compared to looking at billboards and other advertising forms. Three modes of viewing advertisements are identified: the look, the gaze and the glance. Each mode of viewing is marked by the length of time over which it occurs and the kind of cognition and attention deployed. Different modes of viewing are used according to a range of factors; these include the nature of the advertising text, the advertising media form in which it appears, where the advertisement is viewed and individual, environmental and contextual elements. Different modes of viewing suit different advertising forms and viewing circumstances.

Second, the chapter explores how sound functions as an integral part of the advertising message, reinforcing visual imagery or in the case of radio advertising creating the message through sound alone. The sound feature of audio-visual advertising and especially that of television functions in a number of important ways. It draws attention to an advertisement's presence and encourages engagement with a more complete audio-visual experience of advertising, at the same time enabling involvement in other activities to take place. In addition, it co-exists with conversation and becomes drawn into the flow of conversation as general 'advertising talk'. This occurs generally, but is more pronounced in domestic environments. Sound lends a potency and intimacy to advertising form.

Looking, gazing and glancing

The literature on the subject of viewing media imagery is largely organized around discussion of two forms of viewing – the 'glance' primarily associated with television viewing (Ellis 1992 [1982]; Morley 1992; Gray 1992; Wilson 1993) and the 'gaze' associated with cinema viewing (Mulvey 1975; Corner 1995; Sturken & Cartwright 2009; Mitchell 2002; Mirzoeff 2012). Viewing can be interpreted in many different ways: for example, the gaze is associated with a dynamic of desire or fantasy in the work of Jacques Lacan (Sharpe 2014) or with power in the work of Michel Foucault (Kelly 2014). However, for the purpose of advertising studies it is useful in the first instance to establish different modes of viewing in which viewers are encouraged to look at advertisements and the different ways they come to see them. As a starting point it is useful to categorize three modes of viewing: looking, gazing and glancing, which can be applied to a range of advertising presented through a variety of different media

The 'look' can be used as a normative standard of viewing. The look, directed for instance at a billboard, television or mobile device screen, can be defined as a directed and steadfast viewing over a period of time. It is a viewing that enables a reading of an advertisement to develop in order that the advert is recognized as such, its message received and understood. Different advertising texts in different advertising media demand different amounts of time, attention and concentration to allow this to occur. The 'gaze' as a mode of viewing shares with the 'look' a form of 'steadfast and directed viewing'. This controlled assimilation of information over a period of time is an outcome of both modes of viewing. The gaze, however, builds on the normative standard of the look, involves a greater visual and cognitive concentration and usually takes place over a longer period of time. When the 'look' becomes fractured or interrupted it might be compared with the 'glance' in terms of its duration. The 'glance' is a significantly, and on occasion intentionally, shorter period of viewing. As with the other modes of viewing, the glance might be invited by the advertising text, through visual or acoustic hailing, or offered by the subject in the process of becoming a viewer. As a mode of viewing, the defining feature of the 'glance' is its brevity. Cognition associated with the 'glance' will be of a lesser order to that associated with the 'look' and the 'gaze'. In summary, the 'glance' is the shortest amount of viewing and interpretive time that will afford some form of advertising recognition; the 'look', the required amount of time and interpretation for the message to become meaningful; and the 'gaze' offers the longest and most intense period of viewing.

The look

The 'look' as a mode of viewing, explored in relation to outdoor advertising such as billboards, adshells, back-lit panels and scrolling advertisements, highlights certain environmental features of advertising in the urban context. Typically the form and content of billboard design is bold and direct. This is also the case with much mobile advertising such as the UK Border Agency's 'Go home' advertisement mounted on an advan and discussed in Chapter 10 (see Figure 10.2). The look once focused on the advertisement is exposed to the distractions and dislocations associated with the multiple sensory conditions prevalent in the modern urban environment. For the 'look' at a billboard to produce a satisfactory reading it requires relatively uninterrupted sightlines and relatively undisturbed interpretive time. The reading of an urban advertising text potentially takes place within a framework of competing visual and aural stimuli. This is often as a result of the movement and density of vehicles and crowds of people in proximity to the viewer. Street layouts and alignments, the position of buildings and street furniture are also important to sightlines. The advertising viewer is in some cases in motion – walking, running, cycling or travelling in a vehicle – and sensory disruption can occur through the crossing of sightlines by traffic and people. This is outside of the control of the viewer. Consequently urban advertisement-viewing conditions can be characterized as ranging from the undistracted, undisturbed view over time, which might encourage the 'look' to develop into a more concentrated advertising gaze. More typically, the urban viewing context creating disruption and interruption may result in the look becoming dislocated. In these circumstances, the glance may become the likely mode of viewing.

In the domestic context, the 'look' as a mode of viewing can be identified in its focus on television and Internet advertising viewing. Applying the look to television advertising suggests a level of attachment and attentiveness but perhaps not with the same level of concentration as applied to television *programmes*. The look usually requires greater visual commitment, attention and consideration than the glance. The glance, in contrast, when applied to television and other screen viewing in the home, suggests the momentary look, the turning towards and the turning away, and only a slight or even distracted engagement.

The gaze

The 'gaze' is a mode of viewing often associated with cinema and originally described as a male form of viewing which 'objectifies' the female as other and as object (Mulvey 1975). More recently the term has come to describe both male and female viewing (Ellis 1992 [1982]; Kaplan 1983; Gammon & Marshment 1988; Gray 1992) and extended to an understanding of the heterosexual controlling gaze in an analysis of homosexual 'queer viewing' (Evans & Gamman 1995). As a mode of viewing it need not be confined to gendered or sexual looking, on the contrary the gaze as a mode of viewing can be applied generally to different advertising media and circumstances. For instance, when applied to cinema-screen advertising it can be seen as a concentrated, highly focused form of looking over a sustained period of viewing and interpretive time. The gaze in this context is a product of the uninterrupted, directed viewing in the cinema environment created by fixed seating, darkened auditoria and the pull of the cinema screen (Hanich 2014). Cinema advertisements, in addition to films, are often viewed in this manner. The gaze can also be applied to the single large-scale outdoor advertisement that captures and sustains interest when the circumstances of the urban environment and space allow. The gaze as applied to advertising viewing describes an engaged and concentrated attachment over time that enables a deep form of textual reading. The look has been identified as the normative mode of viewing. A more sustained attention can be described as a form of concentrated look or gaze.

John Corner draws attention to the importance of viewing circumstances in distinguishing between the gaze and the glance (Corner 1995). The gaze is, as we have seen, often associated with the viewing arrangements of cinema auditoria in which the size and distance of the cinema screen are important. Screens showing advertisements are of various sizes and shapes and are placed at different viewing distances, resulting in different kinds of 'immersions' in screens and creating different relationships between viewer and text (Odin 2012). The size and distance of the cinema screen is important and contrasts with computer, television and especially mobile device screens displaying advertisements. Unlike the cinema, the gaze is the less likely mode of viewing for these screens. Other factors are involved, such as the general nature of segment and flow in television output, the specifics of advertising content and the disposition of the viewer.

Television modes of viewing, usually thought of as the look and the glance, are for Ang more likely to produce a form of resistance to media texts due to the circumstances of domestic reception. This is in contrast to the gaze associated with cinema viewing and the cinema environment (Ang 1996). The domestic context to television advertising viewing is marked by activities that cut into and across the flow of advertisements into the home: 'if the camera pulls us in, the family pulls us out' (Cubitt quoted in Morley, 1986: 19). Ang identifies a freedom of movement within the domestic environment denied to cinema viewers, who, in a controlled environment, are 'trapped in their chairs in the darkened theatre, enforced to keep their gaze directed to the large screen'. This is in contrast to television viewers who 'have the freedom to move around in their own homes when their TV set is on' (Ang 1996: 56). This juxtaposition of viewing contexts leads back to the heart of common-sense assumptions about the media and subjectivity, structure and agency: 'there is no obligation (on the part of the television audience) to keep looking and they can always divert their attention to something else whenever they want to' (Ang 1996: 56).

The glance

Wilson (1993) and Ellis (1992 [1982]) agree that the act of television watching is performed by the 'distracted viewer', and the mode of viewing associated with this can be formulated as the 'glance' rather than the 'fixed gaze'. The glance can be understood as a momentary look, marked by a turning towards and an equally sharp turning away from an advertisement. It is a mode of viewing only occasionally repeated and a short duration is its defining feature. The glance is often marked by an indifferent level of attention (Ellis 1992 [1982]: 137; Wilson 1993: 147), although it may also be a short but incisive attempt to take in vital information. Either way, an impression is formed of an overall, and perhaps detailed, text. The glance can be applied to all forms of advertising and appears to be well suited to the television advertisement. 'If television watching is intermittent, characterised by an often distracted audience which is frequently "absent" from the programme, it is also to be defined by an audience more "present" in its own (often) domestic conditions of viewing' (Wilson 1993: 66). For Wilson this is the guarantee of a 'freedom' from the tyranny of television where the domestic context of television viewing encourages a 'critical spectatorship'. This can be extended to television *advertising* viewing. It may also apply to Internet and mobile-device advertising sharing the same 'communication spaces' as television (Odin 2012: 155).

However, a consideration of the relationship between context and advertising text might emphasize the integration of advertising reception through sound and vision into the discourses of domestic life. This is explored in Chapter 9. Non-screen forms of advertising appearing in newspapers, supplements, magazines and other forms of newsprint media also occur in domestic environments. The look is applied to the continuous or continual reading of texts and viewing of images that make up newsprint advertising, and a more concentrated gaze may be applied to items of special interest or where a critical reading is involved. But the glance is an important element of newsprint reception which often involves intermittent and distracted reading and viewing. Glancing at newsprint and advertising content may be as a result of domestic distractions or it may be a chosen mode of viewing akin to skim reading.

Modes of viewing advertisements are set in motion and sustained by a combination of factors. These include the specific properties of the media presenting the advertisement; the nature of the advertising content and its arrangement as a text; changing contextual aspects of domestic or urban environments as well as the disposition of the viewer. Modes of viewing vary according to a variety of factors but they may become routine aspects of familiar and repeated everyday behaviour, forming a *habit of viewing*. For instance, looking at billboards may be occasioned by the long interpretive time that accompanies a much repeated walk past a poster site. Similarly, occasional glances at television advertisements within the domestic environment may over time also become a 'habit of viewing' – an extension of the self and a way of seeing advertisements.

Sound

The visual tends to dominate analysis of advertising content, with sound elements usually taken for granted. Yet for television, mobile, laptop, tablet and other forms of audio visual advertising, sound is a significant formal element. Radio advertising is of course created by sound alone, made up of a combinations of narrative speech as monologue and dialogue, voice-overs, lyrics, musical scores, jingles, sonic logos and sound effects. Radio advertising sound can involve a live spoken endorsement of a product by a presenter or it might take the form of a pre-recorded advertisement constructed in a similar way to a television or tele-screen advertisement (Andrejevic 2009). It can comprise a narrative and dialogue, and in the absence of visuals music and sound effects often feature prominently. Jingles have long been a feature of commercial radio with sound branding and sound logos more recent inclusions. In addition advertising sound is used in combination with visual form in screen advertisements. Sound in radio advertising and as an element of audio-visual advertising has the ability to convey its message at a distance unconstrained by the direct sightlines required by visual elements of advertising. Radio advertising sound as the single form creating the advertising effect has a singular and distinctive narrative clarity. Projected into domestic and other interior settings, it interweaves with activities and conversations in a similar but more distinctive manner to the sound produced by television and other screen advertising.

The soundtrack is according to Rick Altman a significant feature of television broadcasting 'mediating the relationship between … two flows' of television and of household activity (1987: 567). Domestic viewing is characterized by 'an inseparable mixture of watching and non-watching as a general style of television viewing behaviour' (Altman 1987: 569). Mobile, laptop, PC and tablet advertising is different. There is usually a closer spatial relationship between the viewer and the screen with sound in a close proximity to the screen (Odin 2012).

Television advertising sound can be seen as a means of drawing the distracted spectator back to the full visual and aural presentation of the television advertisement. For an audience only partially engaged with the advertisement, perhaps reading, using other media devices or engaged in conversation, the sound track will 'serve to *label* the menu items' (Altman 1987: 573). Sound then acts as a means of holding and directing attention. It is able to retrieve and return full attention to the complete television experience of sound and vision. It also enables other domestic activities to run concurrently with the television advertisement. Sound according to Altman is, in the western world, incomplete, 'it seems to call for identification with a visible object given as a sound source' (1987: 574). Therefore the intermittent spectator will constantly re-engage with the advertisement's sound source and in so doing re-engage with the advertising imagery. In this process sound draws the receiver to the advertisement. This can be imagined as Althusser's description of ideology metaphorically hailing its subject, 'hey you!'; and in turning towards the sound, the listener becomes a viewer and as Altman puts it 'make[s] those images seem to be made *just for me*' (Altman 1987: 58). This personalization process is described by Paddy Scannell as part of a media process that speaks to a wide audience, at the same time creating the sense of media communication being personally directed. In this the advertising message is transformed from a 'for-anyone structure' into becoming a 'for-anyone-as-someone structure' (Scannell 2000: 5–24).

What are the wider significances and consequences of sound for advertising and contemporary life? The sound of the radio or audio of the television advertisement – its music, sound effects and spoken language – form an aspect of the passage of an advertisement into domestic life. They become part of the familiar experience of the domestic environment, and the repetition of advertisements is an important feature of this. It becomes a 'well-known presence within the viewer's life world' (Wilson 1993: 20). The idea of the 'life world' suggests the rich texture of shared experience by people as domestic or other social groups and is constituted by familiarity and a recurrent sameness of experience. It forms the 'horizon' before which individuals live out the sense of the known, familiar and the predictable. As Scannell and others have pointed out, the media – and for our purposes the sound and vision of advertisements – play a large part in modern societies in constructing 'the everyday' through the notion of 'dailiness' (1996, 2000). Repetition of form and content is of major significance when recognizing the importance advertising has as a radio and screen domestic presence. Mobile and interactive devices are also important in this. Single advertisements are often repeated and advertising slots appear with regularity and merge into a general advertising flow.

Conclusion

Viewing associated with advertisements falls into three modes: the look, the gaze and the glance. These are associated with particular media forms, television with the glance and cinema with the gaze. The look, it has been suggested, is the normative standard against which modes of viewing can be understood. Different modes of viewing are present in both domestic and outdoor viewing environments. The mode of viewing is an encounter involving text, viewer and context. Both the glance and nature of the domestic context may offer some respite from the ideological penetration of advertising texts, but paradoxically this also works to embed television advertising form within the domestic unit and bind the subject more closely to an ideology of consumerism.

This chapter also explored sound as an aspect of radio advertising and as a significant element of television, Internet, tablet, mobile device and other forms of advertising. When operating within the bounded space of the domestic unit, audio-form functions in a number of ways, re-uniting a distracted viewer with the advertising text, drawing the attention of people engaged in other activities and enabling the advert to be followed while domestic tasks are pursued. Internet advertising sound is usually experienced by the individual user and within proximity of the computer or mobile device. Television and radio sound becomes part of domestic arrangements and both contribute to the sense of self within the domestic space, addressing not just 'anyone' but 'someone'.

12 Consumer culture

Introduction

This chapter explores contemporary consumer culture in which commodities, advertising and branding are increasingly significant to the experience of society (Lury 2011). Consumer society was shaped by the largely eighteenth- and nineteenth-century developments of a market economy, industrialization and mass production and consumption. Characterized by the everyday activities associated with the buying and selling of goods, consumer culture involves a broad range of activities and experiences. From the goods and publicity images that saturate urban public spaces to the advertising signs and logos that intervene and weave through private life covering an increasing number of surfaces, the social and economic aspects of a consumer society are ubiquitous. They are part of what has been described as a 'society dominated by consumption' (Ritzer & Jurgenson 2010: 16).

This chapter looks at various threads of consumer culture, recognizing it as a shared way of life to which access depends upon a range of economic and social factors. Social identity is important to it with class, gender, ethnicity and other factors playing a part. Branding as a recent form of advertising has contributed to a deeper and more intense form of concentrated or hyperconsumption. This not only involves reference to needs, wants and satisfactions, but is driven by what Zygmunt Bauman has referred to as the 'consuming desire of consuming' (2001: 13). Urban centres have become potent symbols of consumer culture and the final section of the chapter considers how cities are not only intense places of consumption but have themselves become branded objects and experiences. Place marketing takes the built environment of a city, the history and lived culture of its people and through the branding treatment promotes it as a product. Branding is explored as a series of marketing strategies involving packaging, logos, brand identity and image.

Consumer culture

It is difficult to offer a clear-cut definition of consumer culture. In a very general sense the term can be used 'to describe the modern global economy' (Hovland & Wolburg 2010: 16) and is commonly used to indicate activities and experiences associated with the purchase of consumer items – from buying goods online to the weekly trip to the supermarket. The word *culture* indicates that activities and experiences associated with consumption, including the use of the goods purchased, are set within a more general range of references. For instance, most aspects of contemporary life are accompanied by advertising and promotional signs that reference consumer goods and the activity of consumption. Indeed the ubiquity and concentration of advertising signs in the contemporary world suggest consumption as a total way of life. How people *respond* to advertising and to the goods they purchase is also part of consumer culture. The value and significance placed on consumption and consumer items is important, and this may take different forms from feelings of helplessness in the face of rising prices and limited incomes to a sense of power people perceive they possess as they make their consumer choices. This may be reinforced by an awareness of consumer rights inscribed in law. In essence we might say that a consumer culture describes certain forms of behaviour and thinking that arise from the centrality of consumption to our way of life (Lury 2011; Slater 2008).

Consumer culture is marked by the mass production and consumption of goods which has gathered speed at least since the early days of the industrial period. It became a feature of the twentieth century and for Don Slater the 1920s was the first consumerist decade. This has intensified in the twenty-first century.

Market society to consumer society

Consumer culture is the product of a market society and markets have been a feature of society for many years. The ancient Greek agora was a public space where produce was bought and sold, and Roman towns were served by a variety of markets from the open space of the forum to the purpose-built structures of the macellum. For instance, the city of Rome had cattle, pig and vegetable markets (Holleran 2012: 160). For these, and later feudal societies, markets were important. In precapitalist societies people largely produced their own food, clothing and shelter. Much of what was necessary to sustain life was produced by the household or in close proximity to the home. Markets were what Polyani termed an 'accessory feature' of life (quoted in Spies-Butcher *et al.* 2012: 4). As production increased, more was produced to sell at markets rather than to directly satisfy needs. Markets became more abstract features of society, and people came to relate to these through the price mechanism: receiving a wage for their labour and exchanging it for consumer goods. Economists refer to this as a market society, one in which the general economy is defined by the supply and demand of goods and services. Since the nineteenth century, market society has become closely aligned with the mass production of goods and associated processes of industrialism. Consumer culture is a development and an intensification of trends within a market society. Its underlying structure and organization and its social and visible effects such as advertising and branding are widely perceived as pivotal aspects of everyday life.

A market society based on the mass production of goods also required the mass *consumption* of goods, with both profits and wages dependent on this process. As the market economy in Britain became more complex, providing a wider range of goods and services, increasingly consumption became more organized and directed. Advertising and the advertising agencies became more important in channelling consumers towards satisfaction of their needs and the creation of further wants. However, a simple cause-and-effect explanation depicting mass consumption as the direct outcome of mass production is complicated by various factors (Slater 2008; Sassatelli 2007; Lury 2011). Some historical accounts identify changes in patterns of consumption prior to the industrial period, with new products such as tea, coffee and potatoes becoming available in Britain. In addition, new textiles and dyes from the colonies were accompanied by changes in style, fashion and demand. The new goods became an element in the display of wealth and social position. New forms of business and marketing were also important to these developments, with the potter Josiah Wedgewood a leading innovator in this area. Consequently the development of market society in Britain involved a range of factors. By the late nineteenth century it was firmly based on mass industrial production using new forms of transportation, commerce and marketing, but 'consumer culture' as Celia Lury suggests should not be viewed 'as entirely determined by production' (2011: 83).

Consumption became an increasingly important feature of social life. It involved the purchase and consumption of manufactured goods, such as clothes, foodstuffs and luxury items, but also the provision of new services and social experiences. Services for some, at the turn of the nineteenth century, included connections to utilities such as water, gas and electricity, with media services such as broadcast media and telephony following later in the twentieth century. Many social events and experiences were transformed into consumer activities: for instance, the free-of-charge approach to football of preindustrial society gave way to a paid-for visit to a sports ground. Something similar occurred in the experience of culture and art as it moved into the spaces of galleries and museums, often ticketed, where today the experience of the attached gallery shop is as important as any exhibit.

Consumption involves different types of commodities and different kinds of consumption. For instance, the activities of eating and drinking use up and exhaust the commodity in the process of consumption. Other forms of consumption depend on the commodity being retained as a possession, perhaps increasing its value and accruing wealth for the owner over time. Some serve the purpose of aesthetic appreciation or provide leisure and entertainment. These types of commodity can be used and reused over time. As Sassatelli suggests, 'the notion of consumption covers different meanings – from purchase, to use, to waste ... and people are described as consumers because they buy and use, store and maintain, manage and fantasize commodities' (2007: 193).

With the consolidation of consumer society, the act of consumption and indeed the commodities themselves came to take on meanings far wider than those of satisfying basic needs. 'Conspicuous consumption' was a term used by Thorstein Veblen (1899) in the late nineteenth century. It is still in popular use today and describes the status associated with commodities, forms of self-presentation and a perceived distance from the everyday world of productive work. This culminated in a lifestyle of the leisured classes that visibly distinguished them from the working classes. Commodities have continued to signify social status particularly in affluent societies. Galbraith's term the 'affluent society' was applied to the world in the period after the Second World War in the United States and gained ground as a more general description of twentieth-century consumer society and culture (1958).

Consumption and choice are often related to the idea of 'consumer sovereignty' (Hutt 1940). This relates to economics and suggests that the choice the consumer makes in selecting a commodity is all important and determines what is produced and offered by markets. The demand for goods sends a signal to the producers of goods. The process also has an effect on the price mechanism, telling the producer what the consumer is prepared to pay. Consumer sovereignty claims that the decisions individuals make about what they consume are rational and the choice freely made. These ideas can be traced back to the Enlightenment and have philosophical and political associations linked to ideas about individual freedom. This became the ideological cornerstone of the Thatcher and Reagan governments in the UK and US in the 1980s (Odih 2010: 33). They pursued neoliberal policies in which 'consumer choice became the obligatory pattern for all social relations and the template for civic dynamism and freedom' (Slater 2008: 10). In this brand of political thought individuals and families were to make choices as consumers, rather than the state or society doing so on their behalf as citizens. Indeed Mrs Thatcher famously claimed 'there is no such thing as society'. But linking freedom with consumption is not without problems, not least because access to consumer goods is restricted by access to resources. In an era marked by an increasingly unequal distribution of income and wealth, access to goods is a major form of restriction on freedom. Furthermore, consumer choice is not a simple, unproblematic act – one that is freely made. Capitalism constantly attempts to create wants and control prices through the operation of advertising, marketing and related research. As we have seen consumer culture is saturated with advertising and promotional signs, and images of consumption are ubiquitous. These shape the frameworks – the range of possibilities in which people make choices. Marketing impacts on the kind of choices people make and levels of income and wealth also limit that choice. Choice then is made within these limited circumstances, which to paraphrase Marx are not of the consumer's making.

Hyperconsumption

As we have seen, consumer culture is an extension and deepening of trends evident in nineteenth- and early-twentieth-century market society and culture. Consumption has come to be recognized as an increasingly significant element of contemporary society (Baudrillard 1998 [1970]); and consumer culture, according to Ritzer and Jurgenson, 'draws our attention to the norms, values and meanings associated with a society dominated by consumption' (2010: 16). Since the 1980s consumer culture in Britain has appeared in a more vigorous and concentrated form than in earlier decades. This has been encouraged by the privatization of publicly owned utilities and services, nationalized industries and mutual societies. We have noted the volume, spread and intensity of consumer culture throughout contemporary life.

This has taken a number of forms. In the home, online shopping is accompanied by an increasing volume of advertisements, media images and programmes dedicated to consumption and appearing on television, mobile and laptop screens. Outdoors, urban shopping areas and out-of-town shopping malls increase in size, volume and concentration of goods, and are joined by airports, railway stations and other public spaces redesigned to incorporate further retail space. Public and private space is increasingly organized around promotional images, which include 'signs, images, publicity [and] an aestheticisation of commodities and their environments: advertising, packaging, shop display, point of sale material, product design' (Slater 2008: 31). In many urban areas, it has become difficult to find space outside the reach of what might be called a spectacle of consumption in which aural and visual elements arrest the senses and steer the mind. Consumption has taken a prominent hold on more and more aspects of social life, thought and identity.

The centrality of consumption to modern life takes a number of forms in the literature on the subject. For instance, Mike Featherstone (1991) and others identify a new attitude towards consumption with people organizing *themselves* as lifestyle projects. They 'display their individuality and sense of style in the particularity of the assemblies of goods, clothes, practices, experiences, appearances and bodily dispositions they design together into a lifestyle' (Featherstone 1991: 86). Many other contemporary studies of consumer culture stress people's active engagement in the process of consumption, engaging in the selection and choice of goods and making creative decisions according to fashion, taste and lifestyle management (Willis 1990; Lury 2011: 46–55). The idea of the 'active consumer' is usually emphasized here and the choices that are made within consumer culture contribute to a reflexive approach to life which has been described as the 'the ability of human subjects to reflect upon the social conditions of their existence' (Thrift & Glennie 1993: 43). This suggests that individuals use the material that consumer culture makes available to fashion their personal and even political identities. This has been referred to as 'reflexive consumption' (Lash & Urry 1999: 61). These choices constitute what Anthony Giddens refers to as 'life politics' and suggests that people create a sense of identity 'through the signifying practices of consumption choices' (Odih 2010: 199). Celia Lury suggests that this comes down to the fact that 'each of us is increasingly expected to organize our lives in relation to the question "How shall I live?", and seek to answer that question in day-to-day decisions about how to behave, what to wear and what to eat' (2011: 198).

In addition, Zygmunt Bauman draws attention to changes in the very *nature* of consumption. People have always needed to consume to stay alive: they had to be 'fed, shod and sheltered ... a fixed number of "needs" which they had to "satisfy" in order to survive' (Bauman 2001: 12). But modern consumption is no longer about simply satisfying 'needs', it is about perpetuating 'desire', which is never simply satisfied by the consumption of goods. Consumer culture no longer needs to 'justify itself by reference to anything but its own pleasurability ... consumption is its own purpose and so is self-propelling'. Bauman speaks of the 'consuming desire of consuming' – a kind of tension no longer related to representations of goods and services or to their referents (Bauman 2001: 13). This has created an insecurity of the present – what he terms a 'fluidity ... the ultimate solidity' – but one that is tied to maintaining the social order. Consuming desire is ignorant of the past and of the future – it lives for today in which 'the future ... can be grasped only as a succession of "nows"' in what Bauman describes as the eternal present (2001: 22–3).

Identities and consumption

An exploration of consumption and consumer culture that involves a discussion of 'life politics', 'lifestyle projects' and even 'consuming desire' also raises the question of identity in relation to consumer culture. A person's identity is a complex arrangement of elements incorporating aspects from the past and the present but with an eye to future presentations. Identity is experienced primarily by the self and it is also to some extent self-established. At the same time it is observed by others such as family, friends and peers who also ascribe identity. Social institutions like education and health are important, as is the criminal justice system and religious and work organizations in creating the sense of who we are and what we might become. The media and advertising industries also play an important part in creating identities, offering role models, social types and scenarios. Identity is formed through experience and by descriptions, labels and expectations which are applied both by the self and by others.

The term *consumer* as we have seen is one of the main descriptions applied to people in contemporary culture. It has become a form of metanarrative, oversimplifying and even misrepresenting the complexity of experience and awareness people have of themselves and the activities and roles they engage in. Identity as a consumer is just one among many. It can be placed alongside other forms of identity such as that of 'citizen', which involves a broad range of characteristics associated with place and community, rights and obligations. There is a rich literature on the subject of consumers and citizens (Soper 2007; Livingstone, Lunt & Miller 2007; Metykova 2013) with some taking the line that 'the identities of consumer and citizen are continuously in tension since the possessive individualism promoted by consumerism is deeply corrosive of the sense of shared fate and equal entitlement required by a culture of citizenship' (Murdock 2004: 34). For others the identity of 'citizen-consumer' has gained ground, combining citizen rights with that of the interests of the consumer. The nature of identity in a consumer culture requires further exploration.

Marxists, for instance, considered social class based on a person's place in the economic and social order to be the fundamental determinant of identity. This emphasizes a person's relationship to production. Occupation, education and income are likely to follow from this. The idea of 'life chances' came to suggest that experiences and social outcomes were not settled in the early years of life according to the social class people are born into. Life chances could be affected by political decisions about the distribution of wealth, education and the provision of health services and other factors. In recent years, identity has come to be thought of as a complex arrangement involving a range of factors.

The term 'hyphenated identity' has been used to represent people's complex and multiple identities. In a postcolonial country like Britain people feel that they are attached to different cultural groups. Inserting a hyphen between references to two cultural traditions or aspects of lived culture helps create a fuller and more accurate description of identity. For example, the terms Anglo-Caribbean or Scottish-Indian are commonly used. In another sense a hyphen might bring together (or even isolate out) different components of identity in a consumer culture. These might include social class, an indicator of income and other social and cultural aspects, or occupation, gender, age, race, ethnicity and sexuality. Educational attainment is an indicator of a range of cultural and economic factors, as is a person's religion, political adherence or personal code of ethics. Where a person lives and their attachment to local cultures might also be an important component of identity. All in all these amount to *identity components* which may function singly, in pairs or in clusters. A pair of components may have equal value, with for example a person's gender and ethnic background being equally important components of their identity. An identity might be experienced and represented as a cluster of identity components, which might for instance involve being homosexual and engaging in gay culture but with a retired person's status, income and world outlook. Yet the most powerful component of identity for this hypothetical individual might be that of a person of colour. Multiple components of identity easily allow for identities that change over time to be represented as such. Identities are always in process and never completed. Components are added and subtracted or fall out of use according to time and experience.

Identity then, is complex. It *does* involve consumption, in that consumption is a significant aspect of the social framework that guides choice and shapes identities. It may be interwoven with identity at all stages of human development from the way people think to the purchases they make and the way they behave and express themselves. The framework of choice does indeed contain, as Marx writing in the early period of capitalism put it, 'an immense accumulation of commodities'; and these are accompanied by a daunting array of commodity signs, advertisements and brands as more recent theorists such as Baudrillard have pointed out. These fill a large amount of the social space in which people think and make decisions. However, as we have explored, identity is not *reducible* to being a consumer. Within the framework of choice, something akin to what Pierre Bourdieu identifies as 'habitus' occurs, which is neither complete individual freedom to choose nor the allocations of absolute determinacy. Habitus is a form of habit and custom that organizes thoughts and feelings and guides people in the way they act (Bourdieu 1984: 170). This according to Giddens includes a sense of responsiveness and reflexivity to the world.[1] The framework of choice includes elements of taste, aesthetics and social awareness that may surface as fashion in a range of consumer areas and may not be successfully developed elsewhere in people's experiences of life, for no fault of their own. These may of course be heavily manipulated by society or they may be prone to peer group and subcultural challenges, such as Dick Hebdige and others have suggested is present in the alternative styles and identities in music, clothes, speech and behaviour that young people fashion for themselves through subcultural and countercultural activity (Hebdige 1979).

Access to resources in twenty-first-century consumer capitalism is uneven and unequal. Income distribution (wages and salaries) have continued to widen in recent years. Statistics show that in 2002/3 the top 10 per cent of earners received a quarter of the total national income and the top 30 per cent received over a half (Office for National Statistics 2005). Income and wealth (shares, savings, houses and other assets) are fundamental not only to the purchase of commodities and the satisfaction of needs but to participation in consumer culture (Lury 2011: 12). Again according to the ONS half of the UK population in 2001 owned just 5 per cent of the wealth (Office for National Statistics 2005). As we have seen, consumer culture involves a greater number of experiences than merely purchasing commodities, but window shopping, advertising appreciation and delayed gratification can only stretch so far in a society of immediate material value. In the cluster of identity components identified above, income and wealth can be associated with gender, place and other aspects of identity but above all with occupation and social class. Consequently, there is a growing social group whose access to much of consumer culture is restricted to no more than that of the passive observer. This is an experience which in a world of hyperconsumption might be considered a form of alienation. The ONS survey on poverty and social exclusion between 2005 and 2011 reports that of respondents interviewed '[t]hirty-seven per cent said they were unable to meet unexpected expenses and thirty per cent said they could not afford an annual holiday. Five per cent were experiencing severe material deprivation' (Leys 2013: 132).

A person's identity is a complex arrangement of components and the consumer aspects of identity are limited and experienced according to a range of factors, not least levels of income and wealth which are closely associated with social class.

Brands and culture

Brands are a very visible part of consumer culture and social experience and an important aspect of the marketing landscape of the twenty-first century. Brand logos, like the elaborate script chosen in the 1880s to represent Coca-Cola and still in use today, or the stylized swoosh of Nike created more recently in 1971, appear on a wide variety of contemporary surfaces (Danesi 2006). From products and packaging to screens and clothing, the reach of the visual logo surpasses its forerunner the trademark, which itself became a feature of product promotion in the nineteenth century. In recent years the visual logo has been joined by the sonic logo. The sonic logo is composed of a sound fragment or a melody such as the Microsoft Windows start-up sound and has, in conjunction with its visual counterpart, come to be a regular feature of private as well as public space.

Contemporary branding involves more than simply attaching a logo to a product. The literature on the subject suggests that the first stage of the branding process entails associating a name with a product. This might be the name of the manufacturer; an early example is that of George Safford Parker, who designed and labelled his product the

Parker pen in the 1880s. Alternatively the product might be given a name indicating its content, such as the turn of the nineteenth-century beef extract, Oxo. Products are likely to be included in suitably designed packaging, which like the distinctive contour shape of the Coca-Cola bottle becomes part of the Coca-Cola branding effort along with logos and advertising campaigns. This created what is often referred to as the **brand identity** (Anholt 2007: 5; Csaba & Bengtsson 2006). This acts to differentiate products, setting them apart from other similar lines. Originally brands made reference to both the manufacturers of the products and to the goods themselves. Product brands focus on the single or limited range of goods available as part of a label where corporate branding makes reference to a wider product remit and crucially the reputation of the corporation itself (Balmer 2006). In both cases **brand management** is about organizing perceptions of either or both the product and the corporation marketing it. Both are central to creating profit: in the first instance, from the volume of sales of the product, and in the latter from the share price of the corporation (Arvidsson 2005; Goldman & Papson 2006).

Arvidsson makes a distinction between branding and older forms of advertising, with traditional advertising 'primarily directed at imposing a particular structure of needs and tastes on consumers' (2006: 8). Advertising in this form tended to guide the use of products and anchor them in specific circumstances in which consumption takes place. Many advertisements were – and still are – based on realistic representations of time and place and the act of consumption. Often, they promote the product through reference to its qualities and 'establish credibility in speaking to the dilemmas of consumer choice' (Kline 2009: 32). Arvidsson refers to this form of advertising as 'Fordist', associated with the techniques and products of mass production first developed by the Ford Motor Company. Post-Fordist or postmodern branding is based on the rise of information capitalism and the entrenchment of media culture. Products are promoted as symbols to do with social belonging and identity and 'provide part of the context in which products are used' (Arvidsson 2006: 8). They become a context for life and a key component of consumer culture. The idea of immaterial labour is important to this process. Labour is in many ways immaterial in the production of advertising, related as it is to the creation or encoding of ideas and symbols into the advertising process rather than creating the material objects of consumption. Increasingly consumers are expected to provide an input into the process of advertising and branding through active interpretation and the making of meaning as part of the decoding process. This is referred to as 'putting consumers to work – turning them into prosumers' (Ritzer & Jurgenson 2010: 18).

In postmodern branding techniques, the brand is managed as an **identity**. Identity is the term we used earlier in this chapter to discuss our human sense of 'being', which is accompanied by perceptions and recognitions of ourselves and by others. It is also used in marketing, often in an anthropomorphic sense, ascribing human attributes to commodities and business organizations.[2] One effect of this is that brands can appear larger than life.

The process of branding involves a number of stages. The **brand identity** is the expression of core ideas associated with the product through product design, packaging, logos and straplines (Anholt 2007: 5). Brand identity is linked to **brand image** which is about the formation of a public image of the brand (Gardner & Levy 1955). Crucially, this is about how the brand is perceived: the 'perception of the brand that exists in the mind of consumers and audiences' (Anholt 2007: 5; Danesi 2006). The brand identity is what is encoded by the advertiser and the brand image is what is decoded by the receiver and interpreted within a context of decoding. For Lury, the brand in contemporary society is an 'open ended object' and is promoted within certain parameters (quoted in Arvidsson 2005: 244).

Audiences are not limited in their interpretations and uses of the brand image. As the *advertising framework* suggests, decoding is complicated and varied and audiences produce a range of negotiated readings. The brand rarely sends a direct message about the product to consumers but becomes embedded in the shared **brand space** of culture. Through irony and intertextual connections, the brand can take directions and attract meanings not necessarily directly preferred by the brand managers. Consumer culture offers shared experiences and meanings in the widest sense from physical spaces such as Disney theme parks and McDonald's restaurants to more abstract environments including virtual environments, video games and the inclusion of product placements (Arvidsson 2005: 245). As in the past, when customers entered the real material space of a department store, they entered a shared space of sales staff and customers, people of defined age, gender and social class and a space of commodities – a display of specific taste, fashions and values. Today, it is the ubiquitous brands, logos and cultural attachments of the likes of Gap and Nike that have become key aspects of consumer culture. Brands in the widest sense have become a significant feature of the twenty-first-century marketing and cultural landscapes.

Case study – city branding

As we have seen in the exploration of outdoor urban advertising in Chapter 10, contemporary cities are places of hyperconsumption. Consumer activity and the visible signs of consumer culture, advertising and brand images dominate the city streets and walkways, shopping malls and retail parks. Not only are cities places where marketing occurs, they are themselves marketed places – recreated as brands (Dinnie 2011). The primary components of cities are the people who inhabit them and their accumulated histories and cultures. However, city branding almost always entails creating a new image of the city often only loosely connected to the real-life experiences of the people who live there. By taking city branding as a case study we can get an insight into the process of branding as part of contemporary culture and what it claims and what it fails to say about the thing it represents.

City or 'place' branding has become a common experience for many people around the world. Urban centres and regions have been 're-imagined' through branding. This usually occurs in conjunction with economic and cultural regeneration policies (Anholt 2007; Middleton 2011). Branding has occurred in the city of Aalborg and the Oresund region of Denmark in northern Europe (Jensen 2005) and in the French Mediterranean port city of Marseille (Dell'Umbria 2012). In the US, Washington DC underwent similar treatment (Gibson 2005) and New York has long been referred to as the Big Apple (Bendel 2011).

Urban branding is also associated with a number of UK cities, many of which have been involved in the European Capital of Culture programme (ECOC), which has become associated with systematic urban branding. Winners of the title, such as Glasgow in 1990, Liverpool in 2008 and competitors whose bids failed such as Newcastle–Gateshead have been subject to pronounced attempts at re-branding (Wharton, Fenwick & Fawcett 2010; Wharton & Fenwick 2012). Urban economic regeneration, including redesigned urban centres and in some cases population displacement, is associated with projects organized through partnership between the local authority and business. An urban culture based on hyperconsumerism and the idea of a 'party city' focused on café, bar and commercial leisure activity has also been central to this. Tourism played an important part (Hospers 2011) with advertising deployed to convey a new, vibrant image of the city. The accuracy of these representations has often been challenged. Marseilles became ECOC for 2013 and experienced something similar to the northern British cities. In the process of changing its image, Marseille has, according to one account, undergone a 'transformation into a commodity' with its 'inhabitants [becoming] spectators of what used to be their city' (Dell'Umbria 2012: 86–7). The UK government has initiated a similar but separate programme to the ECOC, the UK City of Culture (UKCOC). Northern Ireland's Derry-Londonderry was the 2013 incumbent and Hull is earmarked for 2017.

Southampton provides an interesting example of the UK process of urban branding; it involved a series of partnerships between the city council and groups like the Placebrands agency. With an impressive client portfolio including newly independent countries of Slovenia and Croatia, Placebrands was appointed by Southampton City Council in 2005 to develop a 'brand strategy' for the city. Although acknowledging that Southampton 'never experienced major decline of the order of other port cities such as Glasgow, Liverpool and Newcastle', the council's Communication Department formed a City Identity Group to address 'concern about its future economic position'. An agency was engaged to develop a cultural strategy to counter economic shortcomings 'by changing the way people viewed the city' (Placebrands 2011). Working alongside organizations such as the Port Authority, Chamber of Commerce, City Health Authority and the universities, and deploying the now familiar but often hollow language of 'public and private', the various 'stakeholders' represented by the 'brand leadership team' engaged in 'systemic creativity' on 'brand activities' in order to produce a 'cultural offer'. The 'offer' involved preliminary conceptualizations of the city as 'water city', 'clockwork city' and as a 'magnet for innovation'. However, the 'product label' of 'SeaCity' eventually emerged from the process although people still insist on using the term 'Southampton' to identify the place where they live, work and visit. The re-branding features of Southampton's identity are retained in the term 'CultureSouthampton', the local authority's cultural development trust, and the title 'SeaCity' is the name given to the local museum.

City branding in the UK has in the main been about re-characterizing and redeveloping former industrial conurbations like Glasgow, Liverpool and Newcastle-Gateshead in an attempt to give them new cultural identities. This was driven by regeneration, investment and potential tourism and has relied on consumption as part of the image of the place. Glasgow's historical experience of industrialism – coal, iron, cotton, textiles and shipbuilding – gave shape to its social, cultural and political profile and to the experiences of its people. The political struggles of the early twentieth century created the image of Red Clydeside, and its legacy in the 1970s Upper Clyde Shipbuilders occupation. This gave prominence to radical left-wing politics and a vibrant working-class political culture. Today, Glasgow retains a strong public sector and collectivist ethos. However, the prevailing impression of the city up until the 1980s was of industrial decline, with the dominant media image one of 'street violence and urban decay' (Bianchini & Parkinson 1993; Tucker 2008: 22). In many ways the experiences of Liverpool and Newcastle–Gateshead are similar. Liverpool developed around its river and docks and became one of the British Empire's most important ports. Facing the Atlantic, it traded in cotton and, before the abolition of slavery, people. On the east coast Newcastle-Gateshead's industrial profile was based on coal, iron and shipbuilding. By the late twentieth century, both places were characterized by industrial and economic decline. Regeneration began with the Albert Dock redevelopment in Liverpool and the Quayside in Newcastle, with 'culture' an important symbolic element of both.

Liverpool's decline is the most marked of the three UK former industrial cities. Liverpool lost over 192,000 jobs, a 53 per cent decline in total employment between the early 1970s and mid 1990s, and became one of the European community's poorest cities (Jones & Wilks-Heeg 2004). The 'wageless life' remains a significant element of deprivation and a profound experience for many in Liverpool and elsewhere despite re-branding efforts (Denning 2010). In a report commissioned by the Department for Communities and Local Government, Liverpool was deemed the most deprived area out of England's 354 local authorities. In the year Liverpool became City of Culture, the *Independent* newspaper reported that incapacity benefit levels were 75 per cent higher than, and life expectancy three years below, the national average. As a result, it was a city 'rich in culture and poor nearly everywhere else' (*Independent* 2008).

Liverpool, like Newcastle–Gateshead and Glasgow, had to manage post-industrialism and a city culture which was based on a working-class 'way of life' from which the work and economic background had been stripped away. Even as place marketing took hold, Liverpool retained an image of a city based on 1980s' left-wing politics (represented by the Trotskyist Militant Council of Deputy Leader Derek Hatton), of urban unrest (the 1981 Toxteth riots) and worker solidarity (Dockers' strike 1996–98). Laurier's comments on Glasgow's ECOC experience in 1990 are also applicable to Liverpool: 'There is nothing more useless to a city-seller than a working class city that is still working class' (Laurier 1993: 276).

Urban brand identity

Between 2000 and 2003 Newcastle took on a different look. Its public spaces – streets, motorways and squares – were adorned with banners, flags and drapes hung from lampposts and other city features announcing and advertising aspects of the city, its culture and amenities. This created a visual 'make over', a spectacle of culture intended to represent the 'party city' and provide a backdrop to hyperconsumption. This became a common feature of other European cities, but in Newcastle–Gateshead the display was an extensive marketing exercise rather than a real attempt at street or urban aesthetics (Greenberg 2002; Moore 2003). The new-Newcastle brand identity appeared along the newly created 'boulevards' that swept traffic into the city and the bustling shopping areas, but rarely in the working-class housing estates like Scotswood, soon to be demolished dispersing the existing inhabitants to other parts of the city. The land on which Scotswood stood is now (2014) in the process of being redeveloped to house a well-heeled estate as part of the local authority's regeneration plans. During the re-branding process banners bearing visual and textual statements lined the city centre streets. Slogans, reminiscent of advertising straplines, decorated the banners with exhortations to 'love the buzz' (the 'buzz' was the mythic and spectacular description used by the local authority to describe city life experience) and was far removed from the social and economic urban realities of the city and region. This 'corporate' makeover attempted to create a visual re-brand of the city. In sharp contrast to the official banners adorning the city centre announcing the council's commitment to culture, the ECOC bid and the city's new, re-branded image, Scotswood was draped in homemade banners declaring 'We shall not be moved'.

Brand development

City branding and re-branding is often accompanied by redevelopment of the city landscape. In Liverpool, for example, the focus was not only on the arts, culture and tourism but on building a £1 billion private retail and commercial development known as Liverpool One in the centre of the city. The leasehold of the 42.5 acre site was obtained by the Duke of Westminster's company, Grosvenor, from the local authority with the intention of drawing 'high-class' shoppers into the now privately owned city centre space. Policing of it by a private security force gave rise to fears about maintaining universal access and rights of way from which 'undesirables' might be excluded (*Guardian* 2008). The building project relied on private funding but much of the cultural strategy for ECOC 2008 rested with organizations such as Liverpool Vision and Liverpool Culture Company largely made up of private sector business in partnership with the public sector (Coleman 2004). Coleman identifies this as a feature of the 'neoliberal city' where the focus is on 'revitalising city centres and downtowns and the built in assumption … that these investment-cum-growth strategies will result in a "trickle down" of wealth creation to replenish poorer constituencies' (Coleman 2004: 231). Such a development marked a change in Liverpool regeneration policy, away from direct attempts to alleviate social deprivation in inner-city areas and peripheral sink estates toward 'the promotion of business growth in the city centre' (Jones & Wilks-Heeg 2004: 346). Property prices in the centre of Liverpool reportedly rose by 20 per cent on the day that the ECOC announcement was made, with the local media forecasting increases in property development, investment and tourism in what was referred to, in the local press, as 'Boom Town' (*Liverpool Echo* 2003).

Tourism and advertising

Developing tourism as part of the local and regional economy involves increased deployment of advertising techniques. Advertising is an important element of 'place marketing' and creating the brand image. In 2008, an extensive advertising campaign proclaiming 'This is Liverpool's year. Make yours with a visit' appeared during the summer months in a range of media outlets from London Underground billboards to double-page spreads in the national newsprint media. In one such example, a life-size cast-iron figure from artist Antony Gormley's installation 'Another Place' on the coast at Crosby was juxtaposed with a series of Liverpool cultural signifiers of 'high' culture art exhibitions and a prestige neoclassical building facade. Gazing down the River Mersey the figure looks across a Liverpool city skyline romantically bathed in an orange-yellow glow, but one curiously omitting the ubiquitous contemporary signifiers of city centre reconstruction and regeneration: the cranes and skeletal buildings that dominated Liverpool's skyline at the time. The advert offers the promise of 'chic boutiques ... stunning new shops ... cool bars and eateries'.

Advertising language has been moulded and stretched in order to sell the city. The place marketing slogan 'Newcastle–Gateshead buzzing' appeared as a strapline for the city's advertising strategy with only a hazy relationship with any referent in lived reality. However, Liverpool's slogan 'the world in one city' appeared to refer to some form of tangible reality attached to the city's multicultural experience, based not least on its position as a leading port through which inward and outward migration had taken place, acknowledging the presence of ethnically diverse peoples including black, Chinese, Irish, Somalian and other communities that make up the Liverpool population.

Decoding the brand identity

The image of the city was projected at tourists and investors, but what of the economic and cultural life of the people of Liverpool in 2008 and since? Concern about restrictions in the privatized shopping mall have been noted. Quiggins, an alternative shopping venue, was closed down in 2006 to make way for the development of Liverpool One after a prolonged public campaign on the part of the 50 or so small businesses and their 250 employees. *Nerve*, a grassroots arts and culture magazine on Merseyside, catalogued and represented concerns about the closure of independent galleries and music venues, art studios and bookshops. Paradoxically these were the cultural venues and activities that formed a distinctive local culture that should have been central to the cultural identity of the 'city of culture' (*Nerve* 2004).

In 2013 nearly one in three households in Liverpool was without anyone of working age in employment. A similar number of households are effectively jobless in Glasgow, and in the north-east of England the figure is one in four.[3] In reality working-class life on the edge of the re-branded city remains grim. In Liverpool's redeveloped city centre, Liverpool One, the shopping centre owned by the Duke of Westminster, the country's richest man, flourishes with visitor numbers in 2012 increasing by 5 per cent on 2010 and sales rising by 10 per cent (*Telegraph* 2013).

For residual working-class populations, the experience of economic decline, chronic and endemic unemployment is not confined to UK cities. Marseille, a working-class city that had by the 1980s experienced a collapse of its industrial base, became European Capital of Culture for 2013. The image of Marseille had become one of a city 'in the grip of unemployment, poverty, urban blight and corruption' (Dell'Umbria 2012: 81). Property speculation and neoliberal development around the port area promoted tourism, but it took 'the dismantling of the industrial and port system, the expulsion of tens of thousands of Marseillais to the city's outskirts ... before it could once more be made attractive to a well-heeled clientele' (Dell'Umbria 2012: 85). This is comparable in many ways to the re-branding experiences of Liverpool, Newcastle–Gateshead and other cities. For instance, consumption became a solution to industrial decline and the building of ever bigger shopping centres with concrete and the car at the heart of the consumerist system of roads, bypasses and parking areas. One of the UK's earliest out-of-town shopping centres, Gateshead's Metrocentre (last year re-branded as 'intu Metrocentre'), opened in 1986 claiming to be the largest of its kind in Europe. In 1997, Marseille claimed the title with the opening of its Grand Littoral complex. The branded city has been termed 'the city as merchandise' (Dell'Umbria 2012: 84). Yet in all of these cities questions remain, not least, what is the difference between the new branded city image and the reality of the economic and cultural life for the city's inhabitants?

This new urban image is not only designed as an outward projection to attract investment and tourism, but also inwardly aimed, intended to create a new sense of identity for the post-industrial, working-class inhabitants of these cities. Despite what has amounted to a spectacle of culture in the form of the 'party city', hyperconsumption, culture and advertising, the tourist and leisure economy, life is still experienced, for many people in Britain's northern cities, as uncertainty, conditioned by the national and regional economic effects of the recession. The experience for many in northern Britain is one of declining standards of living, job losses and cuts to health and social services, education and cultural provision. In response to this a more volatile politics of community action, student protest, trades union resistance and direct street action is gaining ground.

Conclusion

This chapter has explored consumer culture as a significant part of contemporary life. Although a feature of earlier times the market society of mass production and consumption has in many parts of the contemporary world reached a volume and intensity that has become known as hyperconsumption. This suggests that social experience is closely enmeshed with consumer culture and has an effect not only on behaviour but also on identity. Although consumer identity is often to the forefront of describing and understanding people in the contemporary world, other components of identity such as citizenship have been explored in this chapter. Access to resources is an important component of this. Brands are important to consumer culture and the process of creating brands has been explored. Branding is not confined to traditional consumer goods but has become attached to a wide range of experiences, such as living in a contemporary urban centre. City branding formed the case study for this chapter and was explored as an attempt to change not only perceptions of places but also of lives lived there and more generally of people's real experience of the world.

Notes

1 Giddens uses the term *structuration*, which includes both the structures that place and guide individual and group actions and the agency and choice they exercise. Structure and agency might be considered alongside Bourdieu's concept of habitus.

2 There is another side to the marketing coin where people are referred to as commodities or depicted as if inanimate objects.

3 In a report comparing levels of government cuts and deprivation compiled by Newcastle City Council, Liverpool had the highest deprivation score of 43.45 and faces cuts of 27.1 per cent. This is compared to Hart District Council in Hampshire with the lowest deprivation score of 4.47 per cent and cuts of 1.5 per cent (*Guardian* 2014).

Bibliography

Adams, P. (2009) *Geographies of Media and Communication*, Malden, MA: Wiley-Blackwell.

Adorno, T. (1991) 'Culture Industry Reconsidered', in J.M. Bernstein (ed.), *The Culture Industry: Selected Essays on Mass Culture*, London: Routledge.

Adorno, T. and Horkheimer, M. (1973) *Dialectic of Enlightenment*, trans. J. Cumming, London: Verso.

——(1997 [1944)] 'The Culture Industry: Enlightenment as Mass Deception', in T. Adorno and M. Horkheimer, *Dialectic of Enlightenment*, trans. J. Cummings, London: Verso.

——(2013 [1944]) *The Culture Industry: Enlightenment as Mass Deception*, New York: Continuum. Available online at www.marxists.org/reference/archive/adorno/1944/culture-industry.htm (accessed 9 December 2013).

Advertising Age (2013) 'Facebook Drops "Sponsored Stories" As It Pares Down Ad Formats'. Available online at http://adage.com/print/241969 (accessed 8 June 2013).

Advertising Standards Authority (2013) *Go Home Advertising Campaign*. Available online at www.asa.org.uk/Rulings/Adjudications/2013/10/Home-Office/SHP_ADJ_237331.aspx (accessed 10 April 2014).

Akwue, J (2012) 'Adland Must Think Creatively to Bolster Diversity', *Campaign*, 9 November.

Allan, G. and Crow, G. (2001) *Families, Households and Society*, London: Palgrave.

Althusser, L. (1971) 'Ideology and Ideological State Apparatuses', in *Lenin and Philosophy and other Essays*, London: New Left Books.

——(1998 [1972]) 'Ideology and Ideological State Apparatuses', in J. Storey (ed.), *Cultural Theory and Popular Culture*, London: Pearson.

Altman, R. (1987) 'Television Sound', in H. Newcomb (ed.), *Television: The Critical View*, Oxford: Oxford University Press, pp. 566–84.

Anderson, P. (2012) 'The Force of the Anomaly', *London Review of Books* 34(8): 3–13.

Andrejevic, M. (2009) 'The Twenty-First Century Telescreen', in G. Turner and J. Tay (eds), *Television Studies after TV: Understanding Television in the Post-Broadcast Era*, London: Routledge.

——(2012) 'Exploitation in the Data Mine', in C. Fuchs, K. Boersma, A. Albrechtslund and M. Sandoval (eds), *Internet and Surveillance*, New York: Routledge.

Ang, I. (1996) *Living Room Wars: Rethinking Media Audiences for a Postmodern World*, London: Routledge.

Angotti, T. (1993) *Metropolis*, London: Routledge.

Anholt, S. (2007) *Competitive Identity*, Basingstoke: Palgrave Macmillan.

Appadurai, A. (1986) *The Social Life of Things: Commodities in Cultural Perspective*, Cambridge: Cambridge University Press.

——(1996) *Modernity at Large: Cultural Dimensions of Globalization*, Minneapolis, MN: University of Minnesota Press.

Armitage, J. (1999) 'From Modernism to Hypermodernism and Beyond: An Interview with Paul Virilio', *Theory Culture and Society* 16(5–6): 25–55.

Arnold, M. (1960 [1869]) *Culture and Anarchy*, London: Cambridge University Press.

Arvidsson, A. (2005) 'Brands: A Critical Perspective', *Journal of Consumer Culture* 5(2): 235–58.

——(2006) *Brands: Meaning and Value in Media Culture*, London: Routledge.

ASA (2013) 'ASA Adjudication on Home Office'. Available online at www.asa.org.uk/Rulings/Adjudications/2013/10/Home-Office/SHP_ADJ_237331.aspx (accessed 10 April 2014).

Ashworth, W.J. (2004) 'Industry and Transport', in C. Williams (ed.), *A Companion to Nineteenth-Century Britain*, Oxford: Blackwell.

Austin, C.G., Zinkhan, G.M. and Song, J.H. (2007) 'Peer-to-Peer Media Opportunities', in G.J. Tellis and T. Ambers (eds), *The Sage Handbook of Advertising*, London: Sage.

Bagdikian, B. (2004) *The New Media Monopoly*, Boston, MA: Beacon Press.

Bainbridge, J. (2013) 'Brands Connect TV and Video Advertising', *Marketing*, 16 January.

Baker, C.E. (1994) *Advertising and a Democratic Press*, Princeton, NJ: Princeton University Press.

Balibar, E. (2002) 'Possessive Individualism Reversed: From Locke to Derrida', *Constellations* 9(3): 299–317.

Balmer, J.M.T. (2006) 'Corporate Brand Cultures and Communities', in J.E. Schroeder and M. Salzer-Morling (eds), *Brand Culture*, Abingdon: Routledge.

Baran, P. and Sweezy, P. (1966) *Monopoly Capital: An Essay on the American Economic and Social Order*, New York: Monthly Review Press.

BARB (2004) *Trends in Television 2004*. Available online at www.barb.co.uk/resources/tv-facts/tv-since-1981 (accessed 19 September 2014).

——(2013) *Trends in Television 2012*. Available online at www.barb.co.uk/resources/tv-facts/trends-in-tv?_s=4 (accessed 21 March 2013).

Bareau, J.W. (1986) *The Hidden Face of Manet*, London: Burlington Magazine.

Barnard, A. (2004) 'The Legacy of the Situationist International: The Production of Situations of Creative Resistance', *Capital and Class* 84: 103–24.

Barthes, R. (1968) *Elements of Semiology*, London: Jonathan Cape.

——(1973) *Mythologies*, trans. A. Lathers, London: Paladin.

——(1977) 'Introduction to the Structural Analysis of Narratives', trans. S. Heath, in his *Image Music Texts*, London: Fontana.

——(1981) 'Introduction to the Structural Analysis of Narratives', in T. Bennett, M. Martin, C. Mercer and J. Woolacott (eds), *Culture, Ideology and Social Process*, Buckingham: Open University.

——(2002) 'The Rhetoric of the Image', N. Mirzoeff (ed.), *The Visual Culture Reader*, London: Routledge.

Bashford, S. (2012) 'Spare Me the Mummy Marketing', *Marketing*, 3 October.

Bassey, J. (2009), 'Advertising and New Media', in H. Powell, J. Hardy, S. Hawkin and I. MacRury (eds), *The Advertising Handbook*, London: Routledge.

Baudelaire, C. (1982) 'The Salon of 1846: On the Heroism of Modern Life', in F. Frascina and C. Harrison (eds), *Modern Art and Modernism: A Critical Anthology*, London: Harper & Row.

Baudrillard, J. (1981) *For a Critique of the Political Economy of the Sign*, St Louis, MO: Telos.

——(1983) *Simulations*, New York: Semiotext(e).

——(1988a) 'For a Critique of the Political Economy of the Sign', in M. Poster (ed.), *Selected Writings*, Cambridge: Polity.

——(1988b) 'Simulacra and Simulations', in M. Poster (ed.), *Selected Writings*, Cambridge: Polity.

——(1994) *Simulacra and Simulation*, trans. S. Glaser, Ann Arbor, MI: University of Michigan Press.

——(1998 [1970]) *The Consumer Society*, London: Sage.

——(2003) *The Consumer Society: Myths and Structures*, London: Sage Press.

Bauman, Z. (2000) *Liquid Modernity*, Cambridge: Polity Press.

——(2001) 'Consuming Life', *The Journal of Consumer Culture* 1(1): 9–29.

Baxandall, M. (1972) *Painting and Experience in Fifteenth-Century Italy*, Oxford: Oxford University Press.

Bayley, S. (1986) *Sex, Drink and Fast Cars: The Creation and Consumption of Images*, London: Faber and Faber.

Beard, M. (2008) *Pompeii: The Life of a Roman Town*, London: Profile.

Bendel, P.R. (2011) 'Branding New York – The Saga of Love New York', in K. Dinnie (ed.), *City Branding: Theory and Cases*, Basingstoke: Palgrave.

Benjamin, W. (1973) 'The Work of Art in the Age of Mechanical Reproduction', in his *Illuminations*, London: Fontana.

Bennett, T. (1986) 'Introduction', in T. Bennett *et al.* (eds), *Popular Culture and Social Relations*, Milton Keynes: Open University Press.

——(1990) *Outside Literature*, New York: Routledge.

Bennett, T. and Woollacott, J. (1987) *Bond and Beyond*, London: Macmillan.

Bennett, T., Martin, M., Mercer, C. and Woollacott, J., eds (1981) *Culture, Ideology and Social Process*, London: Open University Press.

Berelson, B. (1952) *Content Analysis in Communication Research*, Glencoe: Free Press.

Bernstein, J.M. (1991) *Introduction to the Culture Industry*, London: Routledge.

Bettig, R. and Hall, J. (2012) *Big Media, Big Money*, Lanham, MD: Rowman and Littlefield.

Bianchini, F. and Parkinson, M. (1993). *Cultural Policy and Regeneration: The West European Experience*, Manchester: Manchester University Press.

Bignell, J. (2002) *Media Semiotics*, Manchester: Manchester University Press.

Blunt, A. and Dowling, R. (2006) *Home*, Abingdon: Routledge.

Boal, I., Clark, T.J., Matthews, J. and Watts, M. (2005) *Afflicted Powers: Capital and Spectacle in a New Age of War*, London: Verso.

Bolin, G. (2004) 'Spaces of Television: The Structuring of Consumers in a Swedish Shopping Mall', in N. Couldry and A. McCarthy (eds), *MediaSpace: Place, Scale and Culture in a Media Age*, London: Routledge.

Bourdieu, P. (1984) *Distinction: A Social Critique of the Judgement of Taste*, London: Routledge.

Briggs, A. and Burke, P. (2005) *A Social History of the Media: From Gutenberg to the Internet*, Cambridge: Polity.

Bryant, J. and Oliver, M.B., eds (2008) *Media Effects: Advances in Theory and Research*, 3rd edn., London: Routledge.

Buckingham, D. (1998) 'Media Education in the UK: Moving beyond Protectionism', *Journal of Communication*, Winter. Available online at http://journalism.uoregon.edu/~cbybee/j412_u09/ Buckingham Protectionism.pdf (accessed 9 December 2013).

Bull, M. (2004) 'To Each Their Own Bubble: Mobile Spaces of Sound in the City', in N. Couldry and A. McCarthy (eds), *MediaSpace: Place, Scale and Culture in a Media Age,* London: Routledge.

Buttimere, A. (1980) 'Home, Reach and the Sense of Place', in A. Buttimere, and D. Seamon (eds), *The Human Experience of Place and Space*, London: Croom Helm, pp. 166–87.

Byrne, D. (2001) *Understanding the Urban*, Basingstoke: Palgrave.

Campaign (1996) Campaign, 3 May.

——(2011) 'Bisto Launches Promise Ad Campaign', *Campaign*, 25 January.

Caraway, B. (2011) 'Audience Labor in the New Media Environment: A Marxian Revisiting of the Audience Commodity', *Media, Culture and Society* 33(5): 693–708.

Carey, A. (1995) *Taking the Risk Out of Democracy*, Champaign, IL: University of Illinois Press.

Carr, E.H. (1961) *What Is History?* London: Penguin.

Cashmore, E. (2006) *Celebrity/Culture*, London: Routledge.

Castells, M. (1996) *The Information Age: Economy, Society and Culture,* vol. I, *The Rise of the Network Society*, Oxford: Blackwell.

——(1997) *The Information Age: Economy, Society and Culture,* vol. II, *The Power of Identity*, Oxford: Blackwell.

——(1998) *The Information Age: Economy, Society and Culture*, vol. III, *End of Millenium*, Oxford: Blackwell.

——(2008) 'The New Public Sphere: Global Civil Society, Communication Networks and Global Surveillance', *Annals of the American Academy of Political and Social Science* 616(1): 78–93.

Cavanagh, A. and Dennis, A. (2012) 'Behind the News: Framing the Riots', *Capital and Class* 36(3) 375–81.

Cellan-Jones, R. (2012) 'Facebook QandA: The Network Justifies the Cost of Its "Like" Adverts'. Available online at www.bbc.co.uk/news/technology-18816674 (accessed 13 July 2012).

Certeau, M. de (1984) *The Practice of Everyday Life*, Berkeley, CA: University of California Press.

Channel 4 News (2013) 'Home Office Faces Immigration Tactics Investigation', Channel 4 News, 2 August. Available online at www.channel4.com/news/immigration-police-checks-arrests-government-home-office (accessed 10 April 2014).

Chapman, M. (2013) 'Is it Mobiles' Time to Shine?' *Marketing*, 13 February 2013.

Clark, T.J. (2000) *The Painting of Modern Life: Paris in the Art of Manet and His Followers*, London: Thames and Hudson.

Clarke, J.R. (2003) *Art in the Lives of Ordinary Romans: visual Representation and Non-elite Viewers in Italy, 100 BC – AD 315*, Berkeley: University of California Press.

Cobley, P. (1994) 'Throwing Out the Baby: Populism and Active Audience Theory', *Media, Culture and Society* 16: 677–87.

Coleman, R. (2004) *Reclaiming the Streets: Surveillance, Social Control and the City*, Uffcolme Cullompton: Willan Publishing.

Collini, S. (1994) *Matthew Arnold: A Critical Portrait*, Oxford: Clarendon Press.

——(2000) 'An Abiding Sense of the Demonic', *London Review of Books* 22(2): 32–4.

Compton, J. (2004) *The Integrated News Spectacle*, New York: Peter Lang.

Cook, G. (2001) *The Discourse of Advertising*, London: Routledge.

Corner, J. (1995) *Television Form and Public Address*, London: Edward Arnold.

——(2001) 'Ideology: A Note on Conceptual Salvage', *Media Culture and Society* 23: 525–33.

——(2002) 'Why Study Media Form?' in A. Briggs and P. Cobley (eds), *The Media: An Introduction*, Harlow: Longman.

Cosgrove, D. (1989) 'Geography Is Everywhere: Culture and Symbolism in Human Landscapes', in D. Gregory, and R. Walford (eds), *Horizons of Human Geography*, London: Macmillan.

Couldry, N. (2012) *Media, Society, World: Social Theory and Digital Media Practice*, Cambridge: Polity.

Couldry, N. and McCarthy, A. (2004) *MediaSpace: Place, Scale and Culture in a Media Age*, London: Routledge.

Courtois, C. (2012) 'When Two Worlds Meet: An Inter-paradigmatic Mixed Method Approach to Convergent Audiovisual Media Consumption', *Participations: Journal of Audience and Reception Studies* 9(2): 716–42.

Crary, J. (2009) 'Spectacle, Attention, Counter-Memory', in B. Highmore (ed.), *The Design Culture Reader*, London: Routledge.

——(2013) *24/7: Late Capitalism and the Ends of Sleep*, London: Verso.

Croll, A. (2004) 'Popular Leisure and Sport', in C. Williams (ed.), *A Companion to Nineteenth-Century Britain*, Oxford: Blackwell.

Cronin, A. (2006) 'Advertising and the Metabolism of the City: Urban Space Commodity Rhythms', *Environment and Planning D: Society and Space* 24(4): 615–32.

Croteau, D. and Hoynes, W. (2006) *The Business of Media*, 2nd edn., Thousand Oaks, CA: Pine Forge Press.

Cruz, J. and Lewis, J. (1994) 'Reflections upon the Encoding/Decoding Model: An Interview with Stuart Hall', in *Viewing, Reading, Listening: Audiences and Cultural Reception*, Boulder, CO: Westview Press.

Csaba, F.F. and Bengtsson, A. (2006) 'Rethinking Identity in Brand Management', in J.E. Schroeder and M. Salzer-Morling (eds), *Brand Culture*, Abingdon: Routledge.

Csikszentmihalyi, M. (2009) 'Design and Order in Everyday Life', in B. Highmore (ed.), *The Design Culture Reader*, London: Routledge.

Cunliffe, B. (2008) *Europe between the Oceans*, New Haven, CT: Yale University Press.

Curran, J. (1978) 'Advertising and the Press', in J. Curran (ed.), *The British Press: A Manifesto*, London: Macmillan.

——(1986) 'The Impact of Advertising on the British Mass Media', in R. Collins, J. Curran, N. Garnham, P. Scannell and C. Sparks (eds), *Media, Culture and Society: A Critical Reader*, London: Sage.

——(1998) 'Crisis of Public Communication: A Reappraisal', in T. Liebes and J. Curran (eds), *Media, Ritual and Identity*, London: Routledge.

——(2002a) 'The Sociology of the Press', in A. Briggs and P. Cobley (eds), *The Media: An Introduction,* Harlow: Longman.

——(2002b) *Media and Power*, London: Routledge.

Curtin, M. (2003) 'Media Capital: Towards the Study of Spatial Flows', *International Journal of Cultural Studies* 6(2): 202–28.

Danesi, M. (2006) *Brands*, London: Routledge.

Darby, I. (2012) 'Does Ad Industry Value Ethnic Britain?', *Campaign*, 12 October.

Daugherty, T. and Hofffman, E. (2014) 'EWOM and the Importance of Capturing Consumer Attention within Social Media', *Journal of Marketing Communications* 20(1–2): 82–102.

Davies, W. (2014) 'Economics of Insomnia', *New Left Review* 85: 141–6.

Davila, A. (2004) 'The Marketable Neighbourhood', in N. Couldry and A. McCarthy (eds), *MediaSpace: Place, Scale and Culture in a Media Age,* London: Routledge.

Davis, H. (2004) *Understanding Stuart Hall*, Sage: London.

Davis, J. (2008) *The Olympic Games Effect: How Sports Marketing Builds Strong Brands*, London: John Wiley.

Deacon, D., Pickering, M., Golding, P. and Murdock, G. (1999) *Researching Communications*, London: Arnold.

Dean, J. (2012) 'Occupy Wall Street: After the Anarchist Moment', in L. Panitch, G. Albo and V. Chibber (eds), *The Question of Strategy: Socialist Register 2013,* Pontypool: Merlin Press.

Debord, G. (1991) *Comments on the Society of the Spectacle*, London: Verso.

——(1992 [1977]) *The Society of the Spectacle*, London: Rebel Press.

Dell'Umbria, A. (2012) 'The Sinking of Marseilles', *New Left Review* 75: 69–87.

Denning, M. (2010) 'Wageless Life', *New Left Review* 66.

Derrida, J. (1987) *The Truth in Painting*, trans. G. Bennington, Chicago, IL: University of Chicago Press.

Dickens, C. (1854) *Hard Times*, London: Odhams Press.

Dickinson, R., Harindranath, R. and Linne, O. (1998) *Approaches to Audiences: A Reader*, London: Arnold.

Dinnie, K. (2011) 'Introduction to the Theory of City Branding', in K. Dinnie (ed.), *City Branding: Theory and Cases*, Basingstoke: Palgrave.

Doro, P. and Greenhalgh, M. (1992) *Essential Art History*, London: Bloomsbury.

Doyle, G. (2002) *Understanding Media Economics*, London: Sage.

du Gay, P. (1997) *Production of Culture/Cultures of Production*, London: Sage/Open University.

Dwyer, T.(2010) *Media Convergence*, Maidenhead: Open University Press.

Dyer, G. (1982) *Advertising as Communication*, London: Routledge.

Elliott, B. (1962) *A History of English Advertising*, London: Batsford.

Ellis, J. (1992 [1982]) *Visible Fictions: Cinema, Television, Video*, London: Routledge.

——(2000) 'Scheduling: The Last Creative Act in Television?', *Media Culture and Society* 22: 25–38.

Engels, F. (1892) *The Condition of the Working-Class in England in 1844*, London: Swan Sonnenschein.

Enzenberger, H.M. (1974) *The Consciousness Industry: On Literature, Politics and the Media*, New York: Continuum.

Ernest Jones (2012) 'Celebrate Christmas 2012', advertisement, *Guardian*, Saturday supplement, 27 October.

Evans, C. and Gamman, L. (1995) 'The Gaze Revisited, Or Reviewing Queer Viewing', in P. Burston and C. Richardson (eds), *A Queer Romance: Lesbians, Gay Men, and Popular Culture,* New York: Routledge.

Evans, R. (2007) *Transport for London Congestion Charging Scheme: Ex-post Evaluation of the Quantified Impacts of the Original Scheme*, report prepared for Congestion Charging Modelling and Evaluation Team, London: Transport for London.

Ewen, S. (1988) *All Consuming Images,* New York: McGraw-Hill.

——(2001) *Captains of Consciousness: Advertising and the Social Routes of the Consumer Culture*, New York: Basic Books.

Ewen, S. and Ewen, E. (1982) *Channels of Desire*, New York: McGraw-Hill.

Falk, P. (1997) 'The Benetton – Toscani Effect: Testing the Limits of Conventional Advertising', in M. Nava, A. Blake, I. MacRury and B. Richards (eds), *Buy this Book: Studies in Advertising and Consumption*, London: Routledge.

Faraone, R. (2011) 'Economy, Ideology and Advertising', in J. Wasko, G. Murdock and H. Sousa (eds), *The Handbook of Political Economy of Communications*, Oxford: Blackwell Publishing.

Faulconbridge, J.R., Beaverstock, J.V., Nativel, C. and Taylor, P.J. (2011) *The Globalization of Advertising: Agencies, Cities and Spaces of Creativity*, Abingdon: Routledge.

Featherstone, M. (1991) *Consumer Culture and Postmodernism*, London: Routledge.

Fennis, B.M. and Sroebe, W. (2010) *The Psychology of Advertising*, Hove: Taylor & Francis.

Fenton, N. (2000) 'The Problematics of Postmodernism for Feminist Media Studies', *Media, Culture and Society* 22: 723–41.

——(2007) 'Bridging the Mythical Divide: Political Economy and Cultural Studies Approaches to the Analysis of the Media', in E. Devereux (ed.), *Issues and Key Debate in the Media Studies,* London: Sage, pp. 7–31.

Fenwick, J. and Wharton, C. (2013) 'Advertising Research', in C. Wharton (ed.), *Advertising as Culture*, Bristol: Intellect.

Fine, B. and Saad-Filho, A. (2004) *Marx's Capital*, London: Pluto Press.

Fish, S. (1980) *Is There a Text in the Class? The Authority of Interpretive Communities*, Cambridge, MA: Harvard University Press.

Fiske, J. (1986) 'Television: Polysemy and Popularity', in *Critical Studies in Mass Communication* 3(4): 391–408.

——(1987) *Television Culture*, London: Methuen.

——(1989) *Understanding Popular Culture*, Boston, MA: Unwin Hyman.

——(1997) *Television Culture*, London: Routledge.

Florida, R. (2002) *The Rise of the Creative Class*, New York: Basic Books.

Floud, R. (1997) *The People and the British Economy*, Oxford: Oxford University Press.

Foster, H. (1983) *The Anti-Aesthetic: Essays on Postmodern Culture*, Seattle, WA: Bay Press.

Foucault, M. (1977) *Discipline and Punish: The Birth of a Prison*, London: Penguin Books.

Fox, R.F. (2000) *Harvesting Minds: How Television Commercials Control Kids*, Oxford: Greenwood.

Frith, K., Shaw, P. and Cheng, H. (2009) 'The Construction of Beauty: A Cross-Cultural Analysis of Womens's Magazine Advertising', in J. Turow and M.P. McAllister (eds), *The Advertising and Consumer Culture Reader*, London: Routledge.

Fuchs, C. (2012) 'Social Media, Riots and Revolutions', *Capital and Class* 36(3): 383–91.

Fukuyama, F. (1992) *The End of History and the Last Man*, New York: Free Press.

Galbraith, J.K. (1958) *The Affluent Society*, New York: Houghton Mifflin Company.

Gammon, l. and Marshment, M. (1988) *The Female Gaze*, London: The Women's Press.

Gandy, O. (1982) *Beyond Agenda Setting*, Norwood, NJ: Ablex.

——(2000) 'Race, Ethnicity and the Segmentation of Media Markets', in J. Curran and M. Gurevitch (eds), *Mass Media and Society*, 3rd edn, London: Arnold.

——(2004) 'Audiences on Demand', in A. Calabrese and C. Sparks (eds), *Toward a Political Economy of Culture*, Lanham, MD: Rowman and Littlefield.

Gans, H. (1980) *Deciding What's News*, London: Constable.

Gardner, B.B. and Levy, S.J. (1955) 'The Product and the Brand', *Harvard Business Review* (March–April): 33–99.

Garnham, N. (2005) 'From Cultural to Creative Industries: An Analysis of the Implications of the "Creative Industries" Approach to Arts and Media Policy Making in the United Kingdom', *International Journal of Cultural Policy* 11: 1–14.

Garreau, J. (1992) *Edge City*, New York: Doubleday.

Gauntlet, D. (1998) 'Ten Things Wrong with the Media Effects Model', in R. Dickinson, R. Harindranath and O. Linne (eds), *Approaches to Audiences: A Reader*, London: Arnold.

Gee, M. (2013) 'Art and Advertising', in C. Wharton (ed.), *Advertising as Culture*, Bristol: Intellect.

Gerbner, G. (1995) 'Towards Cultural Indicators: The Analysis of Mass Mediated Public Message Systems', in O. Boyd-Barrett and C. Newbold (eds), *Approaches to Media: A Reader*, London: Arnold.

Gerbner, G., Gross, L., Morgan, M. and Signorielli, N. (1980) 'The Mainstreaming of America: Violence Profile No. 11', *The Journal of Communication* 30(3): 10–29.

Ghostsigns (2011) 'Archive'. Available online at www.ghostsigns.co.uk/archive (accessed 11 May 2011).

Gibson, T.A. (2005) 'Selling City Living: Urban Branding Campaigns, Class Power and the Civic Good', *International Journal of Cultural Studies* 8: 259–80.

Giddens, A. (1990) *The Consequences of Modernity*, Stanford, CA: Stanford University Press.

——(1991). *The Consequences of Modernity*, Cambridge: Polity Press.

Giddings, R. (1986) *Matthew Arnold: Between Two Worlds*, London: Vision Press.

Gliserman, S. (1969) 'Mitchell's Newspaper Directory, 1846–1907', *Victorian Periodicals Newsletter* 4, April.

Goldman, R. (1992) *Reading Ads Socially*, London: Routledge.

Goldman, R. and Papson, S. (2006) 'Capital's Brandscapes', *Journal of Consumer Culture* 6(3): 327–53.

Gombrich, E.H. (1979) *Ideals and Idols: Essays on Values in History and in Art*, Oxford: Phaidon.

Goodman, J.R. (2009) 'Flabless is Fabulous', in J. Turow and M.P. McAllister (eds), *The Advertising and Consumer Culture Reader*, London: Routledge.

Goodwin, F. (1991) 'Creativity and Research', *Poster Scene* 11.

Gorman, L. and McLean, D. (2009) *Media and Society into the Twenty-first Century*, Chichester: Wiley-Blackwell.

Gottdiener, M. (1995) *Postmodern Semiotics*, Oxford: Blackwell.

Graham, S. (2010) *Cities under Siege*, London: Verso.

Graham, S. and Marvin, S. (2001) *Splintering Urbanism: Networked Infrastructures, Technological Mobilities and the Urban Condition*, New York: Routledge.

Gray, A. (1992) *Video Playtime: The Gendering of a Leisure Technology*, London: Routledge.

Greenberg, M. (2002) 'Branding Cities: A Social History of the Urban Lifestyle Magazine', *Urban Affairs Review* 36(2): 228–63.

Griffin, E. (2004) 'Audiences on Demand', in A. Calabrese and C. Sparks (eds), *Toward a Political Economy of Culture*, Lanham, MD: Rowman and Littlefield.

——(2010) *A Short History of the British Industrial Revolution*, Basingstoke: Palgrave Macmillan.

Gripsrud, J. (1998) 'Television, Broadcasting, Flow: Key Metaphors in TV Theory', in C. Geraghty and D. Lusted (eds), *The Television Studies Book,* London: Arnold.

Grossberg, L. (1984) 'Strategies of Marxist Cultural Interpretation', in *Critical Studies in Mass Communication* 1: 392–421.

Guardian (2008) 'Policing the Retail Republic', *Guardian*, 28 May.

——(2011) 'England Rioters: Young, Poor and Unemployed', *Guardian* 18 August.

——(2013a) *ABC: National Daily Newspaper Circulation February 2013*. Available online at www.theguardian.com/media/2013/nov/13/abcs-national-newspapers-2013 (accessed 14 April 2014).

——(2013b) 'Council Calls for Withdrawal of Ad Campaign', *Guardian* 27 July.

——(2013c) 'Dhaka: Many Dead', *Guardian* 25 April.

——(2014) 'Local Government Cuts Hitting Poorest Areas', *Guardian* 30 January.

Habermas, J. (1992) *The Structural Transformation of the Public Sphere: An Inquiry into a Category of Bourgeois Society*, Cambridge: Polity Press.

Hall, S. (1972) 'The Determination of News Photographs', in his *Working Papers in Cultural Studies*, Birmingham: Centre for Contemporary Cultural Studies, pp. 53–87.

——(1973) 'Encoding and Decoding in the Television Discourse', in his *Stencilled Occasional Paper*, Birmingham: Centre for Contemporary Cultural Studies.

——(1981a) 'Cultural Studies: Two Paradigms', in T. Bennett, M. Graham, C. Mercer and J. Wollacott (eds), *Culture, Ideology and Social Process*, Buckingham: Open University Press.

——(1981b) 'The Structured Communication of Events' in D. Potter (ed.), *Society and the Social Sciences,* London: Routledge and Kegan Paul.

——(1982) 'The Rediscovery of Ideology', in M. Gurevitch (ed.), *Culture, Society and the Media,* London: Methuen.

——(1983) 'The Problem of Ideology – Marxism without Guarantees', in B. Matthews (ed.), *Marx: A Hundred Years On*, London: Lawrence and Wishart.

——(1985) 'Signification, Representation, Ideology: Althusser and the Post-Structuralist Debates', *Critical Studies in Mass Communication* 2(2): 91–114.

——(1989) 'Ideology and Communication Theory', in E. Ervin (ed.), *Rethinking Communication, Volume 1: Paradigm Issues*, Thousand Oaks, CA: Sage.

——(1991) 'Old and New Identities, Old and New Ethnicities', in A. King (ed.), *Culture, Globalisation and the World System,* Basingstoke: Macmillan.

——(1993a) 'Encoding and Decoding in Television Discourse', in S. During (ed.), *The Cultural Studies Reader,* London: Routledge.

——(1993b) 'Reflections upon the Encoding/Decoding Model: An Interview with Stuart Hall', in J. Cruz. and J. Lewis (eds), *Viewing, Reading, Listening: Audiences and Cultural Reception,* Boulder, CO: Westview.

——(1995) 'Fantasy, Identity, Politics', in E. Carter, J. Donaldson and J. Squires (eds), *Cultural Remix: Theories of Politics and the Popular*, London: Lawrence and Wishart.

——(1996) 'Who Needs "Identity"?', in S. Hall and P. du Guy (eds), *Questions of Cultural Identity,* London: Sage.

——(1997) *Representation: Cultural Representations and Signifying Practices*, London: Sage/Open University.

——(1999) 'Unsettling "The Heritage": Re-imagining the Post-nation', paper presented at Whose Heritage? conference, North West Arts Board, Manchester: Arts Council of England.

——(2006 [1973]) 'Encoding/Decoding', in M.G. Durham and D.M. Kellner (eds), *Media and Cultural Studies: Keyworks*, Oxford: Blackwell.

Hamilton, K. and Hoyle, S. (2005) 'Moving Cities: Transport Connections', in J. Allen, D. Massey, and M. Pryke (eds), *Unsettling Cities*, London: Routledge.

Hanich, J. (2014) 'Watching a Film With Others: Towards a Theory of Collective Spectatorship', *Screen* 55(3): 338–59.

Hansen, A., Cottle, S., Negrine, R. and Newbold, C. (1998) *Mass Communication Research Methods*, London: Macmillan.

Hardt, M. and Negri, A. (2001) *Empire*, Cambridge, MA: Harvard University Press.

——(2011) 'Arabs are Democracy's New Pioneers', *Guardian*, 25 February.

Hardy, J. (2009) 'Advertising Regulation', in H. Powell, J. Hardy, S. Hawkin and I. MacRury (eds), *The Advertising Handbook*, 3rd edn, London: Routledge.

——(2010a) *Cross-Media Promotion*, New York: Peter Lang.

——(2010b) 'The Contribution of Critical Political Economy', in J. Curran (ed.) *Media and Society*, 5th edn, London: Bloomsbury.

——(2013) 'The Changing Relationship between Media and Marketing' in H. Powell (ed.), *Promotional Culture and Convergence: Markets, Methods and Media*, Abingdon: Routledge.

——(2014) *Critical Political Economy of the Media: An Introduction*, Abingdon: Routledge.

Harms, J. and Kellner, D. (1990), 'Toward a Critical Theory of Advertising'. Available online at http://pages.gseis.ucla.edu/faculty/kellner/Illumina%20Folder/kell6.htm (accessed 7 January 2014).

Hart, H. (1979) *Social Theories of the Press: Early German and American Perspectives*, Beverley Hills, CA: Sage.

Harvey, C., Press, J. and Maclean, M. (2011) 'William Morris, Cultural Leadership, and the Dynamics of Taste', *Business History Review* 85: 245–71.

Harvey, D. (1992) *The Condition of Postmodernity: An Enquiry into the Origins of Cultural Change*, Oxford: Blackwell.

Haug, W. (1986) *Critique of Commodity Aesthetics*, Cambridge: Polity.

Heartney, E. (2001) *Postmodernism*, London: Tate Publishing.

Heath, S. (1990) 'Representing Television' in P. Mellencamp (ed.), *Logics of Television,* Bloomington, IN: Indiana University Press, pp. 267–302.

Hebdige, D. (1979) *Subculture: The Meaning of Style*, London: Methuen.

Held, D., McGrew, A., Goldblatt, D. and Perraton, J. (1999) *Global Transformations: Politics, Economics and Culture*, Cambridge: Polity Press.

Helmore, E. (2013) 'America's Fast-food Workers in Vanguard of Growing Protests at Starvation Wages', *Observer*, 11 August.

Herman, E. and Chomsky, N. (2008 [1988]) *Manufacturing Consent: The Political Economy of the Mass Media*, 2nd edn, London: Bodley Head.

Herman, E. and McChesney, R. (1997) *The Global Media*, London: Cassell.

Herzog, H. (1944) 'What Do We Really Know about Daytime Serial Listeners?' in P. Lazarfeld and F. Stanton (eds), *Radio Research 1942–1943*, New York: Duell, Sloane and Pearce.

Hesmondhalgh, D. (2010) 'Media Industry Studies, Media Production Studies', in J. Curran (ed.), *Media and Society*, London: Bloomsbury.

——(2013) *The Cultural Industries*, 3rd edn, London: Sage.

Hill, K. (2012) 'Facebook Will Pay $10 Million to Make Its "Sponsored Stories" Problem Go Away', *Forbes*. Available online at www.forbes.com/sites/kashmirhill/2012/06/18/facebook-will-pay-10-million-to-make-its-sponsored-stories-problem-go-away (accessed 10 April 2014).

Hindley, D. and Hindley, G. (1972) *Advertising in Victorian Britain 1837–1901*, London: Wayland Publishers.

History of Advertising Trust (2014) 'The History of Advertising Trust's Gallery'. Available online at www.hatads.org.uk/about (accessed 18 April 2014).

Hobsbawm, E. (1973) *The Age of Revolution*, London: Cardinal.

——(1987) *The Age of Empire. 1875–1914*, New York: Pantheon Books.

——(1999 [1968]) *Industry and Empire, from 1750 to the Present Day*, London: Penguin.

——(1999) *Industry and Empire: The Birth of the Industrial Revolution*, New York: The New Press.

Hoggart, R. (1957) *The Uses of Literacy*, Fairlawn, NJ: Essential Books.

Holleran, C. (2012) *Shopping in Ancient Rome: The Retail Trade in the Late Republic and the Principate*, Oxford: Oxford University Press.

Hollis, N. (2005) 'Ten Years of Learning How Online Advertising Builds Brands', *Journal of Advertising Research* 45(2).

Holsti, O.R. (1969) *Content Analysis for the Social Sciences and Humanities*, Reading, MA: Addison-Wesley.

Hospers, G. (2011) 'City Branding and the Tourist Gaze', in K. Dinnie (ed.), *City Branding: Theory and Cases*, Basingstoke: Palgrave.

Hovland, R. and Wolburg, J.M. (2010) *Advertising, Society, and Consumer Culture*, London: M.E. Sharpe.

Howe, A. (2004) 'Britain and the World Economy', in C. Williams (ed.), *A Companion to Nineteenth-Century Britain,* Oxford: Blackwell.

Howe, J. (2002) 'Vehicles of Desire', *New Left Review* 15: 105–17.

Huffington Post (2013) 'Pope Francis Condemns "Slave Labor" in Bangladesh'. Available online at www.huffingtonpost.com/2013/05/01/pope-francis-slave-labor_n_3191288.html (accessed 11 April 2014).

Huq, R. (2013) 'This Hunt for Illegal Immigrants Is Revolting', *Guardian*, 3 August.

Hurtz, W. and Durkin, K. (1997) 'Gender Role Stereotyping in Australian Radio Commercials', *Sex Roles* 36(1): 103–14.

Hutt, W.H. (1940) 'The Concept of Consumers' Sovereignty', *The Economic Journal* 50(197): 66–77. Available online at www.jstor.org/discover/10.2307/2225739?uid=3738032anduid=2anduid=4andsid=21103646920191 (accessed 10 August 2013).

Independent (2008) 'City Rich in Culture', *Independent*, 2 May.

Internet Advertising Bureau (2009) *A Guide to Online Behavioural Advertising*. Available online at www.iabuk.net/sites/default/files/publication-download/OnlineBehaviouralAdvertisingHandbook_5455.pdf (accessed 25 January 2010).

Iser, W. (1989) *Prospecting: From Reader Response to Literary Anthropology*, Baltimore, MD: Johns Hopkins University Press.

ITV News – Daybreak (2013) 'Farage Slams "Nasty" Immigration Posters'. Available online at www.itv.com/news/topic/nigel-farage (accessed 15 August 2013).

Jackson, P. and Thrift, N. (1995) 'Geographies of Consumption', in D. Miller (ed.), *Acknowledging Consumption*, London: Routledge, pp. 204–37.

Jameson, F. (1984) 'Postmodernism, or the Cultural Logic of Late Capitalism', *New Left Review* 146: 53–92.

——(1991) *Postmodernism or the Cultural Logic of Late Capitalism*, Durham, NC: Duke University Press.

Jefkins, F. and Yadin, D. (2000) *Advertising*, Harlow: Pearson.

Jenkins, H. (2006) *Convergence Culture: Where Old and New Media Collide*, New York: New York University Press.

Jensen, O. (2005) 'Branding the Contemporary City – Rebranding as Regional Growth Agenda', paper presented at the Regional Studies Association Conference Regional Growth Agendas, Alborg.

Jhally, S. (1990) *The Codes of Advertising*, London: Routledge.

Jones, G.S. (1974) 'Working Class Culture and Working Class Politics in London, 1870–1900: Notes on the Remaking of a Working Class', *Journal of Social History* 7: 460–508.

Jones, P. and Wilks-Heeg, S. (2004). 'Capitalising Culture: Liverpool 2008', *Local Economy* 19(4): 341–60.

Jordanova, L. (2006) *History in Practice*, 2nd edn, London: Hodder Arnold.

Jordin, M. and Brunt, R. (1988) 'Constituting the Television Audience: Problem of Method', in P. Drummond and R. Paterson (eds), *Television and Its Audience: International Research Perspectives*, London: BFI.

Kaplan, E.A. (1983) 'Is the Gaze Male?', in *Women and Film: Both Sides of the Camera*, London: Routledge.

Kasapi, E. (2009) 'Viral Advertising: Internet Entertainment and Virtual Society', in H. Powell, J. Hardy, S. Hawkin and I. MacRury (eds), *The Advertising Handbook*, 3rd edn, London: Routledge.

Kavyta, R. (2012) 'Hyphenated Identities: Negotiating "Indianness" and being Indo-Trinidadian', in G. Hosein and L. Outar (eds), *CRGS* 6: 1–19.

Keller, E. and Fay, B. (2012) 'Word of Mouth Advocacy: A New Key to Advertising Effectiveness', *Journal of Advertising Research* 52(4): 459–64.

Kelly, A., Lawlor, K. and O'Donohoe, S. (2009) 'Encoding Advertisements: The Creative Perspective', in J. Turow and M.P. McAllister (eds), *The Advertising and Consumer Culture Reader*, London: Routledge.

Kelly, M. (2014) 'Michel Foucault', *Internet Encyclopedia of Philosophy*. Available online at www.iep.utm.edu/foucault (accessed 11 April 2014).

Kempson, R., Fernando, T. and Asher, N., eds (2012) *Philosophy of Linguistics*, Oxford: North Holland.

Kimmel, A.T. and Kitchener, P.T. (2014) 'Word of Mouth and Social Media', *Journal of Marketing Communications* 20(1–2): 2–4.

Klein, N. (2010) *No Logo*, 2nd edn, London: Flamingo.

Kline, S. (1993) *Out of the Garden: Toys, TV, and Children's Culture in the Age of Marketing*, London: Verso.

——(2009) 'Ronald's New Dance: A Case Study of Corporate Re-branding in the Age of Integrated Marketing Communications', in H. Powell, J. Hardy, S. Hawkin and I. MacRury (eds), *The Advertising Handbook*, 3rd edn, London: Routledge.

Laclau, E. and Mouffe, C. (1985) *Hegemony and Socialist Strategy*, London: Verso.

Lash, S. and Lury, C. (2007) *Global Culture Industry*, Cambridge: Polity.

Lash, S. and Urry, J. (1994) *Economies of Signs and Space*, London: Sage.

——(1999) *Economies of Signs and Space*, London: Sage.

Lasn, K. (2000) *Culture Jam*, New York: Quill.

Laswell, H. (1936) *Politics: Who Gets What, When, How*, London: McGraw-Hill.

Laswell, H. and Leites, N. (1949) *Language of Politics: Studies in Quantitative Semantics*, Cambridge, MA: MIT Press.

Laurier, E. (1993) 'Tackintosh: Glasgow's Supplementary Gloss', in G. Kearns and C. Philo (eds), *Selling Places: The City as Cultural Capital, Past and Present*, Oxford: Pergamon Press.

Lawrence, C. (2009) *The Cult of Celebrity*, Guilford, CT: Globe Pequot.

Leavis, F.R. and Thompson, D. (1977) *Culture and Environment*, Westport, CT: Greenwood Press.

Lehu, J.-M. (2009) *Branded Entertainment*, London: Kogan Page.

Leibling, D. (2008) 'Car Ownership in Britain – RAC Foundation'. Available online at www.racfoundation.org/assets/rac (accessed 7 January 2014).

Leiss, W., Kline, S. and Jhally, S. (1997) *Social Communication in Advertising: Persons, Products, and Images of Well-being*, 2nd edn, New York: Routledge.

Leiss, W., Kline, S., Jhally, S. and Botterill, J (2005) *Social Communication in Advertising: Consumption in the Mediated Marketplace*, 3rd edn, London: Routledge.

Leslie, D. (1997) 'Flexibly Specialised Agencies? Reflexivity, Identity and the Advertising Industry', *Environment and Planning A* 29: 1017–38.

Levy, M. and Windahl, S. (1985) 'The Concept of Audience Activity', in K.E. Rosengren, L.A. Wenner and P. Palmgreen (eds), *Media Gratifications Research, Current Perspectives*, Beverley Hills, CA: Sage.

Lewis, J. (1997) 'What Counts in Cultural Studies?', *Media, Culture and Society* 19: 83–97.

——(2010) 'The Myth of Commercialism: Why a Market Approach to Broadcasting Does Not Work', in J. Klaehn (ed.), *The Political Economy of Media and Power*, New York: Peter Lang.

Leys, C. (2013) 'The British Ruling Class', in L. Panitch, G. Albo and V. Chibber (eds), *Registering Class: Socialist Register 2014*, London: Merlin Press.

Lilleker, D. and Scullion, R. (2009) 'Political Advertising', in H. Powell, J. Hardy, S. Hawkin and I. MacRury (eds), *The Advertising Handbook* 3rd edn, London: Routledge.

Linsey, C. (2003) 'A Century of Labour Market Change: 1900 to 2000', National Statistics. Available online at www.statistics.gov.uk/cci/article.asp?id=653 (accessed 8 April 2013).

Liverpool Echo (2003) 'Boom Town', *Liverpool Echo* 6 June.

Livingstone, S. (2002) *Young People and the Media*, London: Sage.

Livingstone, S. and Das, R. (2013) 'The End of Audiences?', in J. Hartley, J. Burgess and A. Bruns (eds), *A Companion to New Media Dynamics*, Chichester: John Wiley.

Livingstone, S., Lunt, P. and Miller, L. (2007) 'Citizens, Consumers and the Citizen-consumer: Articulating the Citizen Interest in Media and Communication Regulation', *Discourse and Communication* 1(1): 85–111.

Lovering, J. (1997) 'Global Restructuring and Local Impact', in M. Pacione (ed.), *Britain's Cities*, London: Routledge, pp. 62–87.

Lury, C. (2011) *Consumer Culture*, Cambridge: Polity.

Lury, C. and Warde, A. (1997) 'Investments in the Imaginary Consumer', in M. Nava, A. Blake, I. MacRury and B. Richards, *Buy this Book: Studies in Advertising and Consumption*, London: Routledge, pp. 87–102.

Lyotard, J.-F. (1979) *The Postmodern Condition: A Report on Knowledge*, Manchester: Manchester University Press.

MacCarthy, F. (1995) *William Morris*, London: Faber and Faber.

MacPherson, C.B. (1962) *The Political Theory of Possessive Individualism: From Hobbes to Locke*, Oxford: Oxford University Press.

MacRury, I. (2009a) *Advertising*, London: Routledge.

——(2009b) 'Sponsorship, Advertising and the Olympic Games', in H. Powell, J. Hardy, S. Hawkin and I. MacRury (eds), *The Advertising Handbook*, 3rd edn, London: Routledge.

Mail Online (2013) 'Racial Profiling Row'. Available online at www.dailymail.co.uk/news/article-2383156/Police-arresting-139-illegal-immigrant-aspects-watchdog-launches-probe.html (accessed 14 August 2013).

Maiuri, A. (1960) *Pompeii*, Novara: Instituto Geografico de Agostini.

Mandese, J. (2010) 'Point of View: Commerce Is King', *Admap*, February.

Mansell, N. (1997) 'Rating POSTAR', *Admap*, September.

Marcuse, H. (1968) *One-Dimensional Man*, London: Sphere.

Marketing (2013) 'Benetton Uses Transsexual Model', *Marketing Magazine*, 30 January, p. 9.

Marshall, P.D. (2009) 'Screens: Television's Dispersed "Broadcast"', in G. Turner and J. Tay (eds), *Television Studies after TV: Understanding Television in the Post-broadcast Era*, London: Routledge.

Marx, K. (1935a) *The Communist Manifesto* in *A Handbook of Marxism*, London: Victor Gollancz.

——(1935b) *The Critique of Political Economy* in *A Handbook of Marxism*, London: Victor Gollancz.

——(1978 [1859]) 'Preface to a Contribution to the Critique of Political Economy', in R.C. Tucker (ed.), *The Marx Engels Reader*, London: Norton.

Mason, P. (2012) *Why It's Kicking Off Everywhere: The New Global Revolutions*, London: Verso.

Mattelart, A. (1989) *Advertising International*, London: Routledge.

——(1991) *Advertising International: The Privatisation of Public Space*, London: Routledge.

McAllister, M. (1996) *The Commercialization of American Culture*, Thousand Oaks, CA: Sage.

——(2000) 'From Flick to Flack: The Increased Emphasis on Marketing by Media Entertainment Corporations', in R. Andersen and L. Strate (eds), *Critical Studies in Media Commercialism*, Oxford: Oxford University Press.

——(2002) 'Television News Plugola and the Last Episode of Seinfeld', *Journal of Communication* 52(2): 383–401.

McAllister, M. and West, E. (2013) *The Routledge Companion to Advertising and Promotional Culture*, New York: Routledge.

McCarthy, A. (2001) *Ambient Television: Visual Culture and Public Space*, Durham, NC: Duke University Press.

McChesney, R. (2008) *The Political Economy of Media*, New York: Monthly Review Press.

——(2013) *Digital Disconnect*, New York: The New Press.

McChesney, R., Stole, I., Foster, J.B. and Holleman, H. (2011) 'Advertising and the Genius of Commercial Propaganda', in G. Sussman (ed.), *The Propaganda Society: Promotional Culture and Politics in Global Context*, New York: Peter Lang.

McDonald, C. and Scott, J. (2007) 'A Brief History of Advertising' in G.J. Tellis and T. Ambler (eds), *The Sage Handbook of Advertising*, London: Sage.

McDougall, D. (2008) 'The Hidden Face of Primark Fashion', *Observer*, 22 June.

McElhatton, N. (2012) 'The Ever Changing Face of the Modern Marketer', *Campaign*, 12 October.

McFall, L. (2004) *Advertising: A Cultural Economy*, London: Sage.
——(2011) 'Advertising: Structure, Agency or Agencement?', in M. Deuze (ed.), *Managing Media Work*, London: Sage.
McGuigan, J. (1999) *Modernity and Postmodern Culture*, Buckingham: Open University Press.
——(2006) 'The Politics of Cultural Studies and Cool Capitalism', *Cultural Politics* 2(2).
——(2009) *Cool Capitalism*, London: Pluto Press.
——(2010) *Cultural Analysis*, London: Sage.
——(2012), 'The Coolness of Capitalism Today', *TripleC* 10(2): 425–38. Available online at www.triple-c.at (accessed 23 October 2012).
McKibbin, R. (2010) 'Nothing to Do with the Economy', *London Review of Books* 32(22): 12–13.
McQuail, D. (1969) *Towards a Sociology of Mass Communications*, London: Macmillan.
——(1998) 'Reflections on Uses and Gratifications Research,' in R. Dickinson, R. Harindranath and O. Linne (eds), *Approaches to Audiences: A Reader*, London: Arnold.
——(2002) *McQuail's Reader in Mass Communication Theory*, London: Sage.
——(2010) *Mass Communication Theory: An Introduction*, London: Sage Publications.
McQuire, S. (1999) 'Blinded by the (Speed of) Light', in J. Armitage (ed.), *Theory, Culture and Society* 16(5–6): 143–59.
——(2008) *The Media City*, London: Sage.
McStay, A. (2011) 'Profiling Phorm: An Autopoietic Approach to the Audience-as-commodity', *Surveillance and Society* 8(3): 310–22.
Media *Guardian* (2011) 'Mobile Marketing', *Guardian*, supplement, 13 June.
Meehan, E. (1993) 'Commodity Audience, Actual Audience: The Blindspot Debate', in J. Wasko, V. Mosco and M. Pendakur (eds), *Illuminating the Blindspots: Essays Honouring Dallas W. Smythe*, Norwood, NJ: Ablex.
——(2002) 'Gendering the Commodity Audience: Critical Media Research, Feminism and Political Economy', in E. Meehan, and E. Riordan (eds), *Sex and Money,* Minneapolis, MN: University of Minnesota Press.
——(2005) *Why TV Is Not Our Fault*, Lanham, MD: Rowman and Littlefield.
Meehan, E. and Riordan, E., eds, (2002) *Sex and Money*, Minneapolis, MN: University of Minnesota Press.
Merrell, F. (2001) 'Charles Sanders Peirce's Concept of the Sign', in P. Cobley (ed.), *The Routledge Companion to Semiotics and Linguistics*, London: Routledge.
Metykova, M. (2013) 'Media and Advertising – The Interests of Citizens and Consumers', in C. Wharton (ed.), *Advertising as Culture*, Bristol: Intellect.
Middleton, A.C. (2011) 'City Branding and Inward Investment', in K. Dinnie (ed.), *City Branding: Theory and Cases*, Basingstoke: Palgrave.
Milne, S. (2013) 'In Cameron's Britain', *Guardian*, 7 August.
Mirzoeff, N. (2012) *The Visual Culture Reader*, London: Routledge.
Mitchell, W.J.T. (2002) 'Showing Seeing: A Critique of Visual Culture', in N. Mirzoeff (ed.), *The Visual Culture Reader*, 2nd edn, London: Routledge.
Montgomery, N.V. and Unnava, H.R. (2007) 'The Role of Consumer Memory in Advertising', in G.J. Tellis and T. Ambler (eds), *The Sage Handbook of Advertising*, London: Sage.
Moore, E. (2003) 'Branding Spaces: The Scope of New Marketing', *Journal of Consumer Culture* 3(1): 39–60.
Morley, D. (1980) *The 'Nationwide' Audience*, London: British Film Institute.
——(1981) 'The "Nationwide" Audience: A Critical Postscript', in *Screen Education* 39: 3–14.
——(1986) *Family Television*, London: Routledge.
——(1990) 'Active Audience Theory: Pendulums and Pitfalls', *Journal of Communication* 43(4): 13–19.
——(1992) *Television Audiences and Cultural Studies*, London: Routledge.
——(2000) *Home Territories: Media Mobility and Identity*, London: Routledge.
——(2007) *Media Modernity and Technology*, London: Routledge.

Morris, W. (1896) *Speech against the Abuses of Public Advertising*, 31 January, Society of Arts, John Street, Adelphi, London.

——(2008 [1888]) *Useful Work v. Useless Toil*, London: Penguin.

Mosco, V. (2009) *The Political Economy of Communication*, 2nd edn, London: Sage.

Mullan, J. (2013) 'As if Life Depended on It', *London Review of Books* 35(17): 10–12.

Mullen, A. (2013) 'Selling Politics – the Political Economy of Political Advertising', in C. Wharton (ed.), *Advertising as Culture*, Bristol: Intellect.

Mulvey, L. (1975) 'Visual Pleasure and Narrative Cinema', *Screen* 16(3): 6–18.

Murdock, G. (1978) 'Blindspots about Western Marxism: A Reply to Dallas Smythe', *Canadian Journal of Political and Social Theory* 2 (Spring–Summer): 109–19.

——(2004) 'Building the Digital Commons: Public Broadcasting in the Age of the Internet', the 2004 Spry Memorial Lecture. Available online at www.com.umontreal.ca/spry/spry-gm-lec.htm (accessed 21 July 2011).

——(2011) 'Political Economies as Moral Economies: Commodities, Gifts and Public Goods', in J. Wasko, G. Murdock and H. Sousa (eds), *The Handbook of Political Economy of Communications*, Oxford: Blackwell.

Murdock, G. and Golding, P. (1977) 'Capitalism, Communication, and Class Relations', in J. Curran *et al.* (eds), *Mass Communication and Society*, London: Edward Arnold.

——(2005) 'Culture, Communications and Political Economy', in J. Curran and M. Gurevitch (eds), *Mass Media and Society*, London: Hodder Arnold.

Myers, G. (1999) *Adworlds: Brands, Media, Audiences*, London: Arnold.

Nairn, A. (2013) *Marketing*, 9 January, pp. 10–11.

Napoli, J., Murgolo-Poore, M. and Boudville, I. (2003) 'Female Gender Images in Adolescent Magazine Advertising', *Australian Marketing Journal* 11(1): 60–69.

Nava, M. (1997) 'Framing Advertising: Cultural Analysis and the Incrimination of Visual Texts', in M. Nava, A. Blake, I. MacRury and B. Richards (eds), *Buy this Book: Studies in Advertising and Consumption*, London: Routledge.

Naylor, G. (2004) *William Morris by Himself: Designs and Writings*, London: Time Warner.

Negus, K. (2002) 'The Work of Cultural Intermediaries and the Enduring Distance between Production and Consumption', *Cultural Studies* 16(4): 501–15.

Nerve (2004) 'Liverpool City of Culture', *Nerve* 4 (Autumn).

Nevett, T.R. (1982) *Advertising in Britain: A History*, London: Heineman.

Newbery, A. (2012) 'There Are Many Gay Role Models on TV – Just Not in the Ads', *Campaign*, 19 October.

Nixon, S. (2003) *Advertising Cultures*, London: Sage.

——(2011) 'From Full-Service Agency to 3-D Marketing Consultants: "Creativity" and Organizational Change in Advertising', in M. Deuze (ed.), *Managing Media Work*, London: Sage.

Norris, C. (1993) *The Truth about Postmodernism*, Oxford: Blackwell.

O'Connell, S. (1999) *The Popular Print in Britain*, London: British Museum.

Odih, P. (2010) *Advertising and Cultural Politics in Global Times*, Farnham: Ashgate.

Odin, R. (2012) 'Spectator, Film and the Mobile Phone', in I. Christie (ed.), *Audiences*, Amsterdam: Amsterdam University Press.

O'Donohoe, S. (1997) 'Leaky Boundaries: Intertextuality and Young Adult Experiences of Advertising', in M. Nava *et al.* (eds), *Buy this Book: Studies in Advertising and Consumption*, London: Routledge.

——(2008) Review of *Adland: A Global History of Advertising* by Mark Tungate (2007), *International Journal of Advertising* 27(1): 172–3.

Ofcom (2013a) *International Communications Market Report*, London: Ofcom.

——(2013b) *Ofcom Communications Market Report*. Available online at http://stakeholders.ofcom.org.uk/market-data-research/market-data/communications-market-reports (accessed 5 August 2013).

Office for National Statistics (2005) 'A Summary of *Focus on Social Inequalities*'. Available online at www.ons.gov.uk/ons/rel/social+inequalities (accessed 11 November 2013).

——(2011) 'Families and Households 2001–11'. Available online at www.ons.gov.uk/ons/rel/family-demography/families-and-households/2011/index.html (accessed 18 April 2014).

Office of Fair Trading (2009) 'Review of the Local and Regional Media Merger Regime'. Available online at www.oft.gov.uk/shared_oft/mergers_ea02/oft1091.pdf (accessed 15 April 2014).

Overton, M. (2002) *Agricultural Revolution in England 1500–1850*, Cambridge: Cambridge University Press.

——(2012) 'Crop Yields'. Available online at www.bbc.co.uk/history/british/empire_seapower/agricultural_revolution_01.shtml (accessed 3 September 2013).

Panofsky, E. (1993 [1955]) *Meaning in the Visual Arts*, London: Penguin.

Pantene (2012) Advertisement. Available online at www.youtube.com/watch?v=CzOBGaymHfQ (accessed 1 November 2012).

Papadatos, C. (2012) 'Choose to Believe: Three Coalition Myths', *Media Planet*, 3 December.

Pariser, E. (2011) *The Filter Bubble*, New York: Penguin.

Pecheux, M. (1982) *Language, Semantics and Ideology*, trans. H. Nagpal, Basingstoke: Macmillan.

Peers, D.M. (2004) 'Britain and Empire', in C. Williams (ed.), *A Companion to Nineteenth-Century Britain,* Oxford: Blackwell.

Peirce, C.S. (1958) *Values in a Universe of Chance: Selected Writings*, P. Weiner (ed.), New York: Dover Press.

Petrie, D. (1996) 'Young People, Television and Daily Life', in D. Petrie and J. Willis (eds), *Television and the Household*, London: British Film Institute.

Pew Research Centre Project for Excellence in Journalism (2013) *The State of the News Media 2013*. Available online at http://stateofthemedia.org/2013 (accessed 10 April 2013).

Placebrands (2011) *City Branding: How Cities Compete in the 21st Century*. Available online www.placebrands.net/_files/placebrands_city_branding_book.pdf (accessed 10 March 2011).

Pooke, G. and Whitham, G. (2003) *Teach Yourself Art History*, London: Hodder and Stoughton.

Poon, D. and Prendergast, G. (2006) 'A New Framework for Evaluating Sponsorship Opportunities', *International Journal of Advertising* 35: 169–81.

Poster, M. (1990) *The Mode of Information*, Cambridge: Polity.

Pountain, D. and Robins, D. (2000) *Cool Rules: Anatomy of an Attitude*, London: Reaktion.

Powell, H. (2009) 'Celebrity', in H. Powell, J. Hardy, S. Hawkin and I. MacRury (eds), *The Advertising Handbook*, 3rd edn, London: Routledge.

Powell, H. and Prasad, S. (2010) '"As seen on TV." The Celebrity Expert: How Taste Is Shaped by Lifestyle Media', *Cultural Politics* 6(1): 111–24.

Powell, H., Hardy, J., Hawkins, S. and MacRury, I., eds (2009) *The Advertising Handbook*, 3rd edn, London: Routledge.

Prus, R. and Dawson, L. (1991) 'Shop 'til You Drop: Shopping as Recreational and Laborious Activity', *Canadian Journal of Sociology* 7: 5–16.

Purvis, T. (2013) 'Advertising – A Way of Life' in C. Wharton (ed.), *Advertising as Culture*, Bristol: Intellect.

Radice, H. (2010) 'Confronting the Crisis: A Class Analysis', in L. Panitch, G. Albo and V. Chibber (eds), *The Crisis This Time: Socialist Register 2011*, London: Merlin Press.

Radway, J. (1987) *Reading the Romance: Women, Patriarchy and Popular Literature*, London: Verso.

Reid, D. (2013) 'On-line digi-ads', in C. Wharton (ed.), *Advertising as Culture*, Bristol: Intellect.

Relph, E. (1976) *Place and Placelessness*, London: Pion.

Richards, J. and Murphy, J. (2009 [1996]) 'Economic Censorship and Free Speech: The Circle of Communication between Advertisers, Media and Consumers', in J. Turow and M. McAllister (eds), *The Advertising and Consumer Culture Reader*, New York: Routledge.

Ridell, S. (1996) 'Resistance through Routines', *European Journal of Communication* 11(40): 557–82.

Rifkin, J. (2014) 'Capitalism Is Making Way for the Age of Free', *Guardian*, 1 April.

Ritzer, G. and Jurgenson, N. (2010) 'Production, Consumption, Prosumption: The Nature of Capitalism in the Age of the Digital "Prosumer"', *Journal of Consumer Culture* 10(1): 13–36.

Robin, C. (2012) 'Achieving Disunity', *London Review of Books* 34(20): 23–5.

Rogers, E.M. (1995 [1962]) *Diffusions of Innovations*, New York: Free Press.

Rojek, C. (2003) *Stuart Hall*, London: Polity Press.

——(2004) 'The Consumerist Syndrome in Contemporary Society: An Interview with Zygmunt Bauman', *Journal of Consumer Culture* 4(3): 291–321.

——(2007) *Cultural Studies*, Cambridge: Polity

Romaniuk, J. (2007) 'Word of Mouth and the Viewing of Television Programmes', *Journal of Advertising Research* 47(4): 462–71.

Rosen, E. (2000) *The Anatomy of Buzz: Creating Word-of-Mouth Marketing*, London: Harper Collins Business.

Rucker, D.D., Petty, R.E. and Priester, J.R. (2007) 'Understanding Advertising Effectiveness for a Psychological Perspective: The Importance of Attitudes and Attitude Strength', in G.J. Tellis and T. Ambler (eds), *The Sage Handbook of Advertising*, London: Sage.

Sage, E.T. (1916) 'Advertising among the Romans', *The Classical Weekly* 9 (26): 202–8.

Sarup, M. (1996) *Identity, Culture and the Postmodern World*, Edinburgh: Edinburgh University Press.

Sassatelli, R. (2007) *Consumer Culture: History, Theory and Politics*, London: Sage.

Sassen, S. (1996) 'Rebuilding the Global City', in A. King (ed.), *Re-presenting the City*, Basingstoke: Macmillan.

Saussure, F. de (1974) *Course in General Linguistics*, trans. W. Baskin, London: Fontana.

Scannell, P. (1996) *Radio, Television and Modern Life*, Oxford: Blackwell.

——(2000) 'For-anyone-as-someone Structures' in *Media, Culture and Society* 1(22): 5–24.

——(2009) 'The Liveness of Broadcast Talk', *Journal of Communication* 59(4): E1–E6.

Schiller, H. (1989) *Culture, Inc.*, New York: Oxford University Press.

Schor, J. (2004) *Born to Buy: The Commercialized Child and the New Consumer Culture*, New York: Scribner.

Schudson, M. (1984) *Advertising, the Uneasy Persuasion*, New York: Basic Books.

——(1993) *Advertising, the Uneasy Persuasion: Its Dubious Impact on American Society*, London: Routledge.

Schultz, T. (2000) 'Mass Media and the Concept of Interactivity: An Exploratory Study of Online Forums and Reader E-mail', *Media Culture Society* 22: 205–21.

Scott, J. (2006a) 'Content Analysis', in V. Jupp (ed.), *The Sage Dictionary of Social Research Methods*, London: Sage.

——(2006b) 'Textual Analysis' in V. Jupp (ed.), *The Sage Dictionary of Social Research Methods*, London: Sage.

Seaman, W.R. (1992) 'Active Audience Theory: Pointless Populism', *Media Culture Society* 14: 301–11.

Seltzer, G. (2010) 'Situationism and the Writings of T.J. Clark', *Journal for the Study of Radicalism* 4(1): 121–40.

Sennett, R. (1999) 'Growth and Failure: The New Political Economy and Its Culture', in M. Featherstone and S. Lash (eds), *Spaces of Culture*, London: Sage.

Shaikh, A. (2010) 'The First Great Depression of the 21st Century', in L. Panitch, G. Albo and V. Chibber (eds), *The Crisis This Time: Socialist Register 2011*, London: Merlin Press.

Shapiro, K. (1981) *The Construction of Television Commercials: Four Cases of Interorganizational Problem Solving*, Stanford, CA: Stanford University Press.

Sharpe, A. (2014) 'Jacques Lacan', *Internet Encyclopedia of Philosophy*. Available online at. www.iep.utm.edu/lacweb (accessed 11 April 2014).

Sheller, M. and Urry, J. (2003) 'Mobile Transformations of "Public" and "Private" Life', *Theory, Culture and Society* 20(3): 115–33.

Short, T.L. (2007) *Peirce's Theory of Signs*, Cambridge: Cambridge University Press.

Shuner, G. (2013) 'Polar Inertia', in J. Armitage (ed.), *The Virilio Dictionary*, Edinburgh: Edinburgh University Press.

Silverstein, M.L. (2012) 'The [] Walked Down the Street', *London Review of Books* 34(21): 8.

Silverstone, R. (2004 [1994]) *Television and Everyday Life*, London: Routledge.

Silverstone, R., Hirsch, E. and Morley, D. (1992) 'Information and Communication Technologies and the Moral Economy of the Household', in R. Silverstone and E. Hirsch (eds), *Consuming Technologies: Media and Information in Domestic Spaces*, London: Routledge.

Simmel, G. (1950) 'The Metropolis and Mental Life', trans. H.H. Gerth and C.W. Mills, in K. Wolf (ed.), *The Sociology of George Simmel*, London: Macmillan.

Sinclair, J. (2011) 'Branding and Culture', in J. Wasko, G. Murdock and H. Sousa (eds), *The Handbook of Political Economy of Communications*, Oxford: Blackwell Publishing.

Sivulka, J. (2009) *Ad Women: How They Impact What We Need, Want, and Buy*, Amherst, NY: Prometheus.

Slater, D. (2008 [1997]) *Consumer Culture and Modernity*, Cambridge: Polity.

Smith, P. (2012) 'The Death of the Demographic: A Guide to the Way Audiences Behave', in *Smooth Radio/Marketing*, 17 October.

Smythe, D. (1977) 'Communications: Blindspot of Western Marxism', *Canadian Journal of Political and Social Theory* 1(3): 1–27.

——(1978) 'Rejoinder to Graham Murdock', *Canadian Journal of Political and Social Theory* 2 (Spring–Summer): 120–27.

——(1981) *Dependency Road*, Norwood, NJ: Ablex.

——(1994) *Counterclockwise*, Boulder, CO: Westview Press.

Soar, M. (2000) 'Encoding Advertisements: Ideology and Meaning in Advertising Production', *Mass Communication and Society* 4.

Social Trends (2000) 'Social Trends 30'. Available online at www.ons.gov.uk/ons/rel/social-trends-rd/social-trends (accessed 7 April 2014).

——(2001) 'Social Trends 31'. Available online at www.ons.gov.uk/ons/rel/social-trends-rd/social-trends/no–31–2001-edition/index.html (accessed 15 April 2014).

Soley, L. (2002) *Censorship, Inc.*, New York: Monthly Review Press.

Soper, K. (2007) 'Re-thinking the "Good Life": The Citizenship Dimension of Consumer Disaffection with Consumerism', *Journal of Consumer Culture* 7(2): 205–29.

Spalding, R. and Parker, C. (2007) *Historiography*, Manchester: Manchester University Press.

Sperling, J. (2010) 'Multiples and Reproductions: Prints and Photographs in Nineteenth-Century England – Visual Communities, Cultures and Class', in J. Kromm and S. Benforado (eds), *A History of Visual Culture: Western Civilisation from the 18th to the 21st Century*, Oxford: Berg.

Spies-Butcher, B., Paton, J. and Cahill, D. (2012) *Market Society: History, Theory, Practice*, Melbourne: Cambridge University Press.

Spigel, L. (1992) *Make Room for TV: Television and the Family Ideal in Postwar America*, Chicago, IL: Chicago University Press.

Spourdalakis, M. (2012) 'Left Strategy in the Greek Cauldron: Explaining Syriza's Success', in L. Panitch, G. Albo and V. Chibber (eds), *The Question of Strategy: Socialist Register 2013*, Pontypool: Merlin Press.

Stallabrass, J. (2006) 'Spectacle and Terror', *New Left Review* 37: 87–106.

Statista (2012) 'Olympic Games Viewing Statistics'. Available online at www.statista.com/statistics/236692/total-number-of-tv-viewers-of-olympic-summer-games-worldwide (accessed 5 November 2012).

Stephenson, J. (2013) 'Music and Advertising – A Happy Marriage?', in C. Wharton (ed.), *Advertising as Culture*, Bristol: Intellect.

Stevenson, N. (1996) *Understanding Media Cultures: Social Theory and Mass Communication*, London: Sage.

Stewart, D.W., Morris, J. and Grover, A. (2007) 'Emotions in Advertising', in G.J. Tellis and T. Ambler (eds), *The Sage Handbook of Advertising*, London: Sage.

Stole, I. (2003) 'Televised Consumption: Women, Advertisers and the Early Daytime Television Industry', *Consumption, Markets and Culture* 6(1): 65–80.

——(2006) *Advertising on Trial: Consumer Activism and Corporate Public Relations in the 1930s*, Urbana, IL: University of Illinois Press.

Storey, J., ed. (1998) *Cultural Theory and Popular Culture: A Reader*, Harlow: Pearson.

——(2009) *Cultural Theory and Popular Culture: An Introduction*, Harlow: Pearson.

Strasser, S. (2009) 'The Alien Past – Consumer Culture in Historical Perspective', in J. Turow and M.P. McAllister (eds), *The Advertising and Consumer Culture Reader*, London: Routledge.

Streeck, W. (2012) 'Citizens as Consumers', *New Left Review* 76: 27–42.

Street, S. (2006) *Crossing the Ether: British Public Service Radio and Commercial Competition 1922–1945*, Eastleigh: John Libbey Publishing.

Sturken, M. and Cartwright, L., eds (2009) *Practices of Looking: An Introduction to Visual Culture*, Oxford: Oxford University Press.

Sumner, C. (1979) *Reading Ideologies: An Investigation into the Marxist Theory of Ideologies and Law*, London: Academic Press.

Sussman, G., ed. (2011) *The Propaganda Society: Promotional Culture and Politics in Global Context*, New York: Peter Lang.

Tattersfield, N. (2009) 'A Peculiar Spirit and Fancy', in J. Watkins (ed.), *Thomas Bewick Tale-Pieces*, Manchester: Ikon Gallery/Corner House Publication.

Telegraph (2013) 'Liverpool Has Biggest "Per Home" Unemployment'. Available online at www.telegraph.co.uk/finance/jobs/9003245/Liverpool-has-biggest-per-home-unemployment.html (accessed 16 April 2014).

TeleScope Study (2013) 'TeleScope – Television Licensing Authority Survey'. Available online at www.tvlicensing.co.uk/about/media-centre/news/tv-licensing-reveals-tv-elation-across-the-nation-NEWS65 (accessed 21 March 2013).

Terranova, T. (2000) 'Free Labour: Producing Culture for the Digital Economy', *Social Text* 18(2): 33–58.

Therborn, G. (2012) 'Class in the 21st Century', *New Left Review* 78: 5–29.

——(2014) 'New Masses?', *New Left Review* 85: 7–16.

Thompson, D. (1932) 'Advertising God', *Scrutiny* 3: 241–6.

Thompson, E.P. (1996) *William Morris: Romantic to Revolutionary*, London: Merlin Press.

Thompson, J.B. (1990) *Ideology and Modern Culture*, Cambridge: Polity Press.

——(1995) *The Media and Modernity: A Social Theory of the Media*, London: Polity Press.

Thrift, N. and Glennie, P. (1993) 'Historical Geographies of Urban Life and Modern Consumption', in G. Kearns and C. Philo (eds), *Selling Places: The City as Cultural Capital, Past and Present*, Oxford: Pergamon.

Toffler, A. (1980) *The Third Wave*, New York: Bantam.

Torronen, J. (2001) 'Between Public Good and the Freedom of the Consumer: Negotiating the Space, Orientation and Position of Us in the Reception of Alcohol Policy Editorials', *Media, Culture and Society* 23: 171–193.

Tosh, J. (2006) *The Pursuit of History*, Harlow: Pearson.

Tucker, M. (2008) 'The Cultural Production of Cities: Rhetoric or Reality? Lessons from Glasgow', *Journal of Retail and Leisure Property* 7: 21–33.

Tudor, A. (1999) *Decoding Culture*, London: Sage.

Tungate, M. (2007) *Adland: A Global History of Advertising*, London: Kogan Page.

Turner, G. and Tay, J. (2009) *Television Studies after TV: Understanding Television in the Post-Broadcast Era*, London: Routledge.

Turow, J. (1997) *Breaking up America*, Chicago, IL: Chicago University Press.

——(2010) *Media Today*, New York: Routledge.

——(2011) *The Daily You: How the New Advertising Industry Is Defining Your Identity and Your Worth*, New Haven, CT: Yale University Press.

Turow, J. and McAllister, M. (2009) 'General Introduction', in J. Turow and M. McAllister (eds), *The Advertising and Consumer Culture Reader*, New York: Routledge.

Uglow, J. (2006) *Nature's Engraver: A Life of Thomas Bewick*, London: Faber and Faber.

UK Border Agency (2013) 'Go Home' mobile billboard. Available online at www.ukba.homeoffice.gov.uk/sitecontent/newsarticles/2013/july/50-returns-pilot (accessed 10 April 2014).

VALS (2012) 'US Framework and VALS Types'. Available online at www.strategicbusinessinsights.com/vals/ustypes.shtml (accessed 17 December 2012).

van den Oever, A. (2012) 'The Aesthetics and Viewing Regimes of Cinema and Television, and Their Dialectics', in I. Christie (ed.), *Audiences*, Amsterdam: Amsterdam University Press.

Vazquez-Casielles, R., Suarez-Alvarez, L. and del Rio-Lanza, A. (2013) 'The Word of Mouth Dynamic', *Journal of Advertising Research* 53(1): 43–60.

Veblen, T. (1899) *Theory of the Leisure Class: An Economic Study in the Evolution of Institutions*, New York: Macmillan.

Virilio, P. (1986 [1977]) *Speed and Politics: An Essay on Dromology*, trans. M. Polizzotti, New York: Semiotext(e).

——(2000) *Polar Inertia*, London: Sage.

Viser, V. (1997) 'Mode of Address, Emotion and Stylistics: Images of Children in American Magazine Advertising, 1940–50', *Communication Research* 24: 83–101.

Wainwright, H. (2012) 'Transformative Power: Political Organisation in Transition', in L. Panitch, G. Albo and V. Chibber (eds), *The Question of Strategy: Socialist Register 2013*, Pontypool: Merlin Press.

Wallace-Hadrill, A. (1994) *Houses and Society in Herculaneum*, Princeton, NJ: Princeton University Press.

WARC (2013) 'Global Product Placement Spend Rises', World Advertising Research Centre, 17 April. Available at www.warc.com/Content/News/Global_product_placement_spend_rises.content?ID=281b295f-1ee2-43f1-9899-b64ba5d213ac&q= (accessed 20 April 2013).

Warnke, G. (1987) *Gadamer: Hermeneutics, Tradition and Reason*, Cambridge: Polity Press.

Wasko, J. (2004) 'The Political Economy of Communications', in J.D. Downing (ed.), *The Sage Handbook of Media Studies*, Thousand Oaks, CA: Sage.

Watts, E.K. and Orbe, M.P. (2009) 'The Spectacular Consumption Of "True" African American Culture', in J. Turow and M.P. McAllister (eds), *The Advertising and Consumer Culture Reader*, London: Routledge.

Wernick, A. (1990) *Promotional Culture*, London: Sage.

——(1997) 'Resort to Nostalgia: Mountains, Memories and Myths of Time', in M. Nava, A. Blake, I. MacRury and B. Richards (eds), *Buy this Book: Studies in Advertising and Consumption*, London: Routledge.

West, R. and Turner, L.H. (2010) 'Uses and Gratifications Theory', in *Introducing Communication Theory: Analysis and Application*, Boston, MA: McGraw-Hill.

Wharton, C. (2013) 'Spreads like Butter', in C. Wharton (ed.) *Advertising as Culture*, Bristol: Intellect.

Wharton, C. and Fenwick, J. (2012) 'Real Urban Images: Policy and Culture in Northern Britain', *Culture and Local Governance* 4(1): 1–30.

Wharton, C., Fenwick, J. and Fawcett, H. (2010) 'Public Policy in the Party City – The Spectacle of Culture, Gender and Locality', *International Journal of Public Administration* 33 (14): 779–89.

White, H. (1980) 'The Value of Narrativity in the Representation of Reality', *Critical Inquiry 1*: 5–27.

Williams, R. (1974) *Television, Technology and Cultural Form*, London: Fontana.

——(1980) 'Advertising the Magic System', in his *Problems in Materialism and Culture*, London: Verso.

——(1981) 'Analysis of Culture', in T. Bennett, M. Martin, C. Mercer and J. Woollacott (eds), *Culture, Ideology and Social Process*, London: Open University Press.

——(1983) *Keywords*, London: Fontana.

——(1992) *The Long Revolution*, London: Hogarth Press.

Williamson, J. (1978) *Decoding Advertisements: Ideology and Meaning in Advertising*, London: Boyars.

Williamson, T. (2002) *The Transformation of Rural England: Farming and the Landscape, 1700–1870*, Exeter: Exeter University Press.

Willis, P. (1990) *Common Culture: Symbolic Work at Play in the Everyday Cultures of the Young*, Milton Keynes: Open University Press.

Wilson, A. (1993) *Watching Television: Hermeneutics, Reception and Popular Culture*, Cambridge: Polity Press.

Wilson, P. and Pahl, R. (1988) 'The Changing Sociological Construct of the Family', *The Sociological Review* 36(2): 233–72.

Winston, B. (1990) 'On Counting the Wrong Things', in M. Alvarado and J.B. Thompson (eds), *The Media Reader*, London: British Film Institute.

Wintour, P. (2013) 'May Admits "Go Home" Vans Were a Failure', *Guardian*, 23 October.

Woo, R. (2001) *Art History as Cultural History: Warburg's Projects*, Amsterdam: G + B Arts International.

Wood, A. (1961) *Nineteenth Century Britain*, London: Longman.

Zelizer, B. (2004) *Taking Journalism Seriously*, London: Sage.

Žižek, S. (2011) 'Zero-Degree Protests', *London Review of Books*. Available online at www.lrb.co.uk/2011/08/19/slavoj-zizek/shoplifters-of-the-world-unite (accessed 18 April 2014).

Zukin, S. (1998) 'Urban Lifestyles: Diversity and Standardization', *Space of Consumption in Urban Studies* 35(5–6): 825–39.

Index